Teachers Exploring Tasks i
Language Teaching

Prepublication praise for *Teachers Exploring Tasks in English Language Teaching*

'Jane Willis' and Corony Edwards' edited collection of papers, *Teachers Exploring Tasks in English Language Teaching,* offers an excellent "making public" of the variety of ways in which teachers use tasks to better understand their teaching and their students' learning. The range of reports – focusing on students, on content, and on classroom communities in a variety of geographical and educational settings – is impressive. In adopting task-based teaching, as Willis and Edwards define it, the contributors to this collection write about their classroom practices from a common point of view, creating in a sense a shared "grammar" of the classroom. This approach then makes their accounts both very readable and, I would think, highly replicable by readers. Clearly, classroom teaching generally, and ELT teaching in particular, is coming of age as teachers explore what and how their students learn, and articulate the understandings that result from their explorations, as they do in this volume.'—Donald Freeman, Dean Language Teacher Education, School for International Training, USA

'ESL teachers in the United States and other English-speaking countries can make effective use of every chapter in the book'—Betty Lou Leaver, Dean, New York Institute of Technology in Amman, Jordan

'High quality, extremely readable and accessible ... I anticipate that this volume will be extremely popular with classroom teachers. I found it refreshing, and even exciting, to read accounts of professional practice by people who have not hitherto been widely published. The volume will be useful not only on MA courses but also on a wide range of in-service courses ... an exciting and innovative project.'—Professor David Nunan, The English Centre, Hong Kong

'Classroom teaching and learning ordinarily center on specific language tasks. Instruction becomes more effective when teachers understand the role of language tasks, recognize their students' needs, and apply both

types of information in a sound, creative way. With better task-based instruction as a goal, current and future teachers will benefit from the enlightening explorations in this book. In addition, researchers will find that this book can inform and enrich many classroom investigations.'
—Professor Rebecca Oxford, University of Maryland, USA

Teachers Exploring Tasks in English Language Teaching

Edited by

Corony Edwards
Senior Lecturer in Applied English Linguistics, Centre for English language Studies, University of Birmingham, UK

and

Jane Willis
Honorary Visiting Fellow, Department of Languages and European Studies, Aston University, UK

First published 2005 by
PALGRAVE MACMILLAN
Houndmills, Basingstoke, Hampshire RG21 6XS and
175 Fifth Avenue, New York, N.Y. 10010
Companies and representatives throughout the world.

PALGRAVE MACMILLAN is the global academic imprint of the Palgrave Macmillan division of St. Martin's Press, LLC and of Palgrave Macmillan Ltd. Macmillan® is a registered trademark in the United States, United Kingdom and other countries. Palgrave is registered trademark in the European Union and other countries.

ISBN 1–4039–4556–X hardback
ISBN 1–4039–4557–8 paperback

This book is printed on paper suitable for recycling and made from fully managed and sustained forest sources.

A catalogue record for this book is available from the British Library.

Library of Congress Cataloging-in-Publication Data
Teachers exploring tasks in English language teaching / edited by Corony Edwards, Jane Willis.
p.cm.
Includes bibliographical references and index.
ISBN 1–4039–4556–X (cloth)–ISBN 1–4039–4557–8 (paper)
1. English language – Study and teaching – Foreign speakers.
I. Edwards, Corony, 1959– II. Willis, Jane R. (Jane Rosemary), 1944–

PE1128.A2T373 2005
428'.071'1—dc22

2004048935

10 9 8 7 6 5 4 3 2 1
14 13 12 11 10 09 08 07 06 05

Transferred to Digital Printing in 2005

Contents

About the Contributors

Corony Edwards is from Britain and is a senior lecturer at the University of Birmingham where she is Director of Learning and Teaching for the School of Humanities, and a course tutor for their distance MA TES/FL programme. She has taught English language since 1986 and has run numerous EFL teacher training courses and workshops in the UK and many other countries. She is co-editor of *English Language Teacher Education and Development* journal, has published in academic journals and books, and has written conventional and web-based teacher development materials. In 2003 she was shortlisted for a National Teaching Fellowship Award.

Jane Willis is from Britain but has worked extensively overseas as an English teacher and trainer. She has written several prize-winning books including *A Framework for Task-based Learning* (Longman), and *English for Primary Teachers*, co-authored with Mary Slattery (OUP) and has edited, with Betty Lou Leaver, *Task-based Instruction in Foreign Language Education: practices and programs* (Georgetown University Press). She has recently retired from Aston University, Birmingham, UK, where she taught on their Masters in TESOL & TESP programmes. She continues to work as a writer and ELT consultant and travels widely.

Maggie Baigent is British, has an MSc in TESOL from Aston University and is currently working at the University of Bologna, teaching students of all levels. She carried out this research at the British Council, Bologna, Italy. She has contributed teaching materials to the coursebook series *Clockwise and Natural English* (OUP).

Gregory Charles Birch is from Canada and lives in Japan. He received his MSc in TESOL from Aston University. He currently works at Seisen Women's College. He completed this study while working at Nagano National College of Technology.

David Coulson is British (MA Japanese Studies, Essex University; MSc TESOL, Aston University) and works with lower intermediate levels and above in the British and American Studies Department of Niigata Women's College in north-west Japan. He is currently pursuing a PhD in vocabulary acquisition at Swansea University, UK.

David Cox is British and has an MSc in TESOL (Aston University). He has taught in Australia, Japan and the UK. He carried out the research for this paper when working for GEOS Language System in a school in Nara, Japan. He is now back in the UK where he is working on the opportunities offered by Webcam technology for language tuition.

Antigone Djapoura is Greek Cypriot and works in a Private Language Institute in Cyprus, teaching mainly 14–15-year-old learners. She holds an MA in TEFL/TESL from the University of Birmingham and loves being involved in anything that deals with the practical issues of teaching.

William Essig is from the USA and is currently teaching in a Japanese university in Osaka. He holds an MA TEFL/TESL from the University of Birmingham. His main interests include implementing TBL and developing practical materials for classroom use.

James Hobbs, from England, has an MSc in TESOL from Aston University. He now teaches at Iwate Medical University, but conducted this research while teaching lower-intermediate English major students at a private Japanese university. He is continuing research into various aspects of task-based learning.

Craig Johnston, from Canada, is working towards an MSc in TESOL from Aston University and teaches at Kansai Gaidai College in Osaka, Japan. He is interested in TBL and lexical approaches to language learning.

Patrick Kiernan is from Britain and has been an English teacher in Japan since 1990. He has an MA in TEFL/TESL from Birmingham University. He is now teaching at Tokyo Denki University and working on a cross-linguistic analysis of conversational narrative for his PhD studies in Applied Linguistics at Birmingham University.

Seung-Min Lee (Steve) is Korean and worked as a primary school teacher for 10 years. He has since become a teacher trainer and now works at the Korea National University of Education where he took his PhD in Primary English Education. He also has an MA in TES/TEFL (University of Birmingham).

Maria Leedham is from Britain. She has taught Japanese and mixed-nationality groups since working in Japan in 1989. She is now a teacher and teacher trainer at both Universities in Oxford and an MSc student at Aston University in Birmingham.

Lamprini Loumpourdi (Lana) is from Greece, where she has worked as a teacher in a private language institution for six years, teaching students of all ages and levels, preparing them for standardized exams. She has an MA in TEFL/TESL from Birmingham University and is currently working on a PhD at Aristotle University, Thessaloniki.

Jason Moser is from Canada. He has an MA in TES/TEFL from the University of Birmingham. He has lived in Japan for over eight years and works at a number of universities in Japan including Osaka University.

Theron Muller is from the USA and is currently working in Japan. He researched this report at 'English for You', a private language school in Nagano, Japan. He is pursuing his MA in TES/TEFL with the University of Birmingham.

Annamaria Pinter is from Britain. She has a PhD in the area of Teaching English to Young Learners from the University of Warwick, where she is currently working as a lecturer at the Centre for English Language Teacher Education (CELTE). Her previous experience was in Hungary, as an English teacher in the lower primary sector, and later as a teacher trainer.

Glen Poupore is a Canadian English Instructor, working in the Department of English, Konkuk University, Seoul, Korea and also for the Konkuk–Illinois Joint TESOL Certification Program, in Seoul. He is currently studying for a PhD in Applied Linguistics at the University of Birmingham.

Patricia Pullin Stark (MA TESOL London) is British. She works for Fribourg University in Switzerland, where she teaches undergraduates. Patricia is currently working on a PhD on social cohesion in workplace communication at Birmingham University.

Raymond Sheehan is from Ireland. He teaches at Higher Colleges of Technology in the United Arab Emirates. His learners are mostly beginner to intermediate level and have recently completed secondary education. He has an MA (NUI), an RSA Diploma in TEFL and an MSc in TESOL (Aston University).

Ali Shehadeh, from Syria, is associate professor at the Department of English, University of Aleppo, Syria, and currently at the College of Languages and Translation, King Saud University, Saudi Arabia. His areas of interest include SLA, teaching methodology and task-based learning and instruction. His work has appeared in the *English Teaching Forum, English Teaching Professional, ELT Journal, TESOL Quarterly, Language Learning,* and *System*. He is an external MA dissertation supervisor on the Open Distance Learning programme of The Centre for English Language Studies at the University of Birmingham.

List of Abbreviations

CAE	Certificate of Advanced English (UCLES Examination)
DDL	Data-driven Learning
EFL	English as a Foreign Language
ELT	English Language Teaching
ESP	English for Specific Purposes
FCE	First Certificate in English (Intermediate level UCLES examination)
IELTS	International English Language Testing Services (UK based language qualification)
L1	first language, mother tongue
L2	second language
NS	native speaker
OHT	overhead transparency/slide
PET	Preliminary English Test
PPP	Presentation, Practice, Production
SLA	Second Language Acquisition
STEP	Socio-cultural, Technological, Economic, and Political
SWOT	Strengths, Weaknesses, Opportunities, Threats
TBI	Task-Based Instruction
TBL	Task-Based Learning
TBLT	Task-Based Language Teaching
TEFL	Teaching English as a Foreign Language
TESOL	Teaching English to Speakers of Other Languages
TESP	Teaching English for Specific Purposes
TOEFL	Test of English as a Foreign Language (ED PSE CHECK) (US-based language qualification)
TT	Team-Talking
UCLES	University of Cambridge Local Examinations Syndicate

Key terms are highlighted in bold where they first appear in the text, or where they are glossed or defined. The references for these items also appear in bold in the index where there are multiple page references.

Acknowledgements

As joint editors, we have thoroughly enjoyed our collaboration on this project. We would like to thank our contributors for their perseverance, their patience and enthusiasm over the 18 months of drafting, writing, revising and checking their papers. Their co-operation has been outstanding.

The whole collection has greatly benefited from the feed-back and constructive suggestions of four anonymous readers who commented, some in great detail, on an early draft. Whoever you are, thank you! Thanks are also due to John Moorcroft for his initial advice in the planning stages, to Jill Lake for her thoughtful feed-back on a near final draft, and to Betty Lou Leaver, Donald Freeman, Rebecca Oxford and David Nunan for their encouraging words about the final script.

We are also grateful for the financial support of our respective Universities, Birmingham and Aston, which enabled us to employ Deborah Yuill of 'WordWright' to provide a thoroughly professional index.

Finally, we both would like to thank our respective husbands, Mohamed and Dave, for doing without us during our late nights at the office and the week-end days we spent at our computers.

Introduction: Aims and Explorations into Tasks and Task-based Teaching

Jane Willis

The aims of this book

This book was written by language teachers for language teachers, with a view to encouraging readers to use more tasks in their lessons, and to explore for themselves various aspects of task-based learning (TBL) and teaching. It gives insights into ways that tasks can be designed, adapted and implemented in a range of teaching contexts and will thus appeal to teachers with little or no previous experience of using tasks themselves. It also illustrates ways in which tasks and task-based learning can be investigated in order to make the whole experience richer and more rewarding. Teachers who are thinking of embarking on a Diploma or Masters course, either on-site or by distance learning, will find lots of useful ideas here for their own classroom-based projects and assignments. Each contributor ends their chapter with practical recommendations and/or advice for other teachers, and many list further ideas that can be carried out in language classes.

This book is not intended to be used as a manual of research techniques, nor is it a treatise on TBL. It makes no attempt to cover every type of task or research process. There are other books that do this. The strength of this book is that it illustrates a range of largely familiar tasks being implemented within various lesson frameworks, a variety of task-based programmes, and task investigations in action, all in normal classroom conditions. It also provides plentiful samples of data from task interactions. Its aims are to complement some of the more formal studies that have been conducted into the use of tasks, and to allow readers to see how other teachers have interpreted the concept of TBL within their own particular educational settings.

Nunan (1989b: 121) and Burns (1999: 181–213), as well as Freeman (1998), all recommend that teachers who carry out small-scale classroom research or action research projects should disseminate their findings. This collection is, in essence, doing just that. We therefore hope that it will serve not only to enrich readers' understanding of task-based approaches to language learning and teaching, but also to provide ideas and insights into exploring and researching classroom learning in a more general sense.

Who are the teachers?

All the teachers who have written for this collection began these particular explorations into tasks and TBL while studying, mostly by distance learning, on Masters programmes in TEFL or TESOL or TESP from English universities. Most contributors are from Aston University and Birmingham University, with one guest contributor from Warwick University. Being distance learners means that they remain in their teaching posts overseas while studying for their Masters degrees with guidance and support from their tutors, supervisors, colleagues and fellow Masters participants. This allowed them to explore their own classrooms as part of their normal teaching day.

Who are the learners and what are the tasks?

The learners taught by our contributors represent all ages and many different types of institution and educational backgrounds. To give an indication of this variety, here are some snapshot scenarios of the learners doing some of the tasks.

Primary age children in Hungary are looking at pictures of rooms in a doll's house and playing 'Spot the Differences' in pairs; others in Korea are listening to directions and drawing on to a street map the routes to various people's homes: a 'Describe and Draw' task. Groups of teenagers in Greece are designing a personality quiz in order to find out how brave people are. Japanese students in the UK, preparing for an oral examination, are doing a problem-solving task: they have a picture of a very bare student room and are deciding together the best way to embellish it. Business students in Switzerland are doing a web-based project: they have each analysed the strengths and weaknesses of an international company and are comparing results. Advanced learners in Italy share their experiences of storms and compare how they feel about them. Elementary adult students in Japan find out about their partner's families and friendships; a class of shy university students exchanges stories about embarrassing incidents that have happened to them, others are researching into Japanese culture as seen through different types of restaurant. In a women's college in Japan, students describe to another group, who then have to draw it unseen, a picture of a cheerful magician sawing his wife in half.

Some of these learners are new to task-based learning, yet all are fully engaged in the tasks they are doing. They are getting their meanings across as best they can in English, trying to understand what others are saying, helping each other as they work towards the agreed goals of the task, and subsequently sharing their experiences of doing the task.

What do we mean by task?

Several different definitions and uses of the term '**task**' exist throughout the literature, ranging from rather general to quite specific, and these are summarized in Chapter 1. Our contributors also use the word 'task' in slightly different ways. So what characteristics do the tasks in this book have in common?

- In carrying out a task the learners' principal focus is on exchanging and understanding meanings, rather than on practice of form or pre-specified forms or patterns.
- There is some kind of purpose or goal set for the task, so that learners know what they are expected to achieve by the end of the task, for example, to write a list of differences, to complete a route map or a picture, to report a solution to a problem, to vote on the best decorated student room or the most interesting/memorable personal anecdote.
- The outcome of the completed task can be shared in some way with others.
- Tasks can involve any or all four skills: listening, speaking, reading and writing.
- The use of tasks does not preclude language-focused study at some points in a TBL lesson, though a focus on specific grammar rules or patterns will not generally come before the task itself, as this could well detract from the real communicative purpose of the subsequent interaction.

What, then, would not count as 'tasks'? Activities requiring learners to use language patterns they have just been taught or been told to use, would not count as tasks in this sense, for example, completing a transformation exercise, acting out dialogues or taking part in role plays with set parts. The principle focus in such activities is not on learners expressing and exchanging their own meanings but on practising pre-specified language forms or functions and displaying their ability to 'produce' these patterns. (See Skehan, 1998: 95–6.)

The task characteristics listed above can apply to many different types of task. While there is no definitive way to classify tasks, a broad classification that is based on cognitive processes consists of six categories: listing tasks; ordering and sorting tasks; comparing tasks; problem solving tasks; sharing personal experiences; and creative tasks (see J. Willis, 1996a). The contributors to this collection have used a range of task-types in their studies. For example, Poupore (Chapter 19) investigates the effects that different types of problem solving tasks have on his students' language production, and Kiernan's students (Chapter 5) engage in narrative tasks where they share embarrassing personal experiences. Shehadeh, in Chapter 1, gives an overview of other ways in which task-types can be categorized for both teaching and research purposes.

The move towards Task-Based Learning (TBL)

In the countries and contexts represented in this book, English is being taught as a Foreign Language with a view to enhancing international communication. However, the examination systems in many of these countries often put a premium on formal accuracy and, as a result, teachers often prioritize the teaching of grammar. Teachers model the target language forms and get students to repeat them, and then ask questions intended to elicit the target forms in response, for example, *What time do you usually get up in the morning?* to elicit: *I usually get up at 7.15*. (Note that *'I don't know really, it depends.'* would not be an acceptable response in this situation.) This approach stems from behaviourist learning theories and the language thus produced is commonly called **'display' language**; students are expected to respond using a word or pattern that conforms to the teacher's expectation of the specific form to be used, rather than on conveying meaning or message (D. Willis, 1996b). The label given to one such approach is **Presentation, Practice, Production**, also known as **PPP**. (For an explanation and discussion of PPP see Shehadeh, Chapter 1 and D. Willis, 1996b: iv–v.) However, we all know that what is taught is not necessarily what is learned. And although PPP lessons are often supplemented with skills lessons, most students taught mainly through conventional approaches such as PPP leave school unable to communicate effectively in English (Stern, 1983). This situation has prompted many

ELT professionals to take note of the findings from second language acquisition (SLA) research studies (see Chapter 1) and to turn towards holistic approaches where meaning is central and where opportunities for language use abound. Task-based learning is one such approach and many of the writers in this book have moved from PPP to TBL. For a fuller account of the move towards TBL see J. Willis, 2004.

A brief overview of the book

The book begins with a chapter summarizing current theories underpinning task-based learning and teaching and reviewing some of the current literature on TBL. It ends with a chapter exploring how teachers – specifically the writers of this book – feel about doing classroom research in general, and presenting their reflections on their projects for this book in particular. It also gives a summary of research methods used in their explorations of tasks.

In between these two chapters there are four parts, A to D. These have been carefully sequenced, beginning with simple descriptions of practice and explorations of aspects of tasks with later chapters going deeper into research and theoretical issues.

Part A contains short accounts where teachers describe their experiences of using tasks in their lessons. These chapters provide models, or offer further ideas, for other similar types of task or TBL procedures.

Chapters in Parts B and C delve deeper, and each explores one particular aspect of tasks or task-based learning. These are illustrated with extracts of data from recordings of tasks in action, which give insights into the ways learners interact with each other and into the use of language in tasks. The procedures followed are clearly described, so that readers could carry out parallel investigations or explore similar features.

Chapters in Part D research the effects of different task types or of different stages in a task-based lesson, and also look at what happens when teachers change the way in which they set up their tasks.

Table 1 at the end of this Introduction describes in more detail what each teacher investigated and why, thus giving a more detailed overview of the whole book.

Routes through the book: from theory to practice or practice to theory?

This is a book you can dip into and read in any order – how you approach it will depend upon where your interests lie, what is of most relevance to your teaching context and what is best for your own professional development at this point in your career.

If you want to broaden and deepen your understanding of the current theories and rationale supporting TBL, start with Chapter 1, and then read other chapters, thus working from theory into practice. This route would help you appreciate the theories and rationale underlying each chapter which are not explicitly stated in the chapters themselves.

But if you are fairly new to the practical side of task-based learning, you might like to start with Part A and gain insights into different practices in TBL. These would form a useful base for understanding the rationale and reflecting on the relevance of theories when you go back and read Chapter 1.

If you have limited time or want to select chapters that are most applicable to your teaching context, we suggest you read the overview in Table 1 which follows this Introduction. If you want to read chapters which use particular types of research methods, you can begin with Appendix 2 at the end of the Epilogue.

Classroom research and action research – what could you do?

With the exception of the first and last chapters, all the contributions to this volume could be considered as examples of classroom research and are mainly qualitative in nature, in that they tend to describe and analyse rather than count and quantify. **Classroom research** does not entail a specific approach or set of techniques; as Nunan (1992: 91) says, it is 'a research context ... rather than ... a particular method'. Indeed, methods described by Nunan (*ibid.*) range from formal experiments to techniques to stimulate recall of events, to observation schemes, with the only common element being that they are conducted in or about classrooms. Some of the teachers in this volume, eg Loumpourdi, Chapter 2, report on informal, small-scale explorations of practice or experiments in their classrooms with little formal data collection, not 'research' in the sense that some would recognize it, but nevertheless moving towards this (this issue is discussed in Edwards, Epilogue). Others, eg Poupore in Chapter 19, use a much more systematic and formalized approach, recording and transcribing data prior to analysis. Others still, eg Moser, Chapter 7, adopt an **action research** cycle, setting out to investigate and solve a particular challenge or problem by following a series of stages, which can be described simply as: develop an action plan to improve a situation; act to implement the plan; observe the effects of action; reflect on these effects; repeat the cycle (see Wallace, 1998 or Burns, 1999 or Edge, 2001 for a fuller account of action research).

Some teachers in this book have used several methods to investigate what is going on in their lessons (Appendix 2 of the Epilogue gives a complete list). These range from informal to more formal methods, and are qualitative in approach.

Informal research methods would include such things as

- observing how learners react to the task instructions,
- watching group interaction to see if all learners are taking part,
- discussing with the class after a task cycle what they thought about the task.

By making notes after (or even during) the lesson on what you observed, or of what students said about the task, you are beginning to make it a little more formal. If you keep a notebook where you regularly write down your observations, you can read back through it after a period of time, reflect on it and begin to notice patterns of responses or behaviours. This is the beginning of real research, and where it starts to get interesting.

To find out more accurately what learners thought of a task, you may need to get individual feedback. Even primary learners can draw smiley faces or unhappy faces on a small slip of paper that they fold and pass up to you. Older learners can be asked to write how they did the task, or to put two things they liked about doing the task and one thing they did not like (tell them they need not put their names). You will need to record the results each time in your note-book, and make sure you include the date, type of task and other details that might be significant.

Such note-books are sometimes referred to as teacher journals. However, in this book, one teacher, Moser (Chapter 7), got his learners to write their own 'learning journal' during the course of each task-based lesson. This showed him how far they understood where they were in the task cycle, and what language they were trying to work with.

More **formal research** methods include

- interviews with learners to get individual feed-back, but this can be time-consuming and learners may be too shy to say what they really think, especially if you are recording the interview,
- questionnaires; these are often used by institutions to get general course feedback, as mentioned by Moser. They can also be used for specific investigations, as in Edwards, Epilogue, However, they are not easy to design and need very careful piloting before being used to gather data.

- recording lessons or parts of lessons, on audio or on video, and then transcribing and analysing relevant extracts.

All these methods and others are fully described in Holliday (2002) and Richards (2003) who both give excellent introductions to this kind of qualitative inquiry and contrast this with quantitative studies. The latter tend to be more formal studies involving statistical measures which necessitate controlling variables in order to make formal comparisons or to prove something specific. This has not been a main objective of any of the studies in this collection, which aim simply to shed light on and deepen our understanding of what happens in TBL in our specific contexts.

One way of beginning to do research is to replicate someone else's research project with your own learners. This is called a replication study. You use the same methods as the original researcher did and find out whether your results were similar to or different from the original study. In this book, Djapoura's study replicates aspects of Foster's 1996 study on the effects of allowing learners pre-task planning time on their task performance.

What methods you use depend partly on what aspects you are interested in investigating. If you are interested in finding out what language is used during the task, or in studying aspects of your learners' interaction, you will need to get your students accustomed to being recorded, or even to tape-recording themselves. Many teachers in this book have done this with interesting results, as you will notice when you see the extracts from their data.

So, as you read the chapters in this book, make a note of what methods the teachers used to gather their data, and what they thought of these. Notice too how the transcriptions and analyses have been done. Reflect on what methods you and/or your colleagues might use. Above all, reflect on what aspects of task-based learning and teaching you, or your learners, think would be interesting to explore.

Over to you

We hope you will enjoy this book as much as we all enjoyed exploring the tasks and writing the chapters. Through reading each others' chapters we, as writers, have all gained a deeper understanding of task-based learning and teaching, and we hope you will too. We also hope (three *hopes* for luck!) that you will feel inspired to experiment in your classes and contribute to the ever-growing and much needed field of research into tasks in language teaching.

If you wish to select chapters to read on the basis of one or more of themes that recur throughout the book, refer to the codes in the second column.

Key to theme codes

Sp&L = speaking & listening tasks
Gr = grammar/Focus on form
Real = 'real-life' tasks
Wr&R = writing & reading tasks
Lex = vocabulary/lexis
Sel = selecting tasks
Com = communication skills & strategies
YL = young learners
Type = exploring task types
Low = low level learners
Var = exploring task variables

Table 1 Summary of the projects

Who did this?	Themes	What did they investigate, and why?
Chapter 2 Lamprini (Lana) Loumpourdi	Gr Sel Var	Lana had noticed that using traditional approaches to teaching grammar confused and bored her students so she wanted to change things a bit. She didn't want to do a formal study, just to make changes in her grammar classes by trying something new (getting students to create quiz questions with multiple choice answers) and observing how well this worked.
Chapter 3 Patricia Pullin Stark	Sp&L Wr&R Real	Patricia was involved in designing a new syllabus for business students, and she incorporated a number of longer, project- type task sequences into this. Like Lana and Theron, she was doing what she would do anyway in the course of her work, the only difference being that she decided to write up what she did as a report.
Chapter 4 Raymond Sheehan	Gr	Raymond found that conventional reference works like grammar books were often unsatisfactory when it came to answering students' linguistic queries, so he wanted to try out using concordances as an alternative.
Chapter 5 Patrick Kiernan	Sp&L Real	Patrick wanted to investigate whether storytelling tasks would help his low level learners develop their fluency and confidence to speak in English. He planned from the outset to record the students' performances throughout the project. Although this is another example of a teacher designing activities to meet his students' needs, it also bears some trademarks of more formal research because of his systematic recording and analysis of data.

Table 1 Continued

Who did this?	Themes	What did they investigate, and why?
Chapter 6 Theron Muller	Sp&L Gr Low Sel	Theron wanted to move away from the PPP approach that prevailed in the set textbook he was using for his beginner level conversation class. Without the time to design new materials from scratch, he decided to adapt units from the book to incorporate tasks.
Chapter 7 Jason Moser	Sp&L Wr&R Gr	Jason felt that in his speaking classes, his students tended to neglect language form for the sake of meaning. He devised a 'lesson journal' sheet that, by requiring them to take notes at each stage of the lesson, drew the students' attention to form. Jason describes his project as *action research*, and in his report we clearly see the plan, act, observe and reflect stages that he went through (although he only reports on one such cycle, instead of the more usual series of cycles typical of action research).
Chapter 8 Maria Leedham	Sp&L Gr Com Var	Maria noticed that her Japanese students employed unusually long turns, often speaking in complete sentences, when practicing for their First Certificate in English speaking exam. This gave an unnatural effect. To help them become aware that this is not how people usually interact in English, she had them compare transcripts of themselves doing tasks with those of native speakers of English, before giving them a chance to repeat the task.
Chapter 9 Seung-Min Lee	Sp&L Com YL	Seung-Min had observed that his young learners tended not to use meaning negotiation skills when they did speaking tasks in English classes, which seemed to lead to communication problems. He set up an experiment to see if teaching such skills had a positive effect on their subsequent task performance. Since he had both an experimental group (who received training) and a control group (who received no training), whom he could compare, his study clearly falls in to the 'formal research' category.
Chapter 10 Annamaria Pinter	Com YL Low Var	Annamaria was interested in the effects of repeating tasks with her young learners. She had read about other studies that did this, but realized that these had been carried out with relatively high level, adult learners. She wanted to do a similar study to see if young, low level learners would benefit in the same way as the adults had.

Chapter 11 David Coulson	Sp&L Com Real	David had sent his students out on an assignment to converse with other international students on their campus, but they came back complaining that their more proficient interlocutors would 'take over' the conversations. To investigate what was happening, David got the students to record their attempted conversations, and noticed that in some cases, groups of his Japanese students were working together to try to maintain the conversation collaboratively. This seemed a good strategy, so he developed this idea of 'Team-Talking' with his class, and recorded the results.
Chapter 12 James Hobbs	Sp&L Lex	James had observed that when his learners did tasks, they often failed to use the sorts of interactive phrases normally used by fluent speakers. Instead, they reverted to their native Japanese to request repetition, comment on an answer, etc. Rather than relying on his native intuition of what phrases they needed to do this in English he recorded native speakers doing tasks, and from his recordings identified all the interactive phrases. He was then able to use these as the basis for a syllabus of interactive phrases.
Chapter 13 Maggie Baigent	Sp&L Lex Type	Maggie had read about the use of multi-word chunks by fluent speakers. She felt that her advanced level students (L1 Italian) were handicapped in their production of natural-sounding spoken English by a lack of these, so she wanted to find out if her hunch was correct. She recorded some of her learners, so she could compare the results with those for native speakers doing the same task.
Chapter 14 David Cox	Gr Lex	David was intrigued by the claim that in genuine tasks, the language needed to perform the task cannot be predicted. He tested this by asking a number of experienced teachers to predict the language they would expect to be used for five tasks, and compared their predictions with the language actually produced when native speakers did the tasks.
Chapter 15 Craig Johnston	Sp&L Gr	Craig had read that including a public report stage in a task-based lesson is meant to help learners improve the quality of their language output. He wanted to see if this was true for his students, who tended to complete tasks using various communication strategies that in some cases meant they hardly used English at all. He compared recordings of them doing tasks, and later giving their reports of these tasks, to see if there was any difference in the quality of their spoken language in the two stages.

Table 1 Continued

Who did this?	Themes	What did they investigate, and why?
Chapter 16 William Essig	Sp&L Real Var	Bill, like Craig, wanted to investigate how far the claims made for task-based learning held true with his students, this time with story-telling tasks. He came up with eight hypotheses concerning the effects of task repetition, planning time and context, and to test these he set up an experiment involving two groups of students, telling and retelling stories under different conditions (one group did this in private, the other in public). Bill recorded all these tasks so he could see if his hypotheses were correct.
Chapter 17 Antigone Djapoura	Sp&L Var	Antigone was also inspired to test one of the claims made for tasks, but this time in relation to the supposed benefits of pre-task planning time and instruction. She divided her class into three groups, which each did three tasks, once each with no planning, unguided planning, and guided planning. Antigone compared the nine transcribed recordings of the groups doing the tasks to find out whether her four hypotheses concerning planned and guided tasks were correct.
Chapter 18 Greg Birch	Sp&L Gr Low Sel Var	Greg was keen to see whether Skehan's suggestion, that selecting tasks with particular characteristics can direct students' attention to either accuracy, or fluency, or complexity of language, worked with his large class of false-beginners. He recorded some of his students doing two different tasks, with different groups doing these under different conditions, so he could look for any differences in the quality of output.
Chapter 19 Glen Poupore	Sp&L Com Type	Glen had been encouraged by his students' positive response to a task-based approach, but he wanted to know if it was really helping their language development. To find out, he devised a study in which his students did a number of different types of task, and looked at the recordings of these to see if they contained any instances of the types of interaction that may be indicative of second language acquisition in progress. Glen links his analysis closely with published theory and research reports, and makes some interesting new observations in relation to these.

1

Task-based Language Learning and Teaching: Theories and Applications

Ali Shehadeh

Background: does teaching lead to learning?

Task-based language teaching is not new. Prabhu[1] used a task-based approach with secondary school classes in Bangalore, India, on his Communicational Teaching Project, beginning in 1979. American Government Language Institutions switched to task-based instruction (TBI) for foreign languages for adults in the early 1980s.[2] Some of the teachers writing for this book have been using task-based learning (TBL) for many years and all are convinced of its value. Other teachers and institutions are following suit. So why are people making this change to TBL?

It is often because they realize that most language learners taught by methods that emphasize mastery of grammar do not achieve an acceptable level of competency in the target language. Language learning in the classroom is usually based on the belief that language is a system of wordings governed by a grammar and a lexicon. However it is more productive to see language primarily as a meaning system. Halliday's (1975) description of his young son's acquisition of his first language is significantly entitled *Learning How to Mean*. We need to recognize that learners are also striving to mean. In the process of these strivings they are prompted to develop a lexico-grammar that will enable them to realize the meanings they want. Without this incentive they are much less likely to develop a usable language system. Furthermore, it is commonly accepted that it is the process of struggling to communicate that stimulates language development. However, even so-called meaning-based, 'communicative' syllabuses, such as functional, situational, thematic or content syllabuses, are often no more effective than structural syllabuses in achieving satisfactory results when delivered via a presentation methodology (see below).

Apart from highly gifted and motivated students, most learners working within a structure-based approach fail to attain a usable level of fluency and proficiency in the second language (L2) even after years of instruction (Skehan, 1996b: 18). In India, Prabhu (1987: 11) notes that the structure-based courses required 'a good deal of remedial re-teaching which, in turn, led to similarly unsatisfactory results', with school leavers unable to deploy the English they had been taught, even though many could form grammatically correct sentences in the classroom. American Government Language Institutions found that with task-based instruction and authentic materials, learners made far more rapid progress and were able to use their new foreign language in real-world circumstances with a reasonable level of efficiency after quite short courses. They were able to operate an effective meaning system, ie to express what they wanted to say, even though their grammar and lexis were often far from perfect (Leaver and Kaplan, forthcoming 2004).

There are several types of form-based instruction, but in Europe, as well as other countries like Brazil,[3] there is one established approach to second language teaching which is, as Loumpourdi explains in Chapter 2, 'well established and difficult to shake'. Commonly referred to as **PPP**, this advocates three stages for teaching new language: **presentation**, **practice** and **production**. **Presentation** often focuses on a single point of grammar, or the realization of a function, usually presented explicitly in a context. This stage is assumed to develop an understanding of the language point in the learner. Presentation is followed by **controlled practice**, presumed to enable learners to use and automatize the newly grasped rule or pattern. At the **production** stage, often called the **'free stage'**, the learner is expected to reproduce the target language more spontaneously and flexibly, for example in a communication task or a role-play activity. But as J. Willis (1996a: 135) points out:

> The irony is that the goal of the final P – free production – is often not achieved. How can production be free if students are required to produce forms that have been specified in advance?

As many practitioners have noticed, one of two things happens at this production stage: either learners 'conform' to teachers' wishes (Willis, D. 1996a) and focus primarily on form, making sentences with the new item (paramount to continuing with the second Practice stage) or they focus primarily on meaning and often accomplish the task successfully without incorporating the new item at all. Interestingly, the latter situation provides an excellent argument for TBL: why not then start with the task, let learners deploy whatever language they have already, and look for ways of building on that, of improving and expanding on their current language capabilities (Willis. D., 2003). This is a far more positive proposition.

So far we have looked at aspects of *teaching*. But what about language *learning?* Grammar-based (structural) approaches have also been criticized in that they are not based on sound theoretical background or empirical evidence. PPP is based on the assumption that students will learn what is taught in the same order in which it was taught, but there is no evidence that this happens (Skehan, 1996b: 18). Indeed, second language acquisition (SLA) research has shown that teaching does not determine the way the learners' language will develop. Insights obtained from SLA research show that the strategies and cognitive processes employed by learners are largely independent of the way learners are taught. Therefore, the rationale that teaching a particular grammar point leads to learning no longer carries much credibility. Instead, the current view posits that language learning is largely determined by learner-internal, rather than external, factors. For instance, Skehan (1996a: 18) points out that:

> The contemporary view of language development is that learning is constrained by internal processes. Learners do not simply acquire the language to which they are exposed, however carefully that the exposure may be orchestrated by the teacher. It is not simply a matter of converting input into output.

According to this view learning is promoted by activating acquisition processes in learners. What is needed, therefore, is an approach to L2 learning and teaching that provides a context that activates these processes.

Rationale for task-based language teaching

Task-based language teaching (TBLT) proposes the use of tasks as a central component in the language classroom because they provide better contexts for activating learner acquisition processes and promoting L2 learning. TBLT is thus based on a theory of language learning rather than a theory of language structure. Richards and Rodgers (2001: 228) suggest that this is because 'tasks are believed to foster processes of negotiation, modification, rephrasing, and experimentation that are at the heart of second language learning.' These are processes mentioned by several writers in Part D of this book, especially Poupore, Chapter 19.

What are, then, the basic assumptions of TBLT? Feez (1998: 17) summarizes these as follows:

- The focus of instruction is on process rather than product.
- Basic elements are purposeful activities and tasks that emphasize communication and meaning.
- Learners learn language by interacting communicatively and purposefully while engaged in meaningful activities and tasks.
- Activities and tasks can be either:
  - those that learners might need to achieve in real life (see Sheehan, Chapter 4);
  - those that have a pedagogical purpose specific to the classroom.
- Activities and tasks of a task-based syllabus can be sequenced according to difficulty.
- The difficulty of a task depends on a range of factors including the previous experience of the learner, the complexity of the tasks, and the degree of support available. (Quoted in Richards and Rodgers, 2001: 224.)

TBLT initially emphasized fluency in communication at the expense of other aspects of language like accuracy and complexity (as did Krashen and Terrell's 1983 Natural Approach, and Prabhu's (1987) arguments against an explicit focus on grammar). It was thought that the ability to use the L2 (knowing how) would develop automatically, hence the experiments with immersion classes in Canada (Swain 1988), where English-speaking children were educated in French-speaking schools to allow them to acquire French naturally. However, it was found that they needed to be encouraged to focus on various points of grammar to achieve the level of accuracy required.

So this position was challenged; a **focus on form** and **grammar** is now seen as essential for efficient learning and effective communication. For example, Nunan (1989a: 13) states that 'there is value in language activities which require learners to focus on form [and that] grammar is an essential resource in using language communicatively.' Several papers in this volume also emphasize the importance of focus on form for language learning (see, eg, Loumpourdi, Chapter 2; Moser, Chapter 7; Johnston, Chapter 15).

Indeed, TBLT with a focus on form (in the context of meaning) is gathering support from SLA research. Long and Robinson (1998), in particular, stress the importance of focus on form for L2 learning by drawing students' attention to linguistic elements, not as discrete items presented to the learner, but as they arise in a meaningful classroom context. Long and Robinson define focus on form as 'consists[ing] of an occasional shift of attention to linguistic code features ... triggered by perceived problems with comprehension or production' (*ibid.* 23). Focus on form (manifestations of which include *consciousness-raising, form-focused instruction*, or *form-focused intervention*) can also incorporate the modified conversational interactions intended to achieve message comprehensibility by drawing students' attention to relationships of L2 form, meaning, and function (Pica, 2001).

In fact, it is now widely accepted that learning partly depends on learners' ability to attend to the relevant language features (Harley, 1998), to restructure knowledge (Dekeyser, 1998), to focus on form when learners notice a 'hole' or gap in their interlanguage. The term ***interlanguage*** refers to the underlying language system used by the second/foreign language learner at any particular stage in the process of learning the target foreign language (Doughty and Williams, 1998). Learning may also depend on the extent to which noticing is learner-initiated (Long and Robinson, 1998). In other words, all these researchers hold the view that drawing learners' attention to the formal properties of the L2 is also important for language learning, but only if it is done while maintaining emphasis on meaning, communication and fluency. This assumption constitutes one of the basic premises of task-based language teaching.

'Task' defined

Before we proceed to look at the different perspectives and research findings pertaining to task-based learning, we must first specify as clearly as possible what we mean by '**task**'. In her introduction, Jane Willis offers six broad characteristics of tasks. But as we can see from the papers in this book, there is no single definition for 'task'. Ellis (2003: 2–9), for example, offers nine sample definitions. This is because the study and description of task has been approached from different perspectives and for different purposes.

Second language acquisition researchers describe tasks in terms of their usefulness for collecting data and eliciting samples of learners' language for research purposes. For example, Bialystok (1983: 103) suggests that a communication task must (a) stimulate real communicative exchange, (b) provide incentive for the L2 speaker/learner to convey information, (c) provide control for the information items required for investigation and (d) fulfil the needs to be used for the goals of the experiment. Similarly, Pica (1989) argues that tasks should be developed in such as way to 'meet criteria for information control, information flow and goals of the study.'

Others look at tasks from a purely classroom interaction perspective. Some definitions of a classroom task are very specific. For instance, J. Willis (1996b: 53) defines a classroom task as 'a goal-oriented activity in which learners use language to achieve a real outcome.' Willis also suggests that language use in tasks is likely to reflect language use in the outside world. Other definitions are more general. Nunan's (1989a) is one of the most commonly cited pedagogical definitions of a classroom task. Nunan proposes that a communication task

> ... is a piece of classroom work which involves learners in comprehending, manipulating, producing, or interacting in the target language while their attention is principally focused on meaning rather than form (Nunan, 1989a: 10).

Long and Crookes (1991) argue that in addition to being meaning-oriented, classroom tasks must also have a clear relationship with real-world contexts of language use and language need (see Kiernan, Chapter 5).

Skehan (1996a: 20) views classroom and L2 research tasks as 'activities which have meaning as their primary focus. Success in the task is evaluated in terms of achievement of an outcome, and tasks generally bear some resemblance to real-life language use'. Ellis (2003: 9–10) lists six 'criterial features of a task'. He mentions all the aspects listed by Skehan above, and also includes the concept of task as a 'workplan for learner activity', which 'requires learners to employ cognitive processes', and 'can involve any of the four language skills'.

While there is no clear agreement on what should constitute an overarching definition of a task, a consensus seems to be emerging over the central characteristics, in particular for pedagogic (as opposed to purely research) tasks. Although the contributors to this collection use the term **'task'** in a number of slightly different ways, we can use the following as our basic definition:

A language learning task is

- an activity
- that has a non-linguistic purpose or goal

- with a clear outcome
- and that uses any or all of the four language skills in its accomplishment
- by conveying meaning in a way that reflects real-world language use

Task types, task variables and task dimensions

When designing or selecting tasks for use in the language classroom teachers have a number of choices to make in terms of the type of task, the conditions under which students complete the task, and other task properties. Some of these options will be more effective than others. Classroom research into tasks often aims to find out the effects of specific task properties. Ellis (2000: 194) states that 'information about significant task variables acquired through research can assist teachers in deciding what tasks to use and when'. In other words, findings of research into the study of tasks can provide teachers with insights that enable them to make language teaching more effective. In addition, as useful ways of classifying task types emerge, we will be a step further towards establishing the basis on which a task-based syllabus might be effectively organized, a point we return to in the conclusion to this chapter.

Task types can be identified in a number of ways. For example, Nunan (1989a) suggests two broad categories: **real-world tasks** (such as using the telephone) and **pedagogic tasks** (such as information gap activities). These can be further subdivided into other categories, by language function (eg giving instructions, apologizing, making suggestions), or by cognitive processes or knowledge hierarchies (eg listing, ordering and sorting, problem solving, being creative; see J. Willis, 1996a and the introduction to this volume). Others might classify tasks by topic, by the language skills required for completion, or by whether the outcome is **closed** or **open** (sometimes called **divergent** and **convergent** tasks; Long, 1989). Pica, Kanagy and Falodun (1993) take as their starting point the type of interaction that occurs during task completion, eg **one-way** or **two-way** information flow, resulting in five types: jigsaw tasks, information gaps, problem-solving, decision-making, opinion exchange. Richards and Rodgers (2001: 233–5) catalogue others. Distinguishing different task types is important, as it allows researchers to investigate which types most effectively promote learning. In this volume, Baigent (Chapter 13) compares the relative effects of experience-sharing tasks and problem-solving tasks on learners' production of lexical and discourse-organizing chunks; Poupore (Chapter 19) examines the types of interactions that occur during completion of problem solving and jigsaw tasks, and relates these to theories of how such interactions contribute to SLA.

In addition to task types, there are also a number of **task variables** that can be studied. These include task characteristics such as whether the task is structured (eg by providing a series of prompts to direct the interaction, thus assisting task completion), cognitive difficulty and familiarity of the task (including the amount of previous practise of the task-type or repetition of the same or similar tasks). The conditions under which tasks are performed can also be adjusted. Interlocutor familiarity, whether the interlocutor is a native or non-native speaker, planning time and performance conditions (eg public or private) are all examples (see Wigglesworth, 2001: 186 and 190–1). A number of the studies reported in this collection investigate task variables: Kiernan, Leedham, Pinter and Essig all consider an aspect of task repetition, while Essig and Djapoura look into the effects of planning time.

A slightly different way of looking at task characteristics is to see these in terms of a number variable, interacting groups of factors. Robinson (2001: 287) proposes three such groups of factors, which together constitute a set of criteria that can be adopted to design tasks with progressively increasing demands. The resulting triadic framework can also be used for designing research into task characteristics. Robinson distinguishes '**task *complexity*** (the task dependent and proactively manipulable cognitive demands of tasks)' such as planning and reasoning demands, from '**task *difficulty*** (dependent on learner factors such as aptitude, confidence, motivation, etc.) and **task *conditions*** (the interactive demands of tasks)', such as familiarity of participants and whether tasks require one-way or two-way information flow. These three groups of factors 'interact to influence task performance, and learning' (*ibid.* 293–4). Furthermore, the factors that contribute to task *complexity* are represented by Robinson as **dimensions**, or in some cases, continuums, 'along which relatively more of a feature is present or absent' (*ibid.* 293–4). For example, narratives may range from simple to complex, topics from familiar to unfamiliar, and tasks may be completed under variable time limits. The concept of task dimensions is one which Kiernan (Chapter 5) finds useful when investigating his story-telling tasks.

Perspectives to task-based learning

Researchers have approached task-based learning differently and from different perspectives. Some researchers have examined tasks from an interaction perspective, others from an output perspective, others from a cognitive perspective, and still others from a socio-cultural perspective. This section will briefly summarize the main perspectives of studies of task-based learning along with their rationales and their main research findings.

The interaction hypothesis perspective

According to the **interaction hypothesis**, negotiation of meaning provides learners with opportunities for both the provision of **comprehensible input** and the production of **modified output**. These are both believed to be necessary for language development. In particular, Long (1983b, 1996) argues that exchange of information gives learners the opportunity to receive feedback on the level of their comprehension in the L2. This results in negotiated modification of conversation which renders the subsequent interaction more understandable, ie it becomes comprehensible input (Krashen, 1985). Long further argues that negotiation serves to draw learners' attention to linguistic form as they attempt to produce the target language. This attention to linguistic form is believed to be necessary for L2 learning because it creates a favourable context for the negotiation of meaning that 'serves as the means by which learners' 'data needs' can be effectively met' (Ellis, 2000: 199). Tasks can stimulate negotiation of meaning (as exemplified in Lee's Chapter 9 and Poupore's Chapter 19), and thus, it is argued, can provide the conditions necessary for language development to occur.

Research working in this paradigm has sought to identify how the different task types, variables and dimensions may affect the negotiation of meaning, interlanguage modification and feedback to learner output (Pica, Kanagy and Falodun, 1993; see also Poupore, Chapter 19), and on occasions has been able to demonstrate that negotiation does indeed appear to promote L2 acquisition (eg Ellis, Tanaka and Yamazaki, 1994).

Ellis (2003: 79–83) goes into more detail on the interaction hypothesis and negotiation of meaning, and also offers some challenging criticism of this. However, some principles of the interaction hypothesis have been shown to be effective not just with adults and older learners, but with children and younger learners as well (see Lee, Chapter 9).

The output hypothesis perspective

The **output hypothesis** posits that learner output (ie the language a learner produces) must be considered not just a sign of acquired knowledge (Krashen, 1985), but also a sign of learning at work (Swain, 1998, 2000). That is, output is not just a product of acquisition that has already taken place or a means by which to practice one's language for greater fluency, but rather it plays a potentially important role in the acquisition process (Izumi, 2002; Swain, 1998, 2000). Swain, in particular, argues that output 'forces' learners to move from semantic analysis of the target language to a more syntactic analysis of it, to test out hypotheses about the target language, and to reflect consciously on the language they are producing (Swain, 1998: 79). In so doing, learners notice a gap between what they can say and what they want to say, which prompts them to stretch their current interlanguage capacity in order to fill the gap, 'enabling them to control and internalise linguistic knowledge' (Swain, 1995: 126). The language produced as a result of this stretched interlanguage is referred to by Swain as '**pushed output**'. Thus, it is argued that 'the importance of output in learning may be construed in terms of the learners' active deployment of their cognitive resources. [That is,] output requirement presents learners with unique opportunities to process language that may not be decisively necessary for simple comprehension' Izumi (2002: 545).

Research conducted within this theoretical framework has examined, amongst other things, how the different task-types and dimensions can have an impact on the negotiation of meaning, negotiation of form, and opportunities for learners' production of modified/comprehensible output (see Birch, Chapter 18; Poupore, Chapter 19). Researchers have been able to demonstrate that task-type does provide learners with varied opportunities toward modified output (eg Iwashita, 1999; Pica, Holliday, Lewis and Morgenthaler, 1989; Shehadeh, 1999; Swain, 1997; Swain and Lapkin, 1998). Iwashita (1999) for example found that one-way tasks provided learners with greater opportunities to modify their output toward comprehensibility than two-way tasks. Similarly, Shehadeh (1999) found that a picture-description task (one-way task) provided significantly greater opportunities than an opinion-exchange task (two-way task) toward modified output.

Similarly, in a series of studies Swain and her colleagues (eg Swain and Lapkin, 1998) have demonstrated that students were able to solve linguistic problems jointly by negotiating target language forms during the process of achieving a communicative task goal, by determining which form to use in order best to convey their message accurately and coherently (see also Pullin Stark, Chapter 3; Poupore, Chapter 19). Further, it was also found that the solutions reached during collaborative dialogues were retained in the learners' interlanguage system (Swain, 1997). These findings can be interpreted as meaning that if learners' production of modified output was found to be integral to successful

L2 learning (as suggested by Swain, 1998; Swain and Lapkin, 1995), the different task-types, variables and dimensions would have varying effects on the progress and development of the learners' L2 development because they have varying effects on the opportunities for the learners' negotiation of meaning, negotiation of form and learners' output modifications. Indeed, a number of papers in this volume have shown that planning time, task-repetition, and public report (Essig, Chapter 16), task-type and task features (Kiernan, Chapter 6; Poupore, Chapter 19) can considerably affect the comprehensibility of learner output.

Skehan's cognitive perspective

As mentioned by several writers in this volume, Skehan (1998) distinguishes between three aspects of learner performance: fluency, accuracy and complexity. **Fluency** refers to the learner's capacity to communicate in real time, **accuracy** to the ability of the learner to use the target language according to its norms, and **complexity** to the learners' ability to use more elaborate and complex target language structures. Skehan argues that these three aspects of performance can be influenced by engaging learners in different types of production and communication. So, for example, if we want to promote fluency in the learner, we should get the learner engaged in meaning-oriented tasks; conversely, if we want to promote accuracy or complexity in the learner, we should get him/her involved in more form-focused tasks.

What must be done, then, is to discover what task-types, variables and dimensions promote fluency, accuracy or complexity in L2 learners and use these accordingly. Based on his 'cognitive' approach framework and findings from previous experimental studies, Skehan (1998: 129) proposes the following five principles that constitute a model for task-based instruction:

1. Choose a range of target structures.
2. Choose tasks which meet the **utility criterion** (Utility: 'where the use of a particular structure would help the efficiency of the completion of the task, but could be avoided through the use of alternative structures or perhaps through the use of communication strategies (Skehan, 1998: 122)').
3. Select and sequence tasks to achieve balanced goal development.
4. Maximize the chances of focus on form through attentional manipulation.
5. Use **cycles of accountability** ('draw learners into consciously engaging in cycles of evaluation'; Skehan, 1998: 122).

Skehan argues that these principles meet criteria that relate to both effective communication (fluency and accuracy) and to facilitating progress and development of the L2 (complexity): 'These [principles] ... offer some prospects for the systematic development of underlying interlanguage and effective communicative performance' (Skehan 1998: 129).

Several papers in this volume have explored how task-based instruction can promote fluency, accuracy and complexity in learners. For example, Loumpourdi (Chapter 2) found that task-based grammar activities seemed to promote both fluency and accuracy; Muller (Chapter 6), Pullin Stark (Chapter 3), and Coulson (Chapter 11) suggest ways of promoting complexity and the quality of learner output; whereas Djapora (Chapter 17) and Birch (Chapter 18) found that planning time and task-type, respectively, can have a positive effect on fluency, accuracy and complexity of learner language. Johnston (Chapter 15) concludes that planning time and the report phase not only promote accuracy and complexity, but can also fight fossilization.

The socio-cultural perspective

Unlike the perspectives illustrated above, **socio-cultural theory** proposes that learners collaboratively construct knowledge as a joint activity. Activities that learners engage in are co-constructed according to the learners' socio-cultural history and the locally determined goals of these activities. It has been argued that such **co-construction of knowledge** engages learners in cognitive processes that are implicated in L2 learning (Lantolf, 1996).

This perspective, originally inspired by the works of Vygotsky (1987), looks at how tasks are jointly accomplished by learners, and how the process of accomplishing a task can contribute to L2 learning. According to Vygotsky, **dialogic interaction** is an important trigger for language learning. Vygotsky argues that external, social activities in which the learner participates are the main source of mental/cognitive activities. When individuals interact with other people, their cognitive processes awaken. These processes, which occur on the **inter-psychological** (or social) **plane**, are believed to include both cognitive development and language development. Vygotsky further argues that this language development moves from the social plane to the individual's internal mental plane on the assumption that what originates in the social (inter-psychological) sphere will eventually be represented internally, or '**intrapsychologically**', that is, within the individual. In other words, individual learners ultimately internalize language by participating in dialogue with others, and one way to achieve this in the language classroom is through the joint completion of tasks.

Research into dialogic interaction has shown that this enables learners jointly to perform tasks and solve linguistic problems that lie beyond their individual abilities. For example, Donato (1994) demonstrated that learners were able to produce jointly a particular grammatical construction which was beyond their individual abilities. He also provided evidence to suggest that language learning was actually taking place during these dialogic interactions. Similarly, Swain (1997) found that learners in collaborative dialogues, which aimed at solving a certain linguistic point, were able to achieve what none of them was able to achieve individually, and that (as reported above) the solutions students reached during such dialogues were retained in their interlanguage system. Hence, it is assumed that social interaction mediates learning, as explained by Ellis (2000: 209): 'learners first succeed in performing a new function with the assistance of another person and then internalise this function so that they can perform it unassisted,' a process often referred to as ***scaffolding***. As explained above, research has indeed shown that there is a strong tendency for learners to 'stick with' the knowledge they had constructed collaboratively (jointly) on previous occasions (LaPierre 1994; Swain 1998; see also Pullin Stark, Chapter 3).

The socio-cultural position looks at how learners approach and perform the task rather than at the inherent properties of the individual tasks. This is because research has shown that the same task can be performed differently by different learners (and sometimes by the same learners but on different occasions), depending on the learners' interpretation of and approach to the task (Coughlan and Duff 1994; Swain and Lapkin 1998). Learners set their own goals, procedures and the way they collaborate in performing a certain task or activity. So tasks here are considered to be internally rather than externally defined because learners to a large extent construct for themselves the activity they are engaged in (see Cox, Chapter 14).

Several papers in this volume have explored how collaborative tasks can be implemented in a classroom context (Muller, Chapter 6; Pullin Stark, Chapter 3; Coulson, Chapter 11; Poupore, Chapter 19). For instance, Muller and Coulson have found that jointly performed tasks enabled students to correct each other's ill-formed utterances and solve linguistic problems that lay beyond their individual abilities.

Task-based learning and language instruction

How do we implement the principles underlying the various perspectives on task-based learning in a classroom context? Scholars have proposed different models for task-based instruction (eg Nunan, 1989a;

Skehan, 1998; Willis and Willis, 1987). Willis's (more fully described in Willis, J., 1996b), being quite practical and straightforward, is the model most commonly cited and employed by classroom teachers and teacher-researchers. Willis's framework, reproduced here, falls into three main parts: pre-task, the task cycle, and language focus. (Note: T stands for Teacher, Ss for students.)

The **pre-task phase** provides the necessary background, knowledge and procedure, introduces students to – and familiarizes them with – the topic and the task to be performed. In the **task phase**, learners carry out a meaning-focused activity. It does not matter if the task is achieved

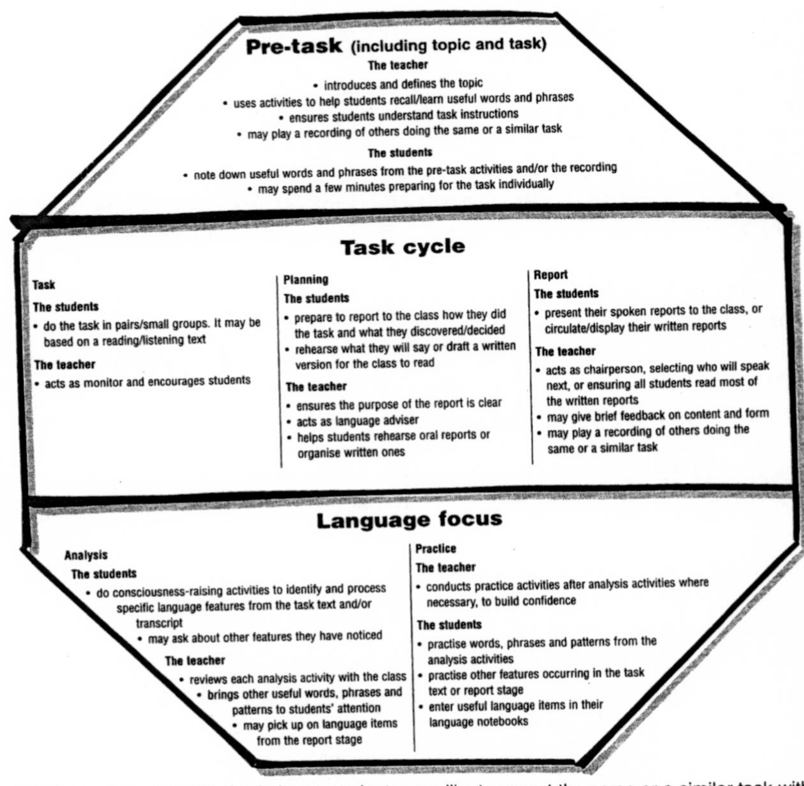

NB: Some time after this final phase, students may like to repeat the same or a similar task with a different partner.

Overview of the TBL **framework** reproduced from page 155 of *A Framework for Task-based Learning*, J. Willis, 1996, reproduced with the permission of Addison Wesley Longman (Pearson Education) Ltd.

through the use of language which is far from the target in terms of accuracy and complexity. They are more likely to concentrate on fluency, producing forms of the language that come readily to them. In the **report phase**, on the other hand, learners are required to present the results of their task phase work to the whole class. Willis and Willis (1987) argue that in this public performance learners will be motivated to produce not only fluent but also accurate language – a more 'prestige' variety. Thus, the report stage ensures 'a smooth transition from private to more public interaction' (Willis, J., 1996b: 56). To enable this transition to happen, learners are given a **planning phase** between task and report. During the planning phase, learners will attend to form in preparation for the report phase based on the assumption that when given planning time, learners will focus on form and try to produce more complex language. As such, this framework provides opportunities for fluency, accuracy and complexity to develop.

As mentioned earlier, several papers in this volume have employed J. Willis's (1996b) framework, singly or in combination with other frameworks – notably Skehan's (1998), in a variety of teaching contexts and techniques. For instance, Johnston (Chapter 15) shows that planning and report stages help combat fossilization and promote accuracy and complexity in learner output/production. Essig (Chapter 16) shows that planning time, task repetition and public performance all have notable effects on learner fluency and accuracy (see also Pinter, Chapter 10 for effect of task repetition on the language of younger learners). Djapora (Chapter 17) demonstrates that pre-task planning time results in better quality output with regard to fluency, accuracy and complexity. Hobbs (Chapter 12) and Baigent (Chapter 13), applying the model to teaching multi-word chunks of language and lexical phrases, find that learners' fluency was promoted at both the lexical level and discourse level. By the same token, task repetition and watching native speakers do the same task was shown to have a positive effect on learner output (Leedham, Chapter 8). Moreover, the model seems to be effective when used not just in general EFL courses, but also in ESP (English for Specific Purposes) courses (Pullin Stark, Chapter 3; Sheehan, Chapter 4; Kiernan, Chapter 5).

The future for task-based learning

The persistence of grammar-based instruction in many teaching contexts in the world, despite its relative failure to produce effective language users, is partly due to the fact that it creates conditions where teachers feel secure as they can predict the language that will be needed and they feel comfortable in their roles as knowers. This goes for teacher training, too. According to Skehan (1998: 94) grammar-based instruction 'has had an excellent relationship with teacher training and teachers' feelings of professionalism. It is comforting and places the teacher firmly in the proceedings' It also 'lends itself to accountability, since it generates clear tangible goals, precise syllabuses, and a comfortingly itemizable basis for the evaluation of effectiveness' (*ibid*). The difficulty in abandoning grammar-based instruction is also in part due to the lack of a clear alternative framework, 'a framework which will translate into classroom organization, teacher training, and accountability and assessment' (Skehan 1998: 94).

Armed with insights from SLA research findings and cognitive psychology, nevertheless, attempts are being made at effecting a transition from grammar-based to task-based instruction not just by researchers (eg Bygate, Skehan and Swain 2001, Ellis 2000, 2003; Skehan 1998, 2003), but also by language teachers and practitioners (see, in particular, Loumpourdi, Chapter 2; Muller, Chapter 6). For instance, Loumpourdi, adopting J. Willis's (1996b) framework for a task-based grammar activity, illustrates ways in which the transition from grammar-based instruction to task-based instruction can be smooth, enjoyable and rewarding for both teachers and learners.

A half-way step would be what Ellis 2003 terms '**task-supported learning**', where tasks are used alongside other more conventional methods, for example to supplement the text book, as described by Muller in Chapter 6. The text book *Cutting Edge* (Cunningham and Moore) is a good example of this, having a task-based strand, with an emphasis on lexis, alongside, but separate from, a grammar and skills syllabus.

Attempts are also being made to develop task-based frameworks into a fully-fledged approach to language teaching. Ellis (2003) describes various ways this can be done, and proposes a **modular syllabus**: beginners start with a purely task-based module, consisting of a range of tasks (linguistically unfocused) to help them acquire naturally as much lexis and grammar as possible; later a separate code-based module is gradually introduced, using focused tasks and explicit grammar teaching, to draw attention to grammar and lexical refinements that learners may not have noticed or acquired earlier.

While the contributors to this volume have focused mainly on individual lessons or short series of lessons, other researchers and practitioners are looking into how to construct complete syllabuses and design task-based language courses. Although this development still has some way to go, some progress has been made. Robinson (2001: 287) argues that sequencing of tasks for syllabus design purposes should be based on the cognitive demands of the tasks (see earlier in this chapter for an outline of his proposed framework). D. Willis (2003) shows how a focus on language can be subsumed within a task-based approach, and on a more practical level, Leaver and Willis (forthcoming 2004) contains around ten case-studies of highly successful foreign language programmes in the USA and South America that have been based on task-based instruction (TBI). In addition, there is work going on exploring task-based assessment and testing, and evaluating task-based pedagogy. See Bygate, Skehan and Swain, 2001 and Ellis, 2003 for illustrations of these.

Several papers in this volume point to the need for further research into task-based language learning and teaching (see, eg, Sheehan, Chapter 4; Essig, Chapter 16; Poupore, Chapter 19). This sentiment is reflected by the debate on tasks in a recent international conference (the IATEFL Conference in Brighton, UK, in April 2003). The debate – still continuing online at the time of writing – brought together researchers, researcher-teachers and professionals in a discussion of the role of tasks in language teaching and learning. Some of the issues addressed include the following:

- In what way are tasks different from exercises?
- Can you learn a language in a 'holistic' way?
- Where does the learning come from in tasks?
- Can we use tasks with learners at all levels?
- Is deeper restructuring of knowledge really taking place with task-based learning? To what degree?
- How do we design task-based language courses?
- What is the methodology of task-based teaching?
- How are learners tested in a task-based language learning/teaching context?
- How do we assess task-based language learning and teaching?

The significance of this debate is that it not only points to the need for more research into this important area in the field of second/foreign language learning and teaching (as do several papers in this volume), but also, like this volume too, it brings researchers and language teachers closer together than ever.

Notes

1. See Prabhu 1987 for a full report of this project.
2. See Leaver and Kaplan forthcoming (2004) for descriptions of TBI on Slavic language programmes.
3. See Lopes (forthcoming 2004), and Passos de Oliveira (*ibid.*).

Part A

Implementing Task-based Learning: Contexts and Purposes

In this first part, teachers in a wide range of different settings give personal accounts of their experiences of using tasks in their lessons. They describe how they set up their tasks and reflect in an exploratory way on the results. Some give suggestions for additional tasks.

Loumpourdi (Chapter 2) introduces tasks into a grammar course for 13-year-old Greek learners in an exam-oriented system, where a very direct teaching of grammar is the norm. Pullin Stark (Chapter 3) describes how task sequences are built into a one-year Business English syllabus for advanced students at a Swiss university. At a Higher College of Technology in the United Arab Emirates, Sheehan (Chapter 4) works with his intermediate learners exploring particular language items using computer generated concordance lines. Kiernan (Chapter 5) and Muller (Chapter 6) both teach low-level learners in Japan: Kiernan describes the narrative tasks he uses to build up his learners' story-telling skills, while Muller illustrates tasks that can be derived from a non-TBL beginner level text book. Finally, Moser (Chapter 7) shows us how he developed a learning journal for use in oral communication lessons, to help learners understand better how the stages of a TBL cycle work, and to get them to focus more carefully on language form.

Class sizes range from 4 to 50 and learner levels include false beginners, elementary–intermediate and advanced. The time taken for doing the actual tasks ranges from one or two minutes (for Muller's low-level learners) to two weeks or more (for Pullin Stark's business projects). Most tasks are set within some kind of task framework, beginning with a pre-task phase, going on to a task cycle which often includes task – planning – report stages (Willis, J., 1996a and 1996b, outlined in Shehadeh, Chapter 1) and a focus on form at some point.

A variety of task types are illustrated. These include listing, ranking, sequencing and simple comparing tasks which are towards the **'closed'** end of a cline, in that they are fairly predictable both in terms of outcomes achieved and language generated. Other tasks are more **open-ended**, for example analysing company performances, sharing life experiences, telling stories and personal anecdotes. Such tasks are less predictable, not just in terms of language used, but also in terms of agenda and procedures followed. Two tasks are **'focused' tasks** (Ellis, 2003) in that an explicit focus on a specific language feature is inherent in the process of achieving the task outcome: Loumpourdi's learners need to explore the meaning potential of the second conditional in order to construct their quiz on personality, and Sheehan's students are exploring the phrase '*due to*' in a set of concordance lines.

Materials used for task data at some point in the task cycle ranged from print materials like textbooks, magazines, quiz books and realia, to video extracts and data collected or sourced by the learners themselves outside class, and the worldwide web.

One course targets effective and appropriate oral communication (Kiernan) while others explore the need for a balance between the promotion of accuracy, fluency and complexity. In the context of oral communication courses, several teachers, including Pullin Stark and Moser, emphasize the importance of a focus on form at some point to develop learner's ability to handle more complex language and push forward their language development.

All teachers set their tasks into the wider context of their overall course design, syllabus or textbook, and give an indication of other tasks that could be tried out by readers.

Learners all seem to have enjoyed their experiences of TBL and most made noticeable progress in their language learning, gaining the confidence to express themselves more fluently in speaking and, in two cases, writing. For the first time in their university course, all Moser's students felt that with TBL their English had improved. Teachers too seem to have found the experiences rewarding and worthwhile.

2

Developing from PPP to TBL: A Focused Grammar Task

Lamprini Loumpourdi

Summary *I teach a grammar module for which teachers in Greece normally use a prescriptive 'Presentation – Practice – Production' approach. Because I wanted to make a smooth shift to teaching grammar through task-based learning, I chose to incorporate tasks selectively into my syllabus. I wanted my students to understand the meaning and use of the second type of conditional, so I assigned a task that involved personal experience: creating their own personality quiz.*

Background: the need for a gradual transition

After teaching English in Greece for several years I have come to two important conclusions. First, the Presentation – Practice – Production (PPP) approach (see Chapter 1), despite the many criticisms it has received, is well established and difficult to shake. It has been used so intensively, and with such persistence, that in some contexts it is considered as maybe the only way to teach, especially with regard to grammar. This happens mainly because PPP aims at accuracy of form.

Secondly, the shift from that approach to task-based learning (TBL) in such a rule-governed learning field as grammar, where accuracy is perceived as being the aim (Foster, 1999), is not going to be smooth or easy. Moreover, in our exam-oriented teaching contexts, where globally recognized language qualifications are seen as necessary for all levels and ages of students, and where students as young as 11 or 12 are coached for public exams intended for adults, some people would find it hard to imagine how tasks could fit into the syllabus. Although tasks seem more fun and keep our students interested, as well as providing more natural learning opportunities, teachers in Greece seem reluctant to adopt them as the basis for a syllabus and to reject PPP altogether.

That is why, when it comes to the hotly contested issue of teaching grammar, I propose a slower transition to tasks so that teachers and students will gradually become acquainted with them.

Context and rationale: incorporating tasks into the syllabus

The task I will describe has been used with my class of intermediate-level students, 12 boys and girls, around the age of 13, studying English at a private language institute in Greece. They follow a six-hour a week course for the academic year, dedicating three hours to the course book, two hours to grammar and one hour to composition each week.

Until recently, the two grammar hours were used for the presentation and practice of grammatical features and rules. However, after noticing how the teaching of just theory and rules confused and bored my students and also failed to achieve the desired results, I chose to change things slightly. I decided to dedicate one of the grammar hours to task-based teaching and keep the second hour as it was – teaching in PPP mode, although in practice, I did not always divide the two grammar hours equally between PPP and TBL each week as I found it more practical to set tasks whenever I felt it necessary. The students were already familiar with tasks, since I had already introduced these into my textbook-based hours, where I used tasks selectively for functional reasons. I chose the grammar task taking into account the functional feature we were examining during the other hour.

This might seem a little risky, or a waste of time for those working on exam-oriented or textbook-based syllabuses which focus mainly on accuracy, but I found that this syllabus is quite flexible and adjustable to students' needs, as it balances both approaches – PPP and TBL. Arranging a whole syllabus around tasks could be rather too challenging in our situation. Thornbury (1999) suggests organizing the syllabus according to **language function** – making an appointment, booking a ticket, etc. – instead of **grammar** features – simple past, conditionals, etc. However, this did not seem realistic for contexts like ours, so what I decided to do was choose tasks that aimed at specific grammar features. These would come into the category of what Ellis (2003) calls **focused tasks.** As Ellis explains, these tasks 'aim to induce learners to process, receptively or productively, some particular linguistic feature, eg a grammatical structure' (2003: 16).

In the grammar module I taught, I quite often detected problems with certain features where the students might have been able to grasp the structure as a form, but nevertheless failed to understand the situations in which it could be used. In such cases I chose to reinforce my teaching with an appropriate task – see samples in Appendix 1. For example, when learning the second conditional, students had difficulty in perceiving the element of the 'unreal' in a statement such as 'If I went on a diet I would lose weight', and how this is expressed with the word 'would'. That happens mainly because in Greek this is achieved with a separate tense. I noticed that they avoided using it in role-plays or free production activities. As a result, I decided to introduce a task, following a task cycle with its different stages as proposed by J. Willis (1996a and 1996b) and described in Shehadeh, Chapter 1 of this volume.

Method: stages of the task cycle

Introduction to topic and task

- I divided the class into two groups of six people. The larger the class is, the more groups you would have to make, while keeping the number of groups even, that is two, four groups, etc. I explained that the aim of the task would be to create a personality quiz with the title 'How courageous are you?' The theme is adaptable. You could choose whatever theme you wished, as long as it is likely to give rise to hypothetical situations. For instance, you could propose 'How honest are you?' or 'How good a friend are you?'
- I asked my students if they had ever done a quiz in a magazine and what it involved. They agreed to the title: 'How courageous are you?', and we brainstormed for ideas that related to the topic, by referring to situations they would consider frightening.

Task

- I asked both groups to create the questions for the quiz by using if-phrases. To help them start I provided a couple myself, using phrases that had come up in the previous stage: 'If I saw a spider ...', or 'If I were alone in a dark house ...'.
- Then, I asked each group to exchange their questions, and create multiple choice answers for the questions they received, using 'would' phrases. I casually demonstrated by providing three possible answers for the questions above. During this stage I just encouraged students to come up with ideas and I monitored their progress.

Planning

- At this stage I asked my groups to choose eight of the questions they found most intriguing within their groups and prepare them for presentation to other groups, by checking them again or re-arranging them. Fortunately, there is a computer room in my school, so students are generally able to produce printed copies of their final drafts, which, in the next stage can be handed out individually. If such a facility is not available, students can either prepare themselves for an oral presentation, or (if you have an overhead projector) write them up neatly on an overhead transparency. During this planning stage I became more involved as I focused on the students' accuracy and correct production of the forms in question, so I circulated and tried to advise them.

Report

- Now, I asked both groups to present their questions and multiple-choice answers by handing out their papers. The whole class had to decide on which of the questions should be included in the final quiz and we ended up with 10 questions (see Appendix 2 for some examples).
- We also decided on how to count the score and I asked both groups to write two small paragraphs each, labelled 'fearless', 'very brave' and 'not so brave', 'chicken', or any other titles students might prefer, that would interpret the results.
- Finally, I asked them to answer the quiz in pairs and report back to me in pairs, because, having only 12 students, the number was manageable. However, if you have larger classes you could divide them into larger groups.

Input

- At this stage, I showed them a similar quiz I had prepared myself, and we discussed this, as a class, comparing it to theirs. I would have preferred to use a quiz from a magazine, but I was unable to find a suitable one. What I would recommend you to do is to collect English magazines or even personality quiz books and compile a 'bank' of materials you can chose from and give to students when a relevant context arises.
- An alternative at this point would be to play a recording of a similar task being carried out by fluent speakers, and discuss any differences they noticed.

Language analysis and practice

- At this stage I explained aspects that I thought students might have questions about, presented the conditional type as a grammatical feature and assigned language focus exercises from their grammar books to boost their confidence. An alternative possibility here, if you have the text of a magazine quiz or a recording of others doing the same task, is to examine some of the language features that occur in these materials, maybe asking students to underline or listen for phrases they find interesting or hard to understand.

Reflection and evaluation

Students engaged wholeheartedly with the task of drafting and discussing the quiz questions and alternative answers. Although they were working with the sentence frames they were given, they were clearly focusing on meanings, on putting their ideas into words. They also had fun doing the quiz themselves at the end and comparing their scores.

After completing the task there was a distinct sense of alertness that gave me the opportunity to hold students' attention a little bit longer and get some feedback from them. This was done mainly informally – through casual conversation, where I asked them if they liked the task and if they would like anything to have been done differently – and how. For instance, one student suggested trying to guess beforehand which category we would fall in and to see if we were correct. Another group remarked that it was fun that for the first time we actually did no grammar in the grammar class (or at least that is what they thought!). Most kept talking about the results, teasing each other for being scared, by actually repeating sentences from the test in English.

Also, throughout the task, I took notes on the students' reactions and occasional comments, in an effort to evaluate the task through observing how it worked and if it served the purposes for which it had been implemented. I began to realize, from personal observations such as these, that asking students to state their own views and make their own choices seemed to raise their self-esteem and boost their confidence. They appeared to feel more valued and perhaps therefore more willing to express themselves. More specifically, a group of boys, who had never really participated in the grammar classes before, came up with the most original ideas and were so eager to utter them first, that they started speaking in English really fast. Another student, who had felt very intimidated by rules and could never recall them, was extremely excited when she found out that she was able to use the second conditional correctly. Finally, a further suggestion to raise motivation would be to propose to students that they put their quiz in the school newspaper.

Basing tasks on learners' personal reactions to situations that occur in everyday life serves two purposes: first of all, it strengthens the students' perception of English as a language not only used in the limited scope of their textbooks, but also to express their own ideas. Secondly, students may subconsciously become familiar with the target features and start to think of them not only as fragments of language governed by rules but also as powerful means of putting their ideas into words.

Further ideas for grammar-focused tasks

There are several tasks that can be used to create the task-based grammar syllabus I referred to in the beginning. For example, you could ask students to tell each other 'The biggest lies I told last year' to work on the simple past tense. When I tried this in class I asked them to find out three lies their partners told last year, write them down and try to decide on the 'top five lies' list. This was a great success. However, my biggest hit was the adaptation of famous TV quizzes in class, such as 'The Gladiator', or 'Who wants to be a millionaire?', where I replaced the questions of general knowledge with questions on English.

Appendix 1

Samples of focused grammar tasks

1. In order to practise tenses you could ask your students to create their own questionnaires and conduct a survey.

   eg For the present simple
   - Divide the students into pairs.
   - Assign the topic for survey, eg The most popular hobby, or how I like spending my weekends.
   - Ask them to make questions about how often their classmates do things they like, eg How often do you play sports? Do you watch TV every night?
   - Ask the same pairs to answer with adverbs of frequency and to count the answers for results.
   - Ask them to report the results, eg around 60 per cent love playing football every day, 10 per cent hardly ever watch TV every day.

You can also practise Future Progressive in a similar way, asking them for example: 'What do you think you will be doing at this time tomorrow/in a week/next year/in 10 years' time? etc.

2. In order to practice modal verbs:

   - Divide learners into groups.
   - Ask each group to come up with a list of 'golden rules' that should be followed if they want to make progress in their studying.
   - Provide the verbs should, shouldn't, must, mustn't, can, could, need, etc.
   - If students cannot come up with many ideas write sentences on the board – 'be on time', 'revise during breaks', etc. and ask students to provide suitable modal verbs for them.
   - Ask the class to choose the 10 best rules by negotiating.
   - Write them on paper and allow students to put them on the wall if they wish.

Appendix 2

Examples from the second conditional quiz

What would you do if an alien spaceship landed in your front yard?

1. I would pack my suitcase as fast as I could.
2. I would freshen up my extra-terrestrial language skills.
3. I would go back to watching the cartoons on TV.

Which would make you most scared?

1. If I had to take a Maths test.
2. If I had to clean my room.
3. If I had to ... well actually nothing scares me!

Acknowledgement

For my father, Dr. N. Loumpourdis, a great scientist and teacher. Without your support, guidance, advice, and most of all love, I would not be the person I am today. Thank you for everything.

3

Integrating Task-based Learning into a Business English Programme

Patricia Pullin Stark

Summary *When I developed a new syllabus for my business students, I wanted to integrate task-based learning into the programme. Here I illustrate how I did this by describing three separate task sequences and explaining the rationale behind each. This approach illustrates ways in which a focus on form can be successfully achieved within a management context.*

Context

The students who took part in the project were at the end of their Business English course in the Faculty of Economics at the University of Fribourg in Switzerland. Students here are mainly Swiss and their mother tongues are French, German and Italian, but there are also many students from other countries. Courses run for two periods a week over one or two academic years with up to 25 students per class. Entry level is lower-intermediate to intermediate, from B1 in the European framework, ie equivalent to Cambridge Preliminary English Test (PET), to B2.1, equivalent to a lower-grade Cambridge First Certificate in English (FCE). Their exit level is upper-intermediate/advanced (B2.2/C1.1[1]) equivalent to a higher grade FCE or Cambridge Certificate in Advanced English (CAE). The aim of the course is for the students to be able to use English as a working language.

Method

Tasks are integrated into the syllabus in several ways. Initially, a number of individual lessons or groups of lessons involve tasks (see Samuda,

2001 on pedagogic sequences in TBLT) and later a task-based project is followed over a number of weeks (see Appendix 1).

Task sequence 1: an analysis of a company

Early in the first semester, learners study general information about companies, building up relevant lexis, and then follow a series of lessons focusing specifically on Nike. I chose this company because it is well-known and very professional, but also because of controversy over its manufacturing practices, which tends to lead to animated debate. Authentic input on video[2] and from the business press covers current issues in relation to the company. These phases act as pre-task or planning activities as they help to provide a wide repertoire of language on which the learners can draw during the task (Skehan and Foster, 2001); it is also generally felt that planning influences complexity and fluency positively (Skehan and Foster, 2001; Skehan, 2003). Subsequently, the core task is set up, culminating in the students carrying out two different analyses on Nike: a STEP analysis (Socio-cultural, Technological, Economic and Political) and a SWOT analysis: (Strengths, Weaknesses, Opportunities, Threats). In this task, early in the course, the focus is on fluency, although emphasis is placed throughout the course on effective communication, ie conveying information succinctly and appropriately whilst ensuring understanding.

The stages involved in the task are:

- Students work in pairs studying information from a specialist website[3] on either STEP or SWOT analyses and discuss their understanding of the concept. They then make notes on key points.
- Students form new pairs consisting of one who has studied the STEP analysis and the other the SWOT. Each student explains what a STEP/SWOT analysis involves and checks his/her partner's understanding by asking or encouraging questions.

A week later, when the students have had sufficient time to assimilate the information and do further research, they work in groups carrying out a SWOT analysis on Nike. Finally, the groups produce a report on their findings. This ties up the activity and gives practical application of work in earlier lessons on text structure and report writing. Working in groups, writing, rewriting and editing their texts creates opportunities for collaborative learning. It is also practical with large classes in that it allows me to correct a limited number of texts quickly and to give rapid feedback. The students feel that they learn a lot in structuring and editing their texts, expanding their active vocabulary and developing formal written style. After correction, the reports are circulated throughout the class so that students can read and compare their findings and report on any differences noticed in style and approach. This also offers them the opportunity to learn useful language and phrases from each other.

Task sequence 2: the History of Production

A further task undertaken during the first semester involves verbally summarizing the history of production. The task draws on a video about Henry Ford's early mass production of cars. One specific aim is to draw learners' attention to form and the relationship between form and function, encouraging them to try out new ways of expressing their meanings and to notice the gap between their own interlanguage and the target language (see Skehan, 2001, 2003 and Chapter 1, this volume). In addition to introducing and reinforcing a limited amount of theme-related vocabulary, the task draws together students' earlier work on summarizing, textual coherence and cohesion and grammar (present perfect and simple past). The similarity between the first and second tasks is deliberate: task **repetition**, provided it is carefully designed and managed, can help to free up attention for focus on form, thus leading to greater accuracy and complexity in performance (Lynch and Maclean, 2001: 158–9).

The stages of the task are:

- Students read texts drawn from an academic textbook on Management,[4] covering some elements of the history of production. This initial input includes work on lexis and a cloze exercise concerning the use of the present perfect and simple past.
- Students watch the video on the history of production, taking notes on the various stages and dates in the development of mass production. They are also free to use other sources.
- Students work in pairs to produce a list of bullet points covering what they each consider to be key developments in the history of manufacturing. Once they have this list, they then work together on identifying a range of linking words to produce coherent and cohesive text. In addition, they are asked to consider which tenses are appropriate to cover the various stages they are going to explain.
- Students then rehearse the task with their current partner, focusing on form. After this, for the final version I get them to focus more on communication. I try to show them that creating interest and

making sure your interlocutor is listening actively is just as important as correct language.

- Students give their talk to another partner with focus on meaning and effective communication. Since they are allowed to weave in their own knowledge, their talks will be different, so they listen to compare versions, and they feed back to each other on various aspects of their talks.
- Students write a summary of the History of Production, which I use for diagnostic purposes to fine-tune further activities and give individual coaching where necessary. The focus here shifts back to language and form, with students producing a polished and condensed version of the History, incorporating new lexis, ensuring they have the right tenses and that they use a range of linking words appropriately. These versions are also read, for purposes of comparison, by other students who seem to like the focus on language at this point.

In classes of relatively mixed ability, weaker students can benefit from the wider range of more advanced students in extending their range and discussing areas of difficulty in grammar. Ellis (2000: 209) refers to the role of '**scaffolding**' through the mediation of social interaction in learning: 'learners first succeed in performing a new function with the assistance of another person and then internalise this function so that they can perform it unassisted'. Incidents of student collaboration during the task point towards such effects. For example, on hearing the more advanced students using cohesive devices they have studied, but do not use, such as 'whereas', the weaker students often begin to experiment with them or simply ask their partners how the expressions 'work'.

Task sequence 3: presenting a company

In the second semester, students form teams and work for several weeks on a project. This involves preparing and giving a presentation on a company. Before the beginning of the project, I give lessons on presentation skills and team work. Diversity within teams is encouraged, ie different gender, origin and mother tongue, to create an opportunity for authentic communication similar to that of the workplace. This diversity also seems to have an impact on students' awareness of their own interlanguage, for example difficulties in understanding arise in such groups, because of their differences in pronunciation.

Initially, I schedule two or three 'meetings', in the form of businesslike but informal discussions, in class time, for the teams to plan their work. These offer considerable opportunity for negotiation of meaning and fluency practice and are useful for me for diagnostic purposes, as they allow me to listen to the students whilst their focus is on meaning rather than form. Subsequently, I can use my findings to fine-tune further tasks to students' specific needs (cf Samuda, 2001 who emphasizes the importance of the teacher's role in TBLT). For example, students tend to avoid more complex structures such as conditionals and modal verbs. In such cases, I address the need to increase range and complexity of language and give examples of simple and more complex language used to express the same concepts. We subsequently work on structure in class, considering form and use and eliciting examples that are personally relevant, for example 'What would you have done if you hadn't come to study in Fribourg?' Finally, when awareness has been raised and the students have worked on 'grammar' outside the class, I set up a simulation which tends to naturally evoke the target structures (see Ellis, 2003 on focused tasks), for example, a meeting to discuss a financial scandal within a company, considering what could have been done to avoid the problem and ways to avoid similar incidents in the future.

To avoid the danger of monotonous presentations, an element of competition is built into the project. The aim of each presentation is to recruit graduates for 'their company' and at the end the audience (classmates) has to vote on which company they would choose and why. This naturally leads to the use of persuasive and enthusiastic language, as they strive towards the goal of effective communication.

In addition, the final practice session before 'performance' in class is filmed. This is followed by brief feedback before the students view the video and compare the feedback with their performance. It is during these practice sessions, that many students begin to become far more aware of their individual strengths and weaknesses and see the personal relevance of many of specific points covered in the course. Students often make notes at key points in the video where errors occur that have been previously highlighted. In particular, this phase seems to be effective in promoting noticing, monitoring and restructuring with students who have improved their accuracy and range overall, but still have areas of weakness such as past tense misuse or habitual syntactic errors.

Reflection

For me, the most valuable aspect of this project concerns the opportunities for individualized feedback. This can be integrated into the project through separate training sessions organized for each team. Such individualisation would normally be difficult with large classes. Skehan (2002: 291) notes that there is '... a need to build opportunities for individualisation of instruction, so that learners who are at different stages can profit in relation to the point which they have reached.' He (2002: 294) also emphasizes the importance of 'personal language systems that ... need development, and personalised feedback that will be the key.'

Lexis and register are two further areas where progress is in many cases striking. First, in the research stage of the task, students read a considerable amount of material, from annual reports to newspaper articles. Subsequently, in team discussions and presentation sessions, they use a much wider range of vocabulary than they previously did, notably extending their range of collocations and formal lexis and actively using specialist lexis studied during the course. Mundane vocabulary such as 'stuff like that', 'do' and 'a big amount', are replaced by more appropriate and formal lexis: 'such issues', 'undertake', 'a major sum'. Secondly, students develop a greater awareness of the differences between written and spoken English. This knowledge develops in terms of 'knowing how' as opposed to simply 'knowing what' as information from written sources has to be adapted appropriately for presentations.

However, there can be pitfalls. For example, one group of students downloaded information from the internet and simply read it out, resulting in such inappropriate language and unprofessional delivery, that the task was abandoned. Had the students' awareness of the differences between spoken and written language been greater, this would not have happened. Criticizing or blaming them is unproductive. Before undertaking research for the project and preparing the presentation I would recommend focusing on practical applications of theoretical knowledge, for example practising transforming short excerpts from dense and formal written text into appropriate spoken language.

Similarly, students need to understand how the task process relates to learning. One student commented that the project had taken a disproportionate amount of time for a five-minute presentation, failing to see that the quality of her language had not simply improved for those five minutes but that in the time devoted to preparing she had gained rich experience in terms of communication skills, increased her active use of specialist vocabulary and gained insights into the importance of adapting language to audience and context. I now review the learning aims of the project before, and again during, the project and ask students at various points how they feel their language and presentation skills have improved. It can also be helpful to tape a first attempt at the task and then compare this with the final video performance, to show tangible proof of progress. In addition, it is important to underline the process as opposed to the end product. I tell the students that they will receive on-going coaching over a period of weeks, and that this is the valuable part of the learning process. The presentation skills demonstrated in the end product will be of value throughout their careers, but in terms of language learning, it is the weeks building up to that point and their focus on language during that period that are of key importance. I also find it useful to ask students for feedback on the project, so that I can fine-tune the organization and ensure that we have a similar understanding of both the aims and the process.

Evaluation and conclusion

Students found the tasks relevant and motivating and probably most importantly, felt they had improved their language skills tangibly. Typical comments include:

> 'I really feel confident about making presentations in English now and working on companies was very interesting.'
>
> 'When I saw myself on the video I thought it was awful, so I really worked hard to sound professional.'
>
> 'Suddenly the work we had done on pronunciation became relevant – everyone looked so confused and we all laughed!'
>
> 'I liked the course, it was all about business and we really used the language.'
>
> 'I liked the group work and discussions and we worked hard on the language but in a practical way.'

They often say that they enjoyed the 'hands-on' nature of the course, for example the simulations of meetings. Interestingly, however, it is often purely language based lessons, such as focus on textual coherence and cohesion, which are listed in the feedback as lessons they most enjoyed. As language teachers, it is important that we do not lose sight of the key aims of our courses, ie increasing the accuracy, range and complexity of our students' interlanguage. We also need to make sure that the students are continually aware of these aims. Integrating this linguistic focus into a task-based specialist business English course has been challenging, but very rewarding.

Further ideas for business English tasks

Materials on company websites and in major business journals such as The Economist (www.economist.com) are ideal for developing tasks.

Many academic management textbooks now also have a list of websites and supporting video and audio materials. Using such materials as the basis for adopting TBLT in business English programmes offers considerable flexibility. Tasks can be adapted to different settings and group sizes. They can provide opportunities for different types of improvement from different learners across a wide proficiency range (Lynch and Maclean, 2001: 155). Many task-based activities such as team work or presentations replicate real world activities, bringing the functions of language and communication to the forefront. The final choice of tasks and the material on which these are based will depend on the precise context and aims of the specific programme.

Notes

1 http://www.unifr.ch/cerle/portfolio
2 Open University *Running the Planet.*
3 http://www.marketing-intelligence.co.uk/aware/resources/mi-help.htm
4 Jones, G. and George, J. (2002) *Contemporary Management* McGraw-Hill/Irwin.

Appendix 1 Overview of the project and its learning outcomes

Group Project – Companies			
Phase	**Language skills**	**Communication skills**	**Intended learning outcomes**
1a Decision on topic for research and presentation	Speaking – giving opinions, arguing for or against particular topics	Team work	
1b Research on a company	Reading – annual reports, web sites, the Press, eg the *Financial Times*		
2 Preparation of Fact Sheets (information sheets suitable for dissemination to the Press & public)	Reading – selecting key information Writing – planning, writing & editing a clear and succinct document Vocabulary – exposure to formal vocabulary, eg in annual reports	Effective written communication	Increased awareness and use of formal vocabulary
3 Preparation of Presentations Target audience – students	Speaking – work on aspects of pronunciation: • rhythm and stress	Presentation skills Work on: • the language of presentations	High level of motivation & consequent increase in work on English – in English – outside

Aim: recruiting graduates	• individual sounds • intonation Speaking/Listening watching and evaluating 'good' and 'poor' presentations	• planning • delivery: clarity & interest; keeping the audience's attention • dealing with equipment • dealing with questions Video filming and feedback on individual language and communication skills	the classroom Increased awareness of individual strengths and weaknesses (noticing), particularly concerning: • pronunciation • grammar • presentation skills Clear progress in all areas Awareness of relevance of training to future needs
4 Presentations in front of the class		Performing under stress	Increase in confidence Acquisition of skills for future careers
5 Writing an article on the company for a student magazine	Writing a formal document		

4
Language as Topic: Learner–Teacher Investigation of Concordances

Raymond Sheehan

Summary *This report describes how I introduced a task-based process with my intermediate level students, wherein teacher explanations of problematic language are replaced by a joint learner–teacher investigation of concordance samples of real language. Thus the topic of the task is an aspect of language itself; exploring the concordance samples generates both spontaneous and planned interaction.*

Background and rationale

'What does *just* mean?' 'What is the difference between *pay* and *cost*?' 'When can you use the idiom *hush-hush*?' How do I as a teacher best deal with such learner-sprung questions about meaning, appropriacy, collocation or structural patterns?

Despite learner expectations of teacher omniscience, the teacher is not a walking thesaurus, a bilingual dictionary, or a grammar. And even these reference sources, along with the extemporizing teacher, may sometimes fail to provide satisfactory answers. There is, however, an interesting alternative to consulting neatly delimited reference books and this, I believe, can offer learners a far richer language learning experience.

The capabilities of computers to provide banks of stored language (***corpora***) and to search and organize these corpora in a systematic format (***concordance** lines*) result in an inexhaustible source of material for task-based learning where learners can explore and induce meanings. (See Appendix 1 for a sample concordance extract.) 'Students need to discover and internalize regularities in the language they are studying.

If we can place students in the position of researchers this will accomplish these goals neatly and economically.' (Willis, 1998: 45)

This report outlines how a group of learners and I worked collaboratively through a task-based research process to see to what extent samples of real language can answer a teacher's and learners' questions. In the following sections I shall describe the initial impetus for the investigation, explain how to access a corpus, show how we worked through a structured task-based research procedure, summarize the results of our research and, finally, offer some suggestions for further classroom research using concordances.

Context

The students I was working with were studying for a Diploma in Business at a Higher College of Technology in the United Arab Emirates. Most were of intermediate level and were recent school leavers. They were required to take English for eight hours a week, mostly as a structured course in general English, but I was also required to help linguistically in a more ad hoc way with the business content aspects of their studies, since they had to compile a portfolio of business communications, write short reports and make presentations.

Method

Establishing a research question

A student brought me a question based on contrasting sentences in a business course, asking about the precise meaning and usage of the word *due*:

- Payment is due *on ...*
- Inflation is due *to ...*

As we discussed the question in class, the students began to see that one sentence clearly related to **time** while the other clearly related to **cause**. Other questions arose, however, from learners' lexical reserves: 'What about *in due course ...*?' and 'Yes, and what about *your library books are due back*?' Clearly, these learners had established for themselves a legitimate field of enquiry.

Here was an opportunity for research where teacher and learners shared a common starting point: an admission of linguistic ignorance.

Identify research sources

Since the ready-made answers in dictionaries often make only a fleeting impression upon learners, I decided to invest research time and energy in a language investigation which might have a more lasting value. The discovery-process would lie, I determined, in **'data-driven learning'** (Johns, 1988) often abbreviated as DDL. Stevens (1995) points out that 'DDL is distinct from other inductive models of learning in that the teacher facilitates student research into the language without knowing in advance what rules or patterns the learners will discover.' The data in this case is from the COBUILD Corpus Concordance Sampler drawn from a bank of 56 million words in contemporary British and American usage, at the time of writing available free on the Internet (COBUILD, 2000). The free sampler version is limited to a maximum display of 40 occurrences of the searched item (see Appendix 1). In fact, however, since you can search for the same word in a British written corpus, a British spoken corpus and an American written corpus, totalling 56 million words, you can increase the displayed occurrences to up to 120 lines. This should provide sufficient authentic data for teachers/learners to make their own linguistic explorations. For an alternative to COBUILD, see Aston (1998). As an alternative to computer-based corpora, Willis (1998) demonstrates how teachers and learners without computer access also have the option to construct their own manageable corpora and concordances of commonly occurring words such as prepositions 'by hand' from texts relevant to students' needs (Willis: 1998).

Establish a research procedure

The planning of the research, the research itself and the reporting back of the research findings required that learners perform a variety of communication tasks as identified in Table 1 below. The table itself is a representation of J. Willis's (1996a, 1996b) TBL framework, chosen because its different stages correspond with the stages of planning, executing and reporting. Willis's stages provided me with a template for making a lesson plan. The details here represent both a plan and a summary. Regarding time, in my lesson learners set the pace, though other teachers may wish to be more rigorous with the timing of pre- and post-task activities. It generally takes longer the first time because learners are becoming familiar with new text and task types. It wasn't just the word *'due'* that they were learning about; they were exposed to a lot of collocations and other useful words and phrases that occurred in the concordance lines, and they wanted to explore these, too. Regarding level, although the investigation procedure seems to work with intermediate levels and above, teachers might want to scale down the corpus, sample concordance and task expectations when dealing with lower language levels. (See Willis, 1998: 55–7 on using concordances with beginners.)

The TBL framework provides not only a structure but also principles. The focus on discovering and negotiating meaning through task fulfilment remains primary and there is no intention to practise pre-taught language. The task, in class, parallels a 'real-world' activity (research and reporting) while retaining an authentic goal within the language classroom. Much of the value of the task is placed on the interaction between learners during the process of shared discovery and reporting. They need, for example, to hypothesize, seek clarification and make amendments. The learners also place considerable value on the completion of the task and its outcome since it is they and not the teacher who have articulated the need to find out about this particular piece of language in the first place.

Table 1 A TBL framework for researching a concordance

Stages	Activities
Pre-task	Learners/teacher discuss the specific language problem. Teacher shows a sample concordance for that word or phrase: asks questions to help students notice features of layout as well as of language. Optional: Learners listen to a recording of colleagues/ more advanced learners discussing a similar concordance. (*Listening worksheet task: What do the speakers find out? Points they agree and disagree about?*)
Task	Learners investigate a sample of real language in groups. The first time, it might be advisable to give each group the same sample. For further concordance tasks, it is more interesting to give different groups different samples and get them to compare findings. Each group gives itself a name. Teacher facilitates by asking quantitative and interpretative questions. For example, *'In how many lines in the concordance is due connected to time? Label the lines "T."'*
Plan Feedback: Teacher as observer, notetaker, language planner…	Teacher gives each learner in the different groups her own colour. All the greens and so on get together from the different groups to compare group findings and build a bigger picture in their new groups. Learners in their new groups prepare an agreed report on what they have found out about the word to feed back to the class, using OHTs, a teacher-prepared data-sheet, notes, etc. They can also be asked to list any other useful words and phrases they have noticed in the concordance lines.

Table 1 Continued

Stages	Activities
Report: Teacher's role as above.	A representative or whole group presents findings, eg as a presentation with handouts. Receiving groups compare findings with their own and ask questions.
Post-task	Consensus among groups. A summary report. Learners write their own grammar/vocab page with 'rules' and examples; write exercises for other groups; write a summary of the discovery procedure for future students to use. Teacher evaluates selected language that learners produced during the 'Task,' 'Plan Feedback' and 'Report' stages in order to upgrade it: a focus on form.

Task outcome/research findings

The discovery process went as follows. Working with this particular COBUILD sample (see Appendix 1), we saw first that *'due to'* occurred in 25/40 instances. Looking at the remainder of *due* + preposition, we saw that *'due **for**'* was followed by a noun/noun phrase; that the only occurrence of *'due **at**'* referred to place (but one learner pointed out that in another sentence, beyond this sample, it could also support a time reference). I suggested that *'to give him his due'* should be classified as a fixed phrase. Then, we revised our *'due to'* tally from 25 to 26 when we noticed that *'due'* and *'to'* were in fact separable: *'due no doubt in part* to ...' We paused to propose a limited list of items that can be inserted between *due* and *to*; for example, *in the main, up to a point; to an extent* – imprecise qualifying expressions with an idea of measurement.

We then noticed that many *'due to'* phrases could be labelled either ***Cause*** (*due to the effects of global warming*) or ***Time*** (*Mr Davis had been due to fly*). I proposed the synonyms *expected* or *scheduled* for *'due to'* in Time sentences, and *because of* in Cause sentences and we all went about labelling lines of the concordance **T** or **C** accordingly. We found that only 9 out of 26 *'due to'* expressions were ***Cause***; the remainder were ***Time***.

Moving from a focus on meaning, I then asked questions to focus on form. *'Due to'* occurred with active verbs 10 out of 26 times (eg *due to go*); with the passive 6 times (*due to be named*). *Due to* can also be followed by a noun/noun phrase (eg *due to characteristics*). However, the *due to* + noun expression necessitated another revision of categories, in that *'due to the bank'* means not *expected*, but *owed to*. Finally, in the phrase *due to the fact that,* we agreed that *the fact that* was not redundant once we saw it allows a subject + verb to be added.

Reflection and evaluation: student response

Students exposed to a new methodology have mixed reactions, as became apparent in an informal feedback discussion about their feelings immediately after the task cycle was complete. It helped that the learners were not new to the task framework itself and not new to research. They had already done discovery-type projects with similar types of researching, language-planning, and reporting-back stages. The only difference was that their perceptions of the task cycle were different because they had not done research into language itself; they were not familiar with a concordanced layout and were initially intimidated by the density of the text (and the small print). Most students were satisfied, however, that they had managed to overcome their initial distaste for what seemed like a user-unfriendly layout, and had succeeded in finding out something valuable for themselves. A few would still have preferred the teacher to simply answer the question for them. It was important to clarify for the whole group that this type of concordance-analysis activity was not designed to replace the more familiar methodologies, but was an extra option that could be used now and then (either with the teacher or independently) to answer questions about language.

Further ideas for TBL concordance tasks

Successful exploitation of concordances depends upon developing ways of noticing, questioning and rationalizing language features. It would perhaps be disingenuous to claim that the teacher and learners are entirely equal partners in the research relationship. They are equal in that they share a discovery process covering new terrain together; wise teachers, however, will spend some time developing some concordance-based noticing, questioning and rationalizing skills to support their own individual explorations of language.

In other classroom investigations using concordancing within a TBL framework, we contrasted printouts for *pay* and *cost*. We explored *hush-hush* collocations both as noun and adjective. When dealing with phrasal verbs, we explored, for example, concordances highlighting *look for, look after* and *look up*. Concordances showing the uses of '*make*' and '*do*' similarly provided real data for linguistic discovery. We explored some differences between written and spoken language.

Further classroom research into concordancing tasks might include the following:

- Learners and teacher identify successful strategies and working styles from studying an audio-video recording of themselves discussing concordance lines.
- Learners transcribe a brief moment of recorded interaction of a concordance-based task. Elicit and give feedback not only on the language but also on the content and communicative efficacy of the transcription. Or see Leedham in this volume: learners develop awareness of communicative turntaking, backchannelling, etc.
- Learners and teacher challenge or supplement the received wisdom of grammar books. *Shall* and *any* are good words with which to start your investigations.

By establishing language itself as the topic for tasks which are executed through research within a clear framework, we may well end up discovering more not only about language but also about classroom interaction and about ourselves as learners.

Appendix 1

Collins COBUILD Concordance for *due*

see things in the same light. Mr Li is	due	at the Airbus headquarters in
the Watts last night. They could be	due	compensation if they can prove their
enveloped in a white-out blizzard. In	due	course, my companion made it to the
How to pay [/h] Council Tax will be	due	for payment from April 1993. Payment
have an existing policy which is not	due	for renewal just yet, you can switch
a new film entitled Pentathalon,	due	for release next year, in which he
Is the Jet-X space telescope,	due	for launch on a soviet space mission
of State since Merry del Val, he was	due	for disappointment. Paul VI did not
000 from a greatest hits collection	due	for release next month, [p]
the screen, lp] Which, to give him his	due,	he does very well. And round about
Pyracantha outside my kitchen window,	due	no doubt in part to the exceptional
them-especially with their first child	due.	Not wanting to move to a new area
sounds utterly astonishing It's	due	out in May. [p] Still on 4AD, The
konjo {f] character). Whenever I was	due	punishment, I was made acutely aware
the danger zone where a test was	due	to take place, [p] For several
are already available, and Winter is	due	to be added shortly. All four '
amount shown In the statement to be	due	to the Bank or £5 (or the full
the River Tames has flooded its banks	due	to the effects of global warming.
hooks are particularly prone to damage	due	to their elongated, ultra fine sharp
this morning. Management and men are	due	to meet in Calais later today, but
Punjab is grim. He said that this is	due	to the fact that Pakistan has now

Most of the price rise has been	due	to speculation In the oil market and
arms reduction in Europe is	due	to be signed. One opportunity for
ELECTIONS [/h] Parliamentary elections	due	to be held in Egypt on Thursday will
eastern Germany. All 380, 000 are	due	to be out by 1994 by agreement. But,
the Interior Ministry. The Sabor is	due	to decide on this in an hour. The "
Nonetheless the Secretary-General is	due	to go to Geneva this weekend and
indigestible South African grass, and,	due	to Roberts' economies, there was *no*t
up. Shortly after that evening I was	due	to see him at his home at Cardiff,
year if it passes certification tests	due	to begin in January, [p] The
State Lottery, [p] Mr Davis had been	due	to fly on to GTech's head office in
the damage or of its being severe was	due	to characteristics of the animal
British Energy, the nuclear company	due	to be sold In mid-summer, Ralltrack
[p] A provisional World Cup 14 is	due	to be named by England either later
police and sheriff's departments	due	to old rivalries. They wouldn't
vanguard of corporate casualties all	due	to unveil lousy figures and the news '
can we expect A greatly enhanced game	due	to its CD-Rom format? Well, there's
[/h] [b] lan Key [/b] [p] A WOMAN	due	to become her city's next Lord Mayor
Derek Hunt, 52. [p] The heatwave –	due	to cool this weekend – took a toll
be a shortfall if the mortgage falls	due	when the stock market is weak. If

Collins COBUILD: Sample concordance for ***due*** *(British written).*

5

Storytelling with Low-level Learners: Developing Narrative Tasks

Patrick Kiernan

Summary *I teach low level learners aged 18–19 in a Japanese university. Here I describe a teaching project where I used narrative tasks with these students, including the problems that arose and ways that I resolved them. I also consider the potential of such tasks for developing general conversational narrative skills.*

Context

I start with the transcript of a student telling a personal anecdote recorded at the end of their first term.

Tomonari:	*So er, get a beer. Uh I'm standing in line. Then uh I uh I I I am ah tap on my back.*
Kouki:	*Oh yeah.*
Tomonari:	*From my back, person, I I turn my back ... uh and then my mother, my mother is standing ...*
Kouki:	*No!*
Tomonari:	*ha, ha. My mother says, uh 'hi, what is, what do you buy?' ah, er*
	[I think 'Oh, no'
Kouki:	[{laughing}
Tomonari:	*I couldn't say nothing*

When I walked into this class at the beginning of the term and began introducing myself in English, Tomonari and Kouki – along with the 30 other Japanese university students in this class – froze. Despite six years of English at school, it was their first experience of a class taught in

English. Who would have thought that by the end of the semester these two machine engineering students with dyed ginger hair who used to protest defensively '*eigo wakarimasen*' (I don't understand English), or Mariko and Noriko, two shy female students of architecture, would be amusing each other with personal anecdotes told in English? This chapter is the story of how these low level learners moved from stunned silence to a babble of chatter.

Background and rationale: why use narratives?

Narrative is a word often associated with the sophisticated world of literary fiction or oral tradition; however, more mundane narratives form an important part of our daily conversation. Through narrative, people rationalize their experiences, creating a coherent sense of self (a life story). In everyday conversation, experiences are shared through anecdotes, or recounts of day to day life. Such narratives are an important way of building and maintaining relationships with others (Ochs & Capps, 2001). A talent for conversational storytelling is also an asset for both amusing and persuading people. Foreign language conversation students therefore have much to gain from developing narrative skills in their target language. One way to prepare learners for conversational situations outside the classroom is through using carefully sequenced narrative tasks, adapted to build conversational skills, and moving towards independent recounts of personal tales, told in pairs or groups, as in the example above.

Narrative tasks have been widely used to elicit learner output in second language acquisition (SLA) studies and, to a lesser extent, in task-based language teaching. In order to make measurable comparisons, narrative tasks have tended to be retellings of picture stories, or videos without words (eg Bygate, 1996 & 2001), rather than elicitations of original anecdotes. Using the same narrative source for a given group of learners allows the teacher to compare student performance, a factor important for assessment and testing of communicative ability. Unlike many other classroom activities, narrative speaking tasks provide opportunities for learners to experience the cognitive demands of real time organization of an extended speaking turn in the target language.

Tasks provide a framework for storytelling which can be manipulated by the task designer or teacher to both support and challenge the learner. We therefore need to look at the possible ways of **grading** narrative tasks, increasing the demands on the narrator as language ability develops. Repeating a very short story based on a familiar text, with preparation time, may be suitable for low-level learners, while spontaneously recounting a personal anecdote to a group of people would be suited to more advanced ones. The problem is how to move from one to the other.

Progression between these two tasks might move in the direction of increasing difficulty on a number of overlapping **dimensions**. Robinson (2001) suggests these dimensions would include the following:

Model narrative structure:

simple language > *complex language (lexically and grammatically)*
simple story > *complex story (many characters, episodes)*
familiar story > *unfamiliar story*

Model narrative mode:

written > *pictures* > *video* > *given theme*
(closed task > open task)

Telling conditions

extensive preparation time > *no planning time*
reference materials (pictures, notes) > *no reference materials*
no time limit > *time pressure*

However, a further dimension of narrative tasks is authenticity. A concern for the relevance of tasks to actual usage has in principle been at the heart of task-based approaches since Prabhu (1987) used railway timetables in his Bangalore project. However, whereas part of Skehan's definition of a pedagogic task is that 'learners are not given other people's meanings to regurgitate' (1998: 95), narrative tasks in course books typically do not call on the learner to create their own story, or talk about a personal experience.

While textbook narratives have tended to be individual retellings of various kinds, conversational research shows that narratives in everyday talk are more interactive and personal, eliciting signs of involvement and interest on the part of the listener(s) (Ochs and Capps, 2001).

Method

Starting with course book activities

As a way of investigating the potential of narrative tasks in building conversational narrative skills I prepared a series of narrative activities to supplement an introductory course in communicative English.

My learners were 120 first-year Japanese university students, divided into four classes of about 30 students each. They were all taking a compulsory English course in the Faculty of Engineering. Although they had studied English in school, they were low-level learners with little experience of having to speak English. For this reason course book style activities were used to build up their confidence. These were sequenced as follows:

1. Retelling very short written stories
2. Retelling from a model conversation
3. Retelling with pictures
4. An information gap story (from Helgesen *et al.*, 1999: 109–10)
5. Retelling from video (Perlman, 1997)
6. Telling a personal story

Among other things, retelling activities 1–4 provided opportunities for learners to practise narrating within a clear-cut framework, before launching them into talking about personal experiences where they would have to organize their own thoughts, thinking of what to say as well as finding the language to express it. The video task (5), although offering a readily comprehensible story, required learners to interpret the story, select and organize their account, and find suitable language to tell it. Finally, task 6 included learners writing their story in advance to allow the maximum support.

All of these tasks were recorded in class using small battery operated tape-recorders (one per pair). Not only did this make it possible to review the simultaneous performance of learners but the tape-recorder itself created some excitement and put pressure on the students to perform in English.

Each task was performed first in L2 then repeated in L1 to check comprehension and compare L1 and L2 performance. Rather than review all these tasks the remainder of this chapter will focus on narratives produced by learners in response to tasks 1, 5 and 6, focusing on one learner in particular *Mariko* – who was fairly typical of learners in her class.

Retelling very short stories

Learners were given a very short story (110 words) to read and retell to a partner. Four stories were prepared altogether, so that each learner could tell a story their partner did not know, thus fostering a need for real communication. The vocabulary and grammar were simplified to facilitate comprehension. The learners were given just enough time to read the story but no time to memorize it (five minutes). The story papers were then collected and the first speaker was directed to tell their story. Although learners may have wanted to recount the story word for word, these conditions made a verbatim recount unlikely. Rather the order of events and salient details were remembered and the learner had to reconstruct them according to their English ability. Below are the final parts of two transcripts where learners are recounting to their partners a variation of the story *Red Riding Hood*.

Mariko:

finally, she looked her mouth

'what teeth, what big teeth you have'

'so I can eat'

the wolf attacked at her

but just then grandmother began shoot the wolf

Tomonari:

So, er, finally, Hanako says, er: 'What, er, what big teeth you have.'

Er, the wolf says 'Yes, er, it's ... I could, er, I can eat you'

And, er, the wolf, jumped up her.

Then, er, Grandfather come back.

And, er, she shot, er, the wolf.

The learner's disfluencies here reflect their developing interlanguage and perhaps personal styles of speech. Tomonari's frequent pauses were also a feature of his L1 repetitions of the same task. Mariko's rephrasing of *what teeth* to *what big teeth* shows that she is constructing the story utterance by utterance. For comparison here is the original story fragment:

> Finally she saw her mouth, 'Grandmother, what big teeth you have!' 'So I can eat you ...' said the wolf and jumped at her. But just then Grandmother came back and shot the Wolf.
>
> [*Hanako* written by the author]

Features such as Mariko's use of *attacked* for *jumped at* illustrate how even the retelling of a short written story is a test of productive skills.

The rewording reflects her correct pragmatic interpretation of a less common phrasal verb as the contextual equivalent of the high frequency verb *attack*.

One problem with this task was that the listeners were rather passive and unresponsive. This may have been because they were rehearsing their own story in their minds, but also because the task did not require learners to listen or remember what they had heard. However when the listeners were told they would have to retell the story they had just heard, write it down or find the differences between two similar stories there was more negotiation of the story content. Establishing a purpose for listening made it more of a genuine task.

Of the four narratives prepared for this task two were variations on well known tales (*Little Red Riding Hood* and *Momotaro*, a Japanese fable), and two were simplifications of (as it turned out) unknown tales (*The King Who loved Stories* and *The Man Who Shot a Rock*, a Zen tale). Although none of the tales were told in their complete form by all learners, all tellers got to the end of the variants of familiar tales. In contrast neither of the obscure tales were told completely by any of the learners and seemed to present comprehension problems. It may be that such short tales do not provide enough of a framework to grasp an unfamiliar tale. In any case this unfortunate result underlined the need for clarity, simplicity, and perhaps elements of familiarity when using written narratives as sources.

Such tasks offer an effective introduction to L2 storytelling especially where the listener is given an active role. They allow low-level learners to experience the cognitive demands of piecing together a story, and sharing it, without the problem of having to think of one.

Retelling from silent video clips

Video narratives with sound but no words are well suited to research into storytelling skills. Retellings of such visual stories offer comparable data that remove the concern of whether learners' understanding has been handicapped by problems of listening comprehension, or reading ability. For this reason such videos have been popular sources of narrative retellings. Bygate (2001) used *Tom and Jerry* animation cartoons; Skehan and Foster (1999) parts of the TV comedy *Mr. Bean;* and Bardovi-Harlig (2000) used the classic silent cinema of Charlie Chaplin's *Hard Times*. For this project I used a seven-minute wordless animation produced by the National Film Board of Canada called *Dinner for Two* (Perlman, 1997).

The story depicts two chameleons that by chance catch the same fly at the same moment. Their attempts to secure the fly soon escalate into a fight, climaxing with them tussling on a breaking branch over some water where two hungry crocodiles wait. Eventually they escape because as one falls the other reaches out to save it, fortuitously leading to both being saved. In a final cathartic scene a frog shares the fly with the two chameleons at a dinner table.

Although using wordless videos ensures comprehension, it also presented these learners with a tough challenge. Not only did they have to find L2 vocabulary to express what they saw, but they also had to rationalize the narrative deciding which bits to report and which to omit.

Before watching, learners were paired and asked to anticipate the story from the title *Dinner for Two* and the picture of the two chameleons on the cover of the video. They were also given a list of animals and asked to circle those that they thought might appear, and to check their answers as they watched. After watching they were given 30 minutes to write what happened and finally compare their interpretations with a partner. The resulting narratives differed considerably as to the details reported, and also in length (from 17 to 98 words in written form). Here are some of the shorter versions:

Shinichi:
There are two chameleon. Then moskeyton [mosquito] appeared. Chameleons try to eat it. But there is one moskeyton.

Hiroaki:
One day blue lizard, green lizard in jungle, blue and green lizard catch the same crab. Then two lizard is battle. Crocodile want to eat lizards but missed it. Then two lizard ran a way, then, two lizard survived.

Yoshinao:
The two chameleons is in the big forest. they are cathing flys by their tongue and eating it. then a big fly is coming in front of them. they start fighting about the big fly. but fighting stop soon owing to the frog. two chameleons and frog eat a big fly.

Even more clearly than the previous task this brought out weaknesses of the learners' grammar, vocabulary and pronunciation and (as we can see here) spelling and punctuation. However the main challenge for learners was how to organize and retell the story. Whereas pedagogic tasks often tend to build structure by, for example, asking learners to put a series of sentences summarizing the narrative in order, here learners had to retell the story in their own words. Below is the story told by Mariko.

> *Two chameleons live in a jungle. They tried to eat a same fly. And caught a same fly. They scrambled for a fly between two tongues. And then two chameleons rised the tree. Two crocodile in the pond under the tree. Two chameleons runaway in a hurry. They let go a fly. Frog caught a fly. Two chameleons stared at a fly and frog. Finally two chameleons and a frog divide a fly.*

While considerably simplified compared with the L1 version she wrote later, this is a reasonable recount. English readers may however find the use of articles random and inappropriate, and the use of 'two chameleons' over-persistent. These are both problems arising directly from the learner's L1 (see Hinds, 1982 for a description of Japanese ellipsis). While these learners may benefit from some overt teaching of the principles of article usage and patterns of ellipsis in English, these activities are a meaningful preparation for this. If learners have already had experiences like this of having to construct a narrative themselves, they may more readily tune into activities that highlight how ellipsis is handled by English speakers or writers.

Telling a personal narrative

If the telling of narratives based on video is a format well suited to research, the telling of personal narratives is a task rather better adapted to the classroom. The personal narratives provided both a chance to tell a story matching their language ability and an opportunity for individual expression. Indeed, while the preparation that went into these narratives made them the least spontaneous, the recordings include laughter and involved more natural interjections from the listener than were found in any of the other recordings. To ensure that all learners participated in this project as fully as possible they were first asked to prepare a personal narrative as a written assignment which would be included in their overall grade for the term. In addition, the telling of the narrative to a partner was made part of an end of term speaking test. The learners were given six titles to choose from derived from those used in a storytelling game on a Japanese chat-show called *Gokigenyo* (literally 'feeling good'):

- a time I felt embarrassed
- an unusual happening
- a time I got really angry

- a scary experience
- a day I will never forget
- my life-story in a nutshell

This broad range of topics with no model to follow caused some initial anxiety, but eventually produced a varied and interesting array of personal stories that would take more than this entire volume to do justice to. Instead the account of this final task will be limited to considering a single tale by Mariko, the architecture student. To encourage involvement, listeners were asked to write a short summary of what they heard, and encouraged to use backchannel phrases introduced during the course such as *I see, right, really?* and *sorry?*

This telling was of particular interest because it was both the most interactive, and the closest to the prepared written version. The similarity is such that she must have gone to considerable trouble to memorize it, yet having done so is able to free up attention to focus on getting the message across to her listener. She was particularly anxious to do this because of difficulties she had experienced understanding her partner's story. Mariko makes careful checks as she tells her story:

Mariko: *uh I was elementary school children*
Noriko: *yes*
Mariko: *I went to a department store with my parents*
Noriko: *yes*
Mariko: *I will talk about this*
Noriko: *ok*
Mariko: *ok?*
Um I don't remember when I was elementary school children
Noriko: *really?* {giggles}
Mariko: *Uh I don't remember when I was elementary school children*
[but I remember about this happening
Noriko: [*unn* {understanding sound} *re, remember?*
Mariko: *Remember.*
Noriko: *yes*
Mariko: *Ok?*
Noriko: *Ok.*

She then goes on to recount an embarrassing childhood incident where she discovered a baby chair in a department store toilet and strapped herself in. Then, realizing she was stuck, she screamed out for her mother.

Mariko: *A few minutes passed*
I wanted to ... get over,
Noriko: *ok*
Mariko: *get over*
But belt [didn't
Noriko: *[ha ha*
Mariko: *[came off*
Noriko: *[ha ha ha ... ha ha*
Mariko: *I confused I shouted*
['Helping mother'
Noriko: [{laughs}
Mariko: *ok?*
Noriko: *ok* {laughing}
Mariko: *and my mother came in my toilet*
Noriko: {continues laughing then stops as next part begins}

Here we can see that the efforts she has made both to memorize her tale and to convey it in a way that is easy for her listener to follow, pay off as her partner recognizes the climax of her tale and laughs. She reproduces the written tale she had submitted previously word for word, with the only real departure being the OKs used for confirmation here, and repetitions at the end of the tale which emphasize her feelings of helplessness while stuck in the chair.

Reflection and evaluation

The project described here represents a first attempt to create a course in spoken narrative. The course was built around tasks of the kind already available in text-books, and following the examples of elicitation techniques used in SLA research. However, a wish to make tasks more authentic in terms of sociolinguistic usage led to the creation of a more learner-centred and open task. Among other things the relative success of using personal narratives was the result of maximizing preparation time and linking the efforts involved to the students' test grades. Moreover the challenge of completing a recorded speaking task during a test created a quite different atmosphere from the usual resigned boredom associated with paper tests.

Not only did the telling of a personal narrative seem to be the most stimulating of the narrative tasks in the classroom context, but the resulting narratives were also the closest to narratives described in the literature on conversational narrative. Stories reflected the outlook of the teller, and stimulated expressions of surprise, amusement and sympathy from the listeners. However there are other aspects of storytelling described in the literature that teachers might wish to incorporate into narrative tasks. Tellers often structure their tale to emphasize the tale's newsworthiness (Labov, 1997), and part of the art of conversational storytelling is to produce a narrative that leads out of the preceding talk so that stories are often told in thematic rounds (Sacks, 1995: Vol. I, 752–83). The ability to blend and adapt to ensuing talk is a particularly difficult thing for language learners to do, but for this reason is something for which classroom based learners need to be gradually prepared. This might be encouraged by putting learners in groups according to the narrative topic they choose, allowing them to share similar experiences. As learners become more skilled, topics could be limited and preparation time gradually reduced.

The use of well structured storytelling tasks is one way to prepare for the telling of personal stories, but it may help to personalize tasks from the outset. Retelling from a video shown in class might be replaced or followed up by a recount of a film, a book, a sporting or musical event or news story chosen by the learner. In addition learners would benefit from looking at typical conversational narrative structure genres in the target language (Eggins and Slade, 1997; Norrick, 2000) and how native speakers go about telling stories in conversation.

Conclusion

Both in SLA research and in the classroom, narrative tasks to date have tended to focus on the cognitive aspects of organizing and telling a narrative. Given that narrative is one of the most important modes of cognitive organization this is an indispensable area of investigation. However at the same time descriptions of conversational narrative, which have all but been ignored in language teaching, indicate that there is good reason to develop tasks which take account of sociolinguistic dimensions of narrative production. This chapter has discussed a project in which traditional narrative tasks were used to prepare low-level learners to tell a personal tale, producing something closer to everyday conversation. However, what has been described here has no more than indicated a general approach applicable to learners in a variety of situations including teaching more advanced learners. This approach is in need of considerable refinement – a challenge which I hope readers of this book will take up and continue.

6
Adding Tasks to Textbooks for Beginner Learners

Theron Muller

Summary *I wanted to introduce task based learning to my small class of false beginners at a private English school in Japan, to give them more opportunities to speak. In this chapter I explain how I adapted a vocabulary-focused lesson from the Presentation Practice Production (PPP)-based textbook that I was using, and suggest some ideas for other tasks that can be generated from non-TBL textbooks.*

Background and rationale: TBL and beginner textbooks

Private EFL language teachers face a dilemma when designing course materials. Many institutions require students to purchase a textbook, often from an international series like Gateways (Frankel & Kimbrough, 1998) or New Interchange (Richards, 2000), which are often based on PPP, a methodology characterized by 'relative failure' (Skehan, 1996a: 17). But for conversation teachers like me, teaching independently of texts is often impractical. As a colleague said, 'There's no way I could possibly come up with my own curriculum, so I use the textbook to provide my syllabus.' TBL may be a preferable alternative to PPP (Skehan, 1996a), so an option open to teachers is to adapt class textbooks to TBL. Also, most TBL material in recent studies is designed for intermediate and advanced students, leaving a paucity of TBL material for beginners. In this chapter I attempt to address both of the above issues by describing how I adapted a beginner-level textbook unit to TBL

In using a TBL approach to language teaching, Skehan (1996a: 22) says educators must balance the three goals of 'accuracy', 'complexity/restructuring', and 'fluency'. Jane Willis (1996a,b) suggests three stages in a cycle that concentrates on fluency first (in the task), complexity/restructuring next (in planning), and finally combines accuracy with fluency (in the report). These stages, and how I adapted them for my class of beginner learners, are further explained below.

Context

The 'Intro' course at English For You, a private language school in Nagano, Japan, is intended to familiarize learners with basic spoken English. Classes are 60 minutes once a week, 46 classes per year. Students range from 18 to 45 years old, and have various motivations and goals. A nurse, Masae, wants to interact with international patients; two housewives, Sanae and Hiromi, study English as a hobby; and a high school student, Atsushi, wants a jump-start on his university English requirement. The class uses New Interchange Intro (Richards, 2000), which was chosen by the school. As false beginners the students can read but have little spoken English ability.

Method

For my classes I adopted J. Willis's (1996a,b) task structure, as follows:

- performing a communicative task;
- planning a report of the performance;
- reporting the task results to the class.

Through switching communication 'context' from private to public performance (Essig, Chapter 16, this volume) Willis's structure encourages focus on fluency (communication) during the task phase, then form (restructuring for complexity and accuracy) during the planning and report phases. Changing communication context involves switching between informal (small group) and formal (class presentation) interaction.

In order to incorporate tasks with a clear link to each unit of the textbook, I took the following steps:

1. I listed vocabulary from each textbook unit;
2. I assigned topics to the vocabulary lists;
3. I listed tasks following J. Willis's (1996a) task-types;
4. I decided in which weeks each unit would be covered.

The results for one such unit are summarized in Table 1.

Table 1 Example integration of speaking tasks with a unit of New Interchange Intro

Unit	Vocabulary	Topics	Pre-Task (type)	Tasks (type)	Week #
2	CD player, *sunglasses*, watch, camera, cell phone, book, eraser, English, dictionary, notebook, a, an, wastebasket, pen, desk, map, table, pencil, bag, board, window, clock, chair, *shoes, wallet, earrings, briefcase, purse, keys*	Classroom objects, traveling	list items to take traveling (listing), rank the items by importance (ranking), discuss what you have lost while traveling (personal experience)	'guess' which item from a group another person is thinking of (problem solving)	4, 5

The task I designed for this unit is loosely based around the dialogue on page 11 of New Interchange Intro (Richards, 2000: 11):

Kate: Oh, no! Where are my car keys?
Joe: Relax, Kate. Are they in your purse?
Kate: No, they're not. They're gone!
Joe: I bet they're still on the table in the restaurant.
Waiter: Excuse me, are these your keys?
Kate: Yes, they are. Thank you!
Joe: See? No problem.
Waiter: And is this your wallet?
Kate: Hmm. No, it's not. Where is your wallet, Joe?
Joe: In my pocket ... Wait a minute! That's my wallet!

I always try to associate loosely the tasks I use with the textbook where possible, though when I use textbook activities I remove suggested phrases from class handouts to avoid setting a 'language agenda' (Edwards, 2003) while still giving students enough help to encourage them to be successful.

A task is 'a goal-oriented activity in which learners use language to achieve a real outcome' (Willis, 1996b: 53). In unit 2 of New Interchange Intro (Richards, 2000) there is a lot of emphasis on singular and plural nouns, and asking yes/no questions with 'be'. To give students opportunities to use singular and plural nouns in an activity with a 'real' outcome, I developed the lesson around the nouns italicized above. The vocabulary items were printed on small laminated cards, with a picture on one side and the word on the other. The goal of the task was to guess which vocabulary item your partner was thinking of. One student wrote the word on a piece of paper, and the other partner had to find out what it was. I linked this task to the book, which has the dialogue set out above, where a couple forget their keys and wallet in a restaurant, by explaining that one partner had 'lost' something of theirs, and wanted it back.

Lesson strategy – pre-task

To introduce the topic of the lesson I conducted a series of pre-tasks which included listing vocabulary items for travel, ranking the items by importance, and talking about things we had lost while travelling. This part of the lesson was teacher-fronted to help students get comfortable talking and to give me better control over the class timeline. The listing and ranking tasks could easily have been performed in pairs, and with intermediate students I probably would ask them to perform these pre-tasks in pairs and then present their findings to the class.

As a final pre-task activity I rehearsed the task with the class as a whole. I wrote down the item I had 'lost', and they asked me questions to discover what it was. I didn't critique student utterances, nor did I correct grammar errors. This pre-task was intended to provide students with a model for task performance and to demonstrate that communication was more important than language form when performing the task. A transcription of this performance appears below.

Teacher-fronted task rehearsal transcript

T: I lost something. I will write it down. Um … I lost something. It's secret. What can you ask me?
M: Have you ever lost something?
T: Have you ever?
S: Shoes?
T: Shoes? No. Not shoes.
A: Wallet?
T: Wallet? Yes. I lost my wallet.
A: Here you are.
T: Thank you.
A: You're welcome.
T: Okay. Good job. Good job.

Learner task performance

While learners were doing the task, I moved between them and assisted with any communication difficulties, though I tried not to correct grammar or pronunciation, instead encouraging them to communicate with as little support as possible. A transcript of one pair performing the task is included below.

Student task performance transcript

A: Purse.
H: No.
A: Bag.
H: No.
A: ???
H: No.
A: Uh ... briefcase.
H: No.
A: Uh ... keys.
H: Yes.

The fact that the learners managed to do this task successfully using single word utterances will be commented on later.

Planning and report

Implementing the planning and report phases with beginners proved the biggest challenge of the lesson and I needed to make some adaptations. While intermediate and advanced students may refine their language when changing context from small groups to class discussion, beginner students may exhibit few differences between speaking in formal and informal contexts, and are often intimidated when speaking before an audience. To encourage a greater contrast between task and report language, and to facilitate successful reports, I asked students to switch from a spoken to a written medium.

After performing the task, in the subsequent planning phase, students were asked to write a 'script' of the task for a role-play performance. They worked in pairs to write their scripts, discussing what language to use, and I moved between the pairs to help them correct language errors. The report phase thus involved a role-play of student-generated scripts. In future classes and at higher levels such scripting may not be appropriate (as Breen & Candlin (2001) note, spoken language should be spoken and written language written), however, at this level, scripting encouraged students to focus on language complexity and improving accuracy.

Written student 'scripts' with corrections

Pair 1

H: What did you ~~lost~~ *lose* ~~something~~?
A: *Um* I lost a bag. This one.
H: This one? OK?
A: *Yes*. Thanks you.
H: You're welcome.

Pair 2:

M: ~~What did you lose something~~? Did you lose something?
S: Yes.
M: ~~Is that~~ ~~Are these~~ keys?
S: No.
M: Is ~~this~~ *it* a wallet?
S: No.
M: Is ~~this~~ *it a* briefcase?
S: No. ~~Wearing~~. ~~No~~. *Something to wear.*
M: Are ~~these~~ *they* sunglasses?
S: Yes.
M: Here you are.
S: Thank you.
M: You're welcome.

Compare the scripts here to the Student Task Performance Transcription above. Even before I corrected the first two lines of the script, there was a shift from single word communication, 'Purse' to an attempt at making complete questions, *'What did you lose something?' and *'What did you lost something?' Sanae, the lowest student in the class, even attempts to help Masae, the highest; when she realizes Yes/No answers aren't working efficiently, she offers a clue: *'No. Wearing. No.' The evidence from this planning stage suggests that Skehan's (1996a: 22) shift from 'fluency' to 'complexity/restructuring' did indeed occur.

To give the students the classroom experience they expect as members of a conversation school, I had them practise and role-play their scripts in front of the class, at the report stage of the lesson. See the transcript of the script role-plays below.

Transcript of Script Role-Plays

Pair 1:

T: OK, so. Atsushi, and Hiromi, please stand up.
H: What did you lose?
A: Um ... I lost a bag. This one.
H: This one? OK?
A: Thank you. Ah ... Yes. Thank you.
H: You're welcome.
T: All right!

Pair 2:

T: OK
M: Did you lose something?
S: Yes.
M: Um ... keys?
S: No.
M: Is it a briefcase?
S: No.
M: Is it a wallet?
S: No. Something to wear.
M: Are they ... sunglasses?
S: Yes.
M: Here you are.
S: Thank you.
M: You're welcome.
T: Oooh ... Good job.

Finally I asked the students to change partners and roles, giving them a chance to experience the different language used during class.

Reflection and evaluation

It is worth noting the differences in how the pairs interpreted and did their tasks. It seems pair 1's goal was to reproducing the 'lost item' scenario while pair 2 was more interested in playing the guessing game (a reproduction of my original demonstration) with a goal of guessing the object. This 'dual' goal probably stems from my attempt to link the activity to the textbook scenario. In future classes it may be preferable to separate the two tasks, perhaps by playing the guessing game as a pre-task, then progressing into the emulation of a real-life scenario as a second task.

Student language during the lesson developed from one-word utterances into more complex forms, and students seemed to gain familiarity with their scripts, showing interest in script correction and practice. Johnston (Chapter 15, this volume) offers a list of possible factors behind the development in student language complexity.

The scripts help demonstrate how much English ability even false beginners bring into the language classroom. Before the lessons I was expecting 'What-questions' exclusively during the task, and that the dialogues of each pair would be linguistically similar. Instead the scripts are varied yet achieve the task successfully.

Whether the language generated in class was retained is a question requiring further study. In the future, the task could be repeated after a gap of weeks or months, and the transcriptions of task performances and scripts could be compared to see if there is an increase in accuracy or complexity during task repetition (see Pinter, Chapter 10 this volume). Even without evidence of language retention, the students were apparently experimenting with their language systems while scripting, a positive sign for the language classroom, and easily contrasted with a classroom where the forms in the book were first drilled then practised, setting a 'language agenda' (Edwards, 2003) that the students would attempt to model throughout the class.

Conclusion

Although the task and the subsequent planning and report stages I have described do not fulfil all the criteria or features of task-based lessons found in the literature, my approach does show how TBL can be used as a starting point for use with very low-level learners who may not be ready for the full version. As these students progress, they will gradually be able tackle tasks, planning and report sessions that are less restricted and more demanding, working within the familiar task – plan – report framework.

Further ideas for beginners' tasks based on books

- Pictures in the text book can be used for games of 'Hide and seek': learners 'hide' an imaginary item (eg a ten dollar note or some keys) in a picture and explain to their partner where to find it. Or their partner has to guess exactly where it is by asking questions like 'is it/are they near the window? High up or low down? Somewhere in the bookcase?' The person 'finding' it after the fewest questions wins.

- Textbook dialogues can be re-written or re-typed on sheets of paper – one for each pair – then cut up into pieces. The learners' task is to arrange them in the proper order, or a possible order. Or they could write their own dialogue, similar to the textbook one, but making some changes to personalize it, or to make it amusing, and cut it up for another pair to arrange.
- Taking the theme in the textbook unit, learners play 'Spot the Lie': learners tell their partners two true things and one lie, and their partner must guess which is the lie. This can also be prepared in pairs for another pair (or the whole class) to listen and guess.
- Memory challenge games can be based on a textbook reading text or a picture. The learners are given a very limited time to look at and remember the people and/or things or actions occurring in a specific picture, or to read the text once through (pre-task stage), then they close their books. In pairs, (task stage), they can write (in note form) a list of as many things as they can remember about the picture or text within a time limit, say in two or three minutes. Then (planning stage) they practise saying these things, and finally (report stage) each pair takes turns reading out an item from their list to the class. If other people have exactly the same item, they must cross it out. The winner is the pair who still has remaining items/things/people that no-one else had. Finally they look back at the text book to make sure all the winner's items are remembered accurately.

7

Using Language-focused Learning Journals on a Task-based Course

Jason Moser

Summary *In my oral communication classes in Japan I noticed that my students tended to neglect language form for the sake of meaning. I designed a framework for a lesson journal for students to write in during the class. The journal format mirrored the TBL sequence to help the students distinguish between the different stages of a TBL lesson. However its main aim was to draw learners' attention to language form by encouraging them to write notes as the lesson progressed.*

Context and rationale

My students in the Faculty of Language and Culture at Osaka University were mainly 'false beginners', non-English majors taking required classes in parallel to their main subject (eg engineering). Their ages spanned an exceptionally wide range, from 18 to 45 (normally 23 is the maximum age found). They had one 90-minute class a week, with between 30 and 50 students in a class. When I first introduced TBL they loved being given the freedom to communicate and it seemed ideal for them. However I soon realized that they were so eager to talk spontaneously that their accuracy suffered. This was true not only of the task stage, but also throughout the planning and reporting stages of the task cycle. Reviewing the literature on TBL, I discovered that Skehan (1996a: 22) has highlighted this same problem. In particular, he contends that task-based interaction favours fluency-based speaking strategies. These strategies consist of accessing memorized 'chunks' of lexicalized language and already familiar language. Certainly, where learners are doing tasks where spontaneous real-time communication is needed, they have little time left for accessing or actively processing grammar. They needed to be made aware that after doing the task, at the reporting back phase, where they present the results of their task to the whole class, it is appropriate to use more accurate language. When preparing what to say at the planning stage before this presentation they needed to make more effort to focus on form, and strive for both accuracy and fluency at the reporting back phase. Baigent, (Chapter 13), reports that her learners had a similar problem.

Another problem I had with TBL is that even if students took notes to prepare for the task or when planning their reports they often wrote in a jumbled way. So I needed to draw students' attention to the kinds of language appropriate for each of the three stages of the task cycle: task, planning and report.

Method

I devised a format for a kind of lesson log, adapted from J. Willis's (1996a, 1996b) TBL framework, into which they could write their notes for each stage of the task-based lesson. I called it a 'learning journal' (see Appendix 1). Students would complete a journal every lesson and, after a period of time, they could look back over these to review their progress (cf Skehan's 'cycles of accountability', 1998: 129). When used regularly, the journals have an important cumulative effect – for learners and for teachers.

We can see from the two journals filled out by learners (Appendix 1) that language from the task-based lesson has in fact been quite well organized and demarcated. In the next section I will describe how this process of writing in the learning journals overcame the lack of form focus problems.

Applying action research principles to the journal project

When I began to use the lesson journals, I incorporated it into an action research project, using one cycle of *plan, act, observe and reflect* (as in Burns, 1999).

Planning

At the planning stage of the action research cycle, I decided that I would hand out to every class a blank 'learning journal' and ask learners to keep written records of the language throughout the three stages of the task framework. I chose the name 'learning journal' because it highlighted the importance of progressive conscious reflection. I hoped that the journal would help learners realize the role that the process of writing plays in achieving a form focus in their TBL lessons.

To make it easier for them to focus on form, I planned some changes to the Willis TBL framework. At the pre-task stage, Willis recommends a teacher–class oral brainstorming session on the topic of the task. However, in my teaching I had found it could be difficult to explore a topic orally with students who are culturally more inclined to listen unless called upon, or who simply do not have a sufficiently high proficiency level to formulate what they want to say in time. In these cases, oral exploration is very time-consuming and ultimately reinforces student-dependence on the teacher. So I decided to let students do their own language planning at the pre-task stage through writing in their learning journals. I decided to do the same with the planning and report stages because, furthermore, writing makes it easier for the students to better recall, and organize, what they talked about. I believed that the effort of doing this should help to stretch their interlanguage and provide an opportunity for what Swain calls 'pushed output' (Ellis, 2003: 72).

I also planned to combine the report stage with a teacher-led language analysis in which I would provide 'public correction'. During student reporting, I would interrupt to clarify, correct, highlight, or add new language, which I would write on the chalkboard, for students to record in the analysis section of their learning journals. I decided on a 'real-time' analysis because I noticed that immediate and timely feedback keeps students focused on language form. Moreover, it is easier for me to utilize my expertise at the moment it is needed, rather then trying to recall and summarize at the end of the reports. Overall it was at this stage where I counted on the journal to be the most helpful, because it was at this stage that students had not been in the habit of taking notes.

Action

At the beginning of each lesson, after handing out the blank learning journals, I introduced open-ended (unfocused) tasks such as the one described in this paper: *Talking about your family and friends*. I did this by briefly writing on the chalkboard such foregrounding techniques as mind-maps, to introduce potential language and ways of approaching the task. After that students prepared for the task for 10 to 15 minutes by writing down whatever language they wanted to use or had available in the *Pre-task Exploration* section of their journals. They could ask each other, use their dictionaries and check out language with me. Even with unguided planning, students managed to use a comprehensive variety of relevant language. Furthermore, they showed great interest in being given such freedom to explore.

During the actual task, students were not allowed to look at their journal or any other material including dictionaries. If they finished quickly, I made everyone change partners at the same time and do it over again. In some cases this resulted in the students doing a task as many as three times with three different partners. Since the tasks were open tasks, the actual information gathered from their new partners was different each time so they did not find this boring. Learners also gained confidence as they talked about their topic for a second or third time; see Lynch and Maclean (2001) for further benefits of task repetition.

When the task finished naturally or at my choosing, students prepared a report of what they had talked about in the *Task Notes* section of their journals. Lower-level students who had trouble writing the report just wrote out their task report in dialogue form (in the same way as in Muller, Chapter 6). This made it easier for them to organize and recall their language and it guaranteed that their reports would contain a variety of responses as well as questions. Finally, during the presentation of their reports, I provided feedback and other explicit form focused instruction which the students recorded in the third section of their journals: *Class Analysis and Summary*. At the end of the lesson I asked them to reflect silently on an aspect of the lesson, and they filled in the bottom of the page: *Today's Reflections*.

Observation and analysis

By reviewing the learning journals throughout the semester, I confirmed that there were grounds for Skehan's warning about learners' overuse of **lexicalized language** (1996a: 22). In the journal examples, complete phrases like *How many people in your family?* were commonly foregrounded and frequently used. Such expressions, like other lexicalized language, can be memorized as 'fixed wholes' or '**chunks**', which means that students are bypassing the underlying grammar that is ultimately crucial for greater language ability and on-going language development.

However, the most common type of language I identified at the pre-task stage, was '**lexical bundles**', such as *Wh*-question fragments (*wh*-question word followed by an auxiliary or modal verb, eg *What are you going to* ...), *Yes-No* question fragments (auxiliary or modal verb followed by a subject pronoun, eg *Have you got any* ...), and finally '**utterance launchers**' (personal pronoun + lexical verb phrase usually followed by a complement clause, eg *I was talking to* ...). What is important to understand is that these, like most lexical bundles, are structurally incomplete and require some form of grammatical competence to use them effectively (see Nattinger & DeCarrico: 1992; Bygate: 1994).

Even with *Wh*—question fragments (see below) that are memorized as complete phrases, there are still grammatical decisions involved when using them. In the sample journals (see Appendix 1), the students try to formulate the questions: *What does he/she do?*, *What is your brother doing?*, *What job does your father do?*, but instead produce, *What does he/she doing?*, *What does your brother/sister doing?*, *What job do your father?* In journal 1, with the first two questions above, there is confusion between the use of the *simple present tense* and *present progressive*. In journal 2, the question about a person's father's job is missing a main verb and there is incorrect subject and verb agreement. The purpose of identifying these errors is that they are grammatically based, and therefore confirm that even with memorized expressions, it is still necessary for students to be familiar with the grammar that is involved in formulating or modifying the questions. In summary the data revealed a more complex picture than Skehan's (1996a) simple dichotomy between syntax and lexicalized language.

The effectiveness of the learning journal and TBL in general is evident in this example: in one journal (not presented here) the student does not use the comparative or the superlative at the pre-task stage, writing *I have one brother who is five years old than I.* Neither partner used these forms at the task stage, saying instead *Old sister is 15 years old and young sister is 10 years,* nor does it appear in the 'task notes'. The errors of omission during the early stages of the lesson probably stem from lack of experience with these grammatical features when talking about one's family. At the report stage the problem became public, and I then provided explicit language instruction which the students could record in the final section of their journals.

Added to the above instruction, I also taught *middle child,* as in *I am a middle child.* Furthermore I explained that besides, *How many people in your family?*, it is also common for pragmatic reasons to use, *Do you have any brothers or sisters?* For details of what they wrote at the final stage, see students' entries in Journal 2 (Appendix 1).

Reflection and evaluation

I gained a number of important insights during this project. First, I realized that Skehan's (1996a) criticism, while important, simplifies the relationship between grammar and lexicalized language. Lexicalized language is for easing cognitive load during conversation, and is also a 'launch pad' for building message and language form, for which ultimately some level of grammatical competence is required. I think the possible explanation for the current emphasis on lexicalized language is a recognition of the need for practice and exposure to this type of language by students. This is credible since students in many EFL environments study languages through methodologies which are overly focused on the rules of grammar.

In addition, the journal, by mirroring the TBL process, made the sequencing of the lesson easier. Most importantly, it helped guide the students' focus of attention from meaning to form and vice versa. The pedagogical sequence of TBL is something that inexperienced EFL students may have trouble understanding, and teachers have trouble articulating, not least because TBL demands a high level of learner autonomy that cannot be presumed in many EFL environments where language learning is still predominately associated with passive learning through rote or habitual methodologies. I believe Skehan's concern may ultimately stem from this fundamental problem, because it is when attention cannot be focused in concert with the TBL sequence that imbalances between meaning and form can occur.

Skehan's (1996a) 'key' to this problem is the same as was first prescribed in the initial planning stage. Namely, it is the recognition that a 'controlled approach' is vital to balance the 'competing pressures' between meaning and form. The idea of the learning journal was to help my learners take a more systematic approach to learning through tasks by raising the profile of language form at specific stages in the task cycle. This I did by ensuring that the writing processes that are beneficial to a focus on form were also highlighted and kept sequential. It succeeded to the point that doing a task became synonymous with using the journal to prepare, report, and then analyse task language. Journal completion was as central to the class as was doing the task itself.

Student feedback

At the end of the semester I conducted a survey to see how the students felt about the journal. Almost all students commented on the importance of getting the opportunity to write down their own ideas before speaking. The students also overwhelmingly indicated that they liked and wanted to continue real-time public correction. Many students remarked that for the first time it felt like they were learning 'real grammar'. Perhaps the most telling information came from the surveys administered by other faculty at the end of the semester. Prior to introducing the journal, 10 per cent of my students regularly indicated that their English had not improved, or that they did not know if it had improved or not. Amazingly this group disappeared! I think the reason for this is that the journal introduced students to the empowering potential of TBL, helped them to be aware of the amount of language they had covered, and showed them that they are just as responsible for their learning as I was.

Conclusion

Using learning journals has helped me achieve with my students what I see as the basic goal of EFL oral communication classes: a 'golden mean' between accuracy, fluency and restructuring to enable students to gain greater language complexity. The key to this balance depends on *student* understanding of this. Furthermore, such journals are likely to prove useful for testers, course directors and for researchers, as they provide a continuous record of the language used and highlighted over the course of a term or a year.

Appendix 1 Samples of learning journals

LEARNING JOURNAL *Name:* *Date:* 10/29

Today's Task: Family / relationships

1 Pre –Task Exploration: ***Think of words, phrases, grammar that will be needed to do the task.***

- How many peaple (are there) in your family? • How many people is there your cosen?
- Do you have any brothe or sister? Do you have any pet?
- How old is your brother or sister?
- what does he/she doing. (your brothe/sister)

2 Task Notes: ***What did you talk about? Write down ideas, words, phrases, grammar, pieces of dialogue***

Do you have a boyfriend?
How many people are there in your family? Do you have a pet?
Do you have any brother or sister? How old is he/she?
What does he/she doing. What is your father's job?
what is your boyfriend name. How about your family?

3 Class Analysis and Summary:

Do you have any pets? Do you live with your family still?
How long have you dated (been together)?
When did you start dating.

Today's Reflection What new wards/gramar did I lorn Today

- 「How about your family」, 「How long have you dated」

I didn't know how to use these words.
But I learned theseword mean by teacher.
So, I understand words mean.

LEARNING JOURNAL Name: Date: 10/29

Today's Task: family / + boyfriend / + gairlfriend

1 Pre –Task Exploration: *Think of words, phrases, grammar that will be needed to do the task.*

There are four people in my family. my father, mother, older brother.
How many people in your family.
I have one brothe who is five years old than I

2 Task Notes: *What did you talk about? Write down ideas, words, phrases, grammar, pieces of dialogue*

- How many people in your family.
- My family is fave people.
- I have father, mother, two sisters and me.
- How old is your sister.
- old sister is 15 years old and young sister is 10 years old

3 Class Analysis and Summary: アメリカ．カナダでは こういう (How many people in your family) と…)

Do you have any brothers or sisters.
There are 5 people in my family including me.
I have a brother and sister.
Is your brother older younger.
I'm a middle child. yongest · oldest middle child

boyfriend バージョン
How long have you been dated / seen / been toger. = when did you start dating seeing eatch other.
when did you break up

Today's Reflection
↳ what new words grammar, did you learn today?

Today I learned new words grammar.
Forexthanple. when asked about family.
" Do you have any brothers or sisters.
There are 4 people in my family including me.

<u>*LEARNING JOURNAL*</u> <u>*Name:*</u> <u>*Date:*</u>

Today's Task: family / boy friend

1 Pre –Task Exploration: ***Think of words, phrases, grammar that will be needed to do the task.***

How many people are in your family?
There are five people in my family
What job do your father?
How old is your mother?
My mother is 43 years old

2 Task Notes: ***What did you talk about? Write down ideas, words, phrases, grammar, pieces of dialogue***

How many people are in your family?
I have five families. Do you have any brothers or sisters?
I have a sister and brother.
I'm a youngest sister in my family
~~Do~~ How old ~~are~~ is your father?
My father is 53 years old.
Do you have any pets?

3 Class Analysis and Summary:

There are 5 people in my family including me.
I'm a middle child (youngest) (oldest)
How long have you been dating (seeing)
Do you have any pets? When did you break up?
Do you have any brothers or (and) sisters?

Today's Reflection What new words grammar did you learn today?

I learnd same how to speak "How many people are in your family?" and "Do you have any brothers or sisters?"
others "There are 5 people in my family including me." I learnd new words

Part B

Exploring Task Interaction: Helping Learners do Better

In this second part, four teachers working in four different countries report on investigations they have carried out to see if they can help their learners do tasks more effectively, use more language and improve their interaction skills. All four recorded their learners doing tasks, and then asked their learners to repeat the task (or rather, do similar style tasks) after doing the first one. They then compared the recordings of their learners' first attempts with later attempts.

The assumption behind all these investigations is that we can intervene to drive our learners' language development forward. This can be achieved by helping learners to make more effective use of the opportunities that tasks offer for them to use the target language to express their own meanings and understand what is being said to them. They will get more confident as they become familiar with the task type, and feel more willing to express themselves more fully. If you are interested in exploring the theories underpinning this assumption before you read Part B, they are summarized in Shehadeh, Chapter 1.

In Chapter 8, Leedham's aim was to help her intermediate Japanese learners in UK do better in an oral interview exam task. She recorded her learners doing exam tasks, and then transcribed them, showing the transcripts to the learners at a language focus stage at the end of the task cycle. She also recorded some native speakers doing the same tasks, and learners looked at transcripts of those too. This enabled learners to compare their efforts with those of native speakers. The thing they immediately noticed was the amount of short speaking turns that native speakers tended to use for this task; there was far more interaction in shorter utterances. Leedham goes on to explore the reasons for the learners using far longer and more sustained speaking turns.

Lee, Chapter 9, working with young learners of around 11–12 years old in Korea, also uses recordings of tasks done by native-speakers to raise learners' awareness of how speakers naturally use devices like confirmation checks, clarification requests and repetition in order to clarify or 'negotiate' the meaning of what is being said. One group of learners had this training, whereas the other group did not, and he explores in what ways the 'trained' learners improved.

Interestingly, Pinter, in Chapter 10, working with slightly younger learners in Hungary, found that her pairs of learners all improved (though to varying degrees) just by repeating the same type of task three times, with no intervention from the teacher and no training at all. Her study focuses closely on the children themselves and explores not only the changes in the task interactions over time, but also how they felt about doing the tasks (it was the first time they had ever used English freely). She discovers they were all aware of the progress they had made and were very happy with the results.

Finally in Chapter 11, Coulson, working at a women's college in Japan, found that when his learners tried to use their English in conversations with international students on campus, they often gave up trying to express what they wanted to say because other more dominant speakers took over the conversation. But when he got his learners to record these conversations, he also found that in some cases another Japanese student present at the time helped the speaker to continue and to get her meaning across. So Coulson developed this idea of peer support into what he calls 'Team-Talking', devising tasks to help train his learners in 'Team-Talking' strategies, so that, working as a team, they could hold their own and keep the floor in cross-cultural conversations.

As well as recording and transcribing their learners' task interactions, three teachers used these transcriptions with their learners in order to raise their awareness of their own interaction strategies and styles. Both Leedham and Lee also recorded native speakers doing tasks and used the transcripts in class, so learners could compare their language with that of fluent speakers. Coulson later got his students to record and transcribe their own interactions in class and outside class, and this process made them even more aware of how far they needed to help each other and explore effective means of doing so. In fact, both learners and teachers made a lot of discoveries through looking closely at task transcripts.

Other research methods used by the teachers included holding interviews after the tasks with learners in pairs (Pinter), discussing with students informally in class (Lee, Leedham and Coulson).

The process of gaining student feedback can also be a task in its own right. Task instructions could be:

> *Think of two or three things you remember about doing the tasks the first/last time. In your pairs/groups make a list of these things (in note form) and prepare to tell the class about them.*

Finally, all the chapters in this section could provide a model for classroom investigations involving task recordings.

8
Exam-oriented Tasks: Transcripts, Turn-taking and Backchannelling

Maria Leedham

Summary *I was working with students who were preparing to take the Cambridge First Certificate of English oral examination, and looking for ways to help them do this. I decided to try a task-based learning cycle which involved recording students doing a task, listening to native speakers doing the same task, and analysing the transcripts, before repeating a similar task. The students appeared to notice some differences between their speech and that of the native speakers, and were able to develop their speaking skills accordingly.*

Context: an exam-oriented course

The two students taking part in this study are young Japanese women in their early twenties. I shall refer to them as Y and S. They are in the last term of a one-year course in British Studies at Oxford University, UK, and both scored 5.5 in a pre-course IELTS test (525 TOEFL equivalent). Being in the UK, they have ample opportunity to talk with native speakers. At the end of the course they will take the Cambridge First Certificate in English (FCE) exam.

In the 15-minute speaking section of this FCE exam, students are tested in pairs. Part 3 of this oral test consists of a three-minute problem-solving task involving the exchange of opinions. After receiving task instructions students have a minute to think before speaking.

Background and rationale

I got involved in this investigation because I wanted to see whether my students benefited from comparing transcripts of their own task interactions with transcripts of native speakers (NS) doing the same task. In particular, did the use of recordings in a TBL cycle help students to notice and use turn-taking and backchannelling features?

Turn-taking, that is, the handing over of talk between speakers, involves less overlapping talk in Japanese as intrusive interruptions are commonly avoided (Murata, 1994). When speaking in English, students allow their partner to finish their contribution and wait for a pause before they give their own opinion. In the oral exam this may well make them appear less fluent than they really are and likely to gain a lower grade. In conversations outside class with other nationalities, Japanese students may appear shy, disfluent or just unwilling to communicate.

The term **backchannel** implies that there are two channels in talk – the main channel of the speaker holding the floor and a backchannel of the listener who contributes to the conversation without gaining the floor (White, 1989). This may take the form of supportive 'mmm' or 'yeah' contributions, and varies in quantity between speakers and nationalities.

In most countries where English is taught as a foreign language students have little or no opportunity to experience English turn-taking and backchannelling patterns since they have little interaction with fluent or native speakers (White, 1989 and own experience). The action research reported here tries to address this issue by highlighting the differences between student and NS (native speaker) language during task performance.

Method

Practice interviews: the problem identified

During practice interviews I noticed that in part 3 Y and S were speaking in long turns of almost equal length. Each student began by agreeing with the previous turn '*I also would ...*' They added something new, then asked '*what do you think?*'. Students maintained fairly complete sentences as they believed this equalled better English and therefore gained a better mark in the test.

They did not build up the topic jointly but considered it in turn, while their partner waited for their turn. Overlapping language was limited to a background '*mmmmm*', which seemed to be a transfer from Japanese 'aizuchi' (backchannelling).

Response

Over two lessons I followed a task-based learning cycle in an effort to help my students respond to each other more naturally. This cycle consisted of task, post-task listening, then repeating the task (see Willis, 1996a: 86).

In lesson one I recorded Y and S completing a FCE part 3 interview question. In lesson two we analysed a transcript of their recording plus a transcript of a NS dyad carrying out the same task.

Two well-known studies consider aspects of task use relevant to this investigation: Bygate (1996) examines the potential benefits of task repetition; and Foster (1996) looks at the effects of including pre-task planning time. Since the students in this research were practising for an imminent exam, I carried out the speaking lessons as mock exam interviews. Students had just one minute of planning time before performing the first task, as in the exam.

Findings and evaluation

Lesson One, Task One: Student performance

The instructions given to the students were as follows:

> Can you look at the picture? Imagine this is your room at college and you are going to live here for a year. What extra things would you need in the room to make it suitable to live in? What would you add? What would you put where? It is not necessary to agree with each other.

(Task rubric based on Practice Tests for FCE, 1998, Morris, S. & Stanton, A, Test 2 part 3.)

These instructions were accompanied by the drawing in Figure 1.

Y and S carried out the task as almost two separate parts with long turns each and little variety of backchannel:

Y: OK ... ahhhh. [I think] the first thing you need [is of] course the desk and chair [and I] want to
S: [mmm] [mmm] [mmm]
Y: put them ahh next to the ahhhh mmmm shelf not shelf ... this [furniture]
S: [ahhh] OK ...
Y: yes, and [ahhh] and also ... mmm mmm if possible I want ... ahhh to put ahh ... um TV
S: [mmmmm]

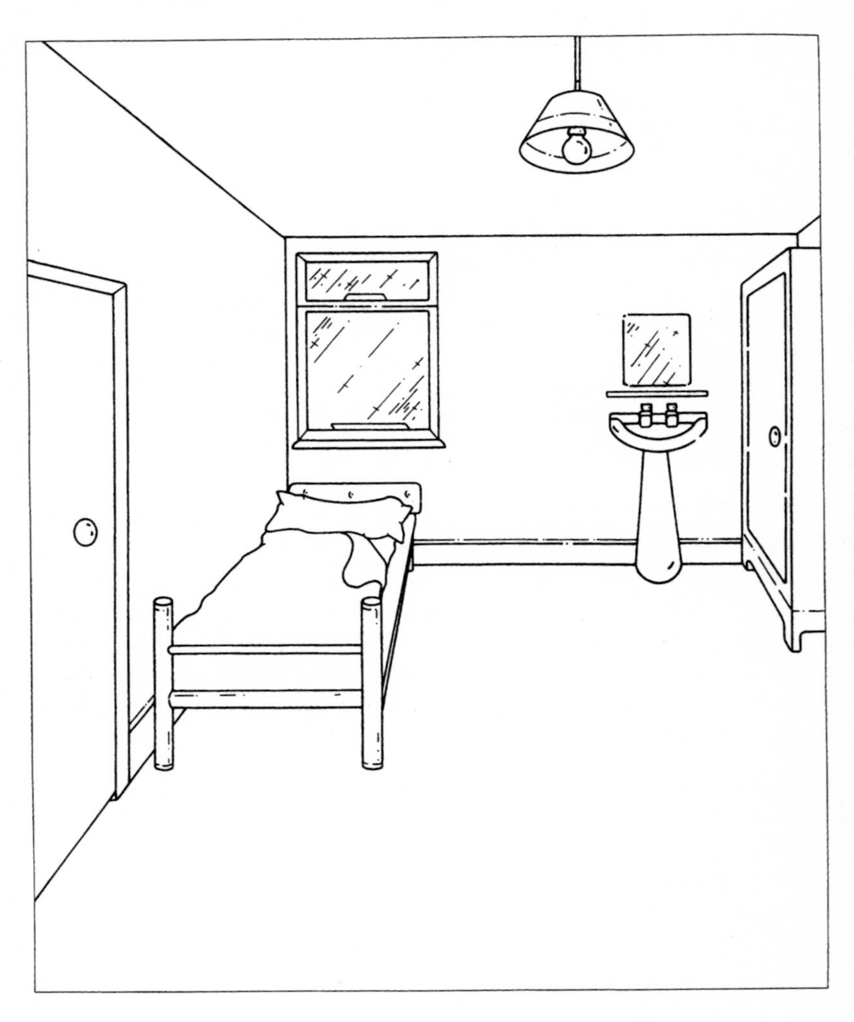

Figure 1

Y: next to mmm ... bed

S: ... I also. I would put first desk and chair ... [then] some entertainment for example TV

Y: [mmm]

S: or [radio],

Y: [yes]

S: maybe put next to the [bed].

Y: [mmm]

S: or useful mmmm [small desk] and on the ... on the desk put TV or radio ... on the desk
Y: [ah kind of mmm]
S: small desk
Y: ... and also I want that the [ahhh] the curtains on the window ... small window [because] mmmm we HAVE to
S: [mmmm]
[mmmm]

Any simultaneous speech is brief and consistently a cooperative interruption (Murata, 1994) serving as listener support. Indeed the use of '*mmm*' as backchannel seems greater each time I listen to the recording and at times is an almost continuous soft background noise. Only once is a question asked towards the end of the three minutes. The two students maintain harmony in their conversation at all times.

Task One: NS performance and comparison with students' talk

The native speaker pair was given exactly the same instructions and line drawing as the students (see above). The overwhelming feeling on listening to the NS dialogue is that it is a real conversation, albeit on a prescribed topic and in front of a tape recorder. The participants respond to each other by asking questions (nine in total) and cooperatively building the topic. Turn-taking is smooth with no discernible pauses between speakers, and sometimes overlapping words, as can be seen from the following extract.

J: but if I'm going to be a student in that room then I think I'd need at least one book[shelf].
V: [mmm]
J: for books
V: mmmm
J: and ermm a toaster ... for late night snacks ... if you're working late and you [just get tired]
V: [but.. would you] not have a kitchen [as well?]
J: [err ...] I think [there'd ....]
V: [Or is this your] own personal toaster?
J: It'd be my own personal [toaster]
V: [(laughs)]
J: and my own personal kettle.

V: what about a ... a rug of some kind? ... I'm not that keen on rugs actually.
J: ... nah ... nah I wouldn't bo- but I definitely wouldn't have a television
V: no
J: too big a distraction
V: not in your bedroom
J: throw it out.

The speakers use few standard EFL 'agreeing words and phrases', and instead show agreement by a limited range of sounds, predominantly '*yeah*', '*mmmm*' and repeating lexical items. This is worth bearing in mind, since textbook lessons featuring ways of agreeing typically concentrate on items such as '*I strongly agree*' which rarely feature in NS talk.

Compared to the student dialogue, the NS turns are on the short side and are punctuated by a variety of feedback from the listener. One speaker makes a suggestion and the other elaborates, justifies or rejects this. eg:

J: it's a bit of a bare room
V: mmm you need some ... some ... plants.
J: plants?
V: (laughs)

Lesson Two: Students compare the transcripts

In the second lesson the students and I compared the two transcripts. I treated this first as a listening exercise and asked them to note down the things each pair wanted to put in the room while listening to the two recordings. I then gave out copies of the transcripts and asked the students to discuss in pairs what they had noticed, followed by a group discussion.

The students commented that they had been worried about finding the right word ('*the ahhh mmmm shelf, not shelf ... this furniture*'), but the NSs seemed unconcerned ('*I don't know what they're called ... it's got big green leaves*'). The students also noticed the NSs' varied use of backchannel and the use of questions and comments. A lot of the talk is incomplete and turns are often very short with lots of listener feedback. The NSs personalized the task and took a wider perspective on it, with frequent digressions.

Task Two: Students

The students then carried out a second, similar task:

> Can you look at the picture? It shows a room where you are going to have a party. I'd like you to talk together and decide what you would do to the room and the things in it before the party to get it ready to receive your guests. What changes would you make to the room? How would you arrange it? It is not necessary to agree with each other.

(Task rubric based on Practice Tests for FCE, 1998, Morris, S. & Stanton, A, Test 4 part 3.)

The accompanying picture is shown in Figure 2.

This time, Y and S asked questions and repeated nouns from each other's speech. Turns are much shorter than in their first lesson and the

Figure 2

conversation is shared, with one student making a suggestion and the other responding.

S: I will keep ... I want to ... to keep a big space much big space .so I will remove chair
Y: chair
S: chair to the other room or [I don't] know how [to say] the table
Y: [uh huh] [mmmm]
S: a kind of table or that put on too and also take take away to a different place
Y: ahhh so you want more space ahh ... I see ... how about books I want to [mmm]
S: [ahhhh]
Y: place replace them to the bookshelf and errr also there is a errr bag from ... shoe ... shoe ... from [shoestore]
S: [mmmm]
Y: so I think [not necessary] we should throw it away and err
S: [not necessary]
this book is errr best kept in the room because someone maybe want to look for the book [and err]
Y: [so you want] to put it some place
S: err not on the floor next to the TV or and the base of TV and errr ...
Y: chest?
S: I don't know ... The table on the lamp and the floor I want to decorate the room look like party party ... party place

The last three lines of the extract above show overlap where Y was trying to help S when the latter hesitated. Earlier in the conversation S carries on despite being unsure over the word. Turns pass from one student to the other more readily:

S: I don't know how to say ... bare room
Y: ahhh ... mmmm ... I prefer a big table to put some dishes on the table
S: [mmmm]
[desk ahhh]
Y: no table ... err necessary to put a lot of dish ... (yes) how to ... on the table put on candle [and] flower

Some improvement may of course be due to repeating a similar task with familiar room and furniture vocabulary and working with the same partner. This familiarity should allow greater attention to turn-taking and backchannelling, as well as lexical or grammatical improvement, since the cognitive load will have been reduced (see Chapter 1).

Evaluation: feedback from the learners

The students felt the task cycle had been useful and seemed to find it motivating. As described above, looking at a transcript of NSs doing the same task generated much discussion on conversation features.

From later discussion with students it seemed the looming exam contributed to their concern with equal-length turns and complete sentences. The former were a concern because students felt they should give their partner equal chance to display their oral ability, and the latter as they felt this is what they would be judged on in FCE. In Japan well-formed sentences are seen as a mark of good English language ability and thus more likely to feature in exam practice.

Conclusion and ideas for other task cycles using transcripts

Students noticed the difference in turn-taking styles and use of backchannel, and made use of this when doing their second task. Longitudinal research would be useful to determine the extent to which they maintain this.

It would be beneficial to continue using transcripts to highlight conversation features over a course of lessons. For example:

- Record students and NSs doing short speaking tasks for other exam interviews, eg Cambridge, TOEFL, end of year exams. Compare transcripts.
- Look at textbook dialogues or the tapescripts in the back of course-books and compare these with spontaneously recorded native or fluent speaker transcripts on a similar task/topic. Do the tapescripts have interruptions, backchannelling?
- Instead of NS speech, use recordings of higher-level students with a lower-level group.
- Students could listen to their own speech and transcribe sections themselves, perhaps in groups. They could compare this with fluent or native speakers' recordings of the same task.

Hobbs (this volume) gives further ideas and advice on making and using recordings.

Since carrying out this research I have encouraged students to record themselves outside class as well as within classes. I have continued to use NS task recordings to highlight features of natural English.

9

Training Young Learners in Meaning Negotiation Skills: Does it Help?

Seung-Min Lee

Summary *In this study I examine the effectiveness of training young learners in meaning negotiation skills. The learners, who were pupils in an English as a foreign language class at a primary school in Korea, showed signs of improved ability to negotiate meaning after training, and were better able to perform speaking tasks.*

Background and rationale

Meaning negotiation skills

Meaning negotiation is a process, in which the participants in a conversation collaborate with each other to problem-solve. To do this, they employ meaning negotiation skills, including **negotiation devices** such as **confirmation checks, comprehension checks, clarification requests, repetition requests,** and repetition. In this way they can achieve successful communication when they anticipate or encounter communication problems. Some examples of negotiation devices are (see also Tsui, 1995):

S1: Where is bookshop?
S2: Uh, next ... next hospital.
S1: *Next hospital?* (Confirmation check)

S1: Where is she from?
S2: She from Korea.
S1: ...
S2: *OK?* (Comprehension check)

S1: England. E, n, g, l, a, n, d.
S2: E, n ... *One more time*. (Repetition request)
S1: E, n, g, l, a, n, d.
(Data from Lee 2002)

Meaning negotiation skills are essential for learning a second or foreign language, in that they can facilitate 'comprehensible input' (Krashen, 1982), 'comprehensible output' (Swain, 1995), and enhance motivation (Larsen-Freeman, 2000). But I had noticed that the primary school pupils who I teach tend not to use such skills when they do speaking tasks in English classes. Some studies (eg Anderson & Lynch, 1988) support my observation: young learners are not good at providing the speaker with feedback to indicate a problem in understanding what is being said, and this may cause communication problems. With these issues in mind, I decided to try to train my young learners in meaning negotiation skills as a means of improving their task performance.

Preliminary recordings of regular classes

During the first week of the three-week project I first observed and video-recorded two regular EFL English classes in a Korean primary school, in order to determine whether primary school pupils did indeed employ any negotiation skills when doing tasks of the kind shown later in this chapter. I found that the most frequent device was repetition of someone else's utterance. Confirmation checks came second. Self-repetition and repetition requests were not used very frequently. Clarification requests and comprehension checks were not used at all. Thus according to the data, it may be said that the pupils do have some negotiation skills and employ them in English classes. But they employ very limited kinds of devices, mainly confirmation checks and repetition.

Another problem was found in the case of confirmation checks. The pupils very often asked another pupil in the same group, who was not the 'informant' for confirmation (only two out of nine confirmation checks were asked of the informant). This 'substitution of the informant' problem (i.e. asking another pupil in the same group instead of the informant) may be serious, because there is a risk of receiving wrong information (or no information!).

The third problem is related to self-repetition and repetition of someone else's utterance:

T: In front of the station, there is a statue. Lisa will be there.

S1: *Statue. Statue.*

S2: *Statue*. Here it is. Here it is.

(Lee, 2002)

Here, S1 and S2 repeated part of the teacher's utterance, but their final answer (given later) was wrong. Thus self-repetition and repetition of someone else's utterance may not be useful negotiation devices, in that they did not seem to help learners perform the tasks successfully. This means that these two devices needed to be excluded from the results. If these two devices and confirmation checks addressed to another pupil who was not an informant are excluded, only three devices remained.

To summarize the problems I found, the children used very limited kinds of negotiation devices. Most of them were rather 'passive' devices, in that they seemed not to help learners to perform the tasks successfully. Thus it can be concluded that the pupils may some have negotiation skills, but they don't employ the full range of them effectively in English classes.

Method

My aim was to examine the development of young learners' negotiation skills when they performed tasks after receiving some training. For this experiment I chose 12 pupils (aged 11–12) from a different primary EFL class. I chose this age-group because the pupils had a sufficient level of basic communicative competence to perform the tasks designed for this study.

In the first session, the 12 pupils performed two tasks in four groups of three, where they could use English in a relaxed and cooperative atmosphere. Half of the pupils (two 'training' groups) then had training sessions in which they worked on their negotiation skills, as I will explain below. Finally, all four groups of pupils did a second, parallel, pair of tasks. These were the same types of tasks, and very similar, but not identical to, the first two tasks. I recorded the pupils doing these tasks over a period of three weeks. During the first week I recorded all four groups doing Task 1A and Task 2A. The second week was for training sessions, which only the two training groups attended. During the third week, I recorded all four groups doing Tasks 1B and 2B.

I designed four tasks to use in training sessions, two of each kind, as follows.

Identifying locations (Task 1A and Task 1B)

These were one-way information gap tasks, where pupils had follow directions to find the house where Tom's birthday party was to be held.

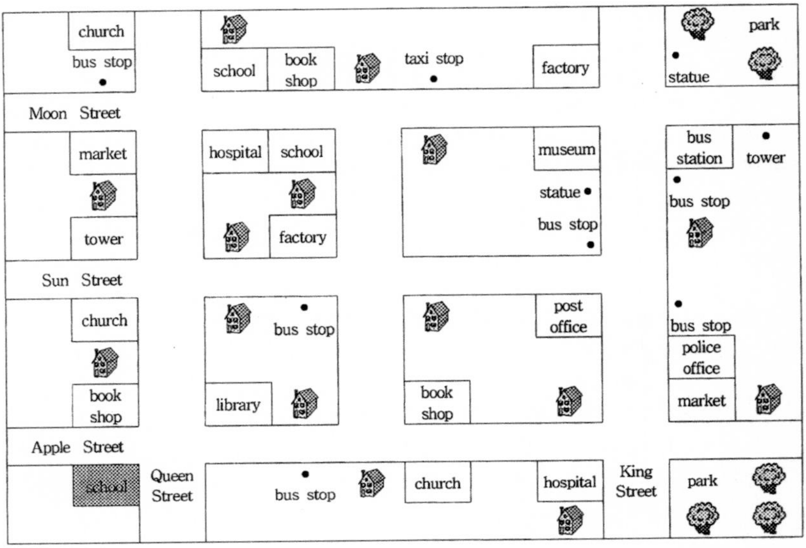

Figure 1 Task 1A

I gave the pupils a map on which they had to mark target places according to the teacher's directions. If they were not sure of the route as I was explaining it, they could ask me for more information during a pause or in fact at any time if it was necessary. Task 1B is slightly different from Task 1A in that the pupils had to find different target places on the same map.

Completing the missing information (Task 2A and Task 2B)

The worksheets for these two-way information gap tasks were divided into two parts, each consisting of complementary information about name, age, job, and country. The students worked in four groups of three (Groups A, B, C and D), and each group was given one of two parts. Without showing their version to the other group, they had to fill in the worksheets by sharing information with the other group. Task 2B is slightly different from Task 2A in that it includes different names, ages, jobs, and countries.

Training sessions

For the training sessions for groups C and D, I got two English teachers to make a recording of themselves doing Task 2A. I asked them to do the

Name			Yujin	
Age	30			
Job		postman	student	actor
Country	U. S. A.	England		Japan

Name	Sue	Tony		Morino
Age		42	13	28
Job	teacher		Korea	
Country				

Figure 2 Task 2A

task as naturally as possible. I used this material for raising the pupils' awareness of the negotiation skills used by fluent speakers doing the task. An example follows:

T1: OK, uh ... who is the man with a moustache? What's his name?
T2: With a moustache? Morino. M, o, r, i, n, o.
T1: Sorry, one more time.
T2: M, o, r, i, n, o. OK?
T1: OK. Uh ... what does he do?
T2: He's an actor.
T1: An actor.

(Lee, 2002)

I held two training sessions during the second week, lasting about an hour each, for the two training groups C and D. My objectives were to help the pupils notice various negotiation devices in the model recording, understand their importance in communication, and be able to use them. In the first session, I showed the worksheets for Task 2A and described the task procedure briefly in Korean. Then I played the model recording to the pupils twice (first the whole of recording, secondly a section). I replayed the tape and, during the second listening, I asked them to listen out for the words and phrases the English teachers used when they were struggling to work out how to do the task. The pupils seemed to understand the task procedure because they had done the same task during the first week, and found some expressions for meaning negotiation with ease. Finally, I stressed the importance of asking for confirmation or clarification when the message is unclear or inadequate (this was also done in Korean). The children also practiced some expressions for meaning negotiation (eg *Sorry, one more time, What do you mean*?, *OK?*, *Do you know what I mean*?) In the second session, the children had targeted practice in using these types of negotiation device during some information-gap tasks, such as finding the number of animals in picture of a farm. In these kinds of task, the pupils needed to use negotiation devices to complete the tasks successfully.

Findings

The effects of meaning negotiation skill training

The extracts below show how pupils (S) in two of the groups, A and C, interacted with the teacher (T) to do Task 1A, that is, their first attempt, before repeating the task or receiving any training. The tendency of the pupils in both groups to repeat all or part of the teacher's preceding utterance is particularly striking (see also Table 1 below). Utterances transcribed in italics have been translated from Korean.

When I analysed the complete transcripts for the four groups, I found the following results for the number of negotiation devices used (see Tables). (For simplicity, I have combined the results for the two non-training groups A and B, and the two training groups C and D.)

Looking at the analysed data, it seems that the training sessions had an appreciable effect. First, the total number of devices used by the trained pupils increased dramatically, more than doubling in the case of Task 2, with confirmation checks accounting for most of this increase. Conversely, repetition of other's utterance decreased. This may be because, after the training sessions, the pupils negotiated for meaning by using more 'active' devices. Secondly, the pupils employed various types of devices. During Task 1A, they used only two types (confirmation

Task 1A Group A	Task 1A Group C
...	...
T: Go straight. You will find a bus station.	T: King Street. Go straight. You will find a bus station.
S: *I think this station is right.*	S: *Here, here it is. Here it is.*
S: *Right.*	S: *Right.*
T: In front of the station, there is a statue.	T: In front of the station, there is a statue. Lisa will be there.
S: (to another S) Statue?	S: *Statue, statue ...*
S: *Yes*, statue.	S: Statue ... *here it is, here it is.*
T: Lisa will be there.	S: Yes.
S: *Here. I think this statue is right.*	T: Then turn left ...
S: *I think so too.*	S: Turn left.
T: Then turn left ...	T: and go straight along Moon Street.
S: Turn left.	S: Moon Street.
T: and go straight along Moon Street.	T: You will find a high school.
S: Moon ... Moon Street ... *here it is.*	S: High school.
T: You will find a high school.	S: *Here it is. Here it is.*
S: High school.	S: (to another S) School?.
S: School, school ... *here ...*	S: *I think this is right.*
T: My house is next to the school.	T: My house is next to the school.
	S: *I think this is right.*
S: *Here it is. Here it is. I got it.*	S: *I think so too.*

Table 1 Number of negotiation devices (Tasks 1A and 1B)

Device Groups	Con	Cla	Rep	Com	Self Rep	Rep (other)	Total
A & B (Task 1A)	5(0/5)	0	0	0	0	22	27
C & D (Task 1A)	11(2/9)	0	0	0	0	12	23
A & B (Task 1B) (repetition only)	3(2/1)	0	0	0	0	14	17
C, D (Task 1B) (training and repetition)	17(13/4)	3	2	0	2	10	34

Key to table 1

Con = Confirmation checks
Rep = Repetition requests
Self = Self-repetition
Cla = Clarification requests
Com = Comprehension checks
Rep (other) = Repetition of other's utterance

Table 2 Number of negotiation devices (Tasks 2A and 2B)

Device Group	Con	Cla	Rep	Com	Self	Rep (other)	Total
A & B (Task 2A)	5(0/5)	0	1	0	1	7	14
C, D (Task 2A)	4(1/3)	0	0	0	4	7	15
A & B (Task 2B) (repetition only)	2(1/1)	0	0	0	1	8	11
C, D (Task 2B) (training and repetition)	20 (19/1)	0	4	0	3	4	31

Key to table 2

Con = Confirmation checks
Rep = Repetition requests
Self = Self-repetition
Cla = Clarification requests
Com = Comprehension checks
Rep (other) = Repetition of other's utterance

checks and repetition of other's utterance). But during Task 1B they employed clarification requests, repetition requests and self-repetition as well as confirmation checks and repetition of other's utterance. This improvement was also found in the transcripts for Task 2B. In the case of control Groups A and B, the total number of negotiation devices used by the students actually decreased in the second tasks; this may be because the children were repeating very similar tasks, so did not perceive as many breakdowns or problems in the communication as for their first tasks.

The most dramatic improvement was observed in the area of confirmation. Before training, only 3 cases out of 15 confirmation checks were addressed to the informant. After training, 32 cases out of 37 cases were addressed to the informant. In the two transcript extracts below, we can see how control Group A (no training) continued to rely on repeating the teacher's utterance (cf. the extract for Task 1A above), while pupils in Group C (who received training) used a range of devices, highlighted here in bold.

Another interesting finding is that this improvement appeared to influence the task results directly. Table 3 shows the number of correct task results for all four groups. From the data, it certainly looks as though the training sessions also improved the task results. In both tasks, the number of right answers increased for the groups that had received training. Although these numbers are too small to provide conclusive evidence, they nevertheless indicate a trend that would merit further investigation.

Task 1B Group A (task repetition without training)	**Task 1B Group C (task repetition after training)**
T: Go straight. You will find a post office. In front of the post office, there is a bus stop. Lisa will be there. S: Bus stop, bus stop. T: Go straight and then turn left. Now you are on Moon Street. S: Moon Street. T: Go straight along Moon Street. S: Moon Street. T: You will find a high school. S: High school, school. T: My house is next to the school. S: Next to the school, school ... *Here it is.* S: *Right.* T: My house is next to the school. S: *Across from ...* S: *Here it is.* S: *No. It means* behind the school S: Behind? *No,* next, next ... *I'm right.*	T: The bookshop is not far from here. Jane's house is next to the bookshop. S: **One more time.** T: One more time? OK. Go straight. You will find a bookshop. It's on Apple Street, a bookshop. S: (to T) *On the left?* T: Yes, it's on the left. Jane's house is next to the bookshop. S: (to another S) **Left?** S: Next, next to the bookshop. S: (to T) **Next?** T: Next, next to the bookshop. S: Next ... *it means beside* S: *Here it is.* T: OK? S: Yes.

Table 3 Numbers of correct task results (All groups)

Task Group	Task 1A	Task 1B	Task 2A	Task 2B
A	2	1	5	6
B	2	2	5	5
Total for A & B	**4**	**3**	**10**	**11**
C	1	3	4	8
D	1	2	8	8
Total for C & D	**2**	**5**	**12**	**16**

Conclusion

Some pedagogical implications for teaching English as a second or foreign language can be derived from this study. First, this small-scale research suggests that it is possible to train young learners in meaning negotiation skills. In particular, teachers need to encourage them to use more active negotiation devices such as confirmation checks, repetition requests and clarification requests. Concerning the substitution of the informant problem (where learners tended to ask another student, rather than their interlocutor), this may be related to their reluctance to speak in English in front of peers. So teachers need to design tasks that can help them not only to use negotiation devices, but also to increase their confidence in speaking English, this may be largely a matter of practice and familiarisation through task repetition. Secondly, this research suggests some useful activities for training young learners in meaning negotiation skills. But this study was carried out for only three weeks and with small numbers. So longer-term research into this issue (eg a longer period of training sessions and meaning negotiation skills) with a larger number of learners would be useful.

10
Task Repetition with 10-year-old Children

Annamaria Pinter

Summary *In this paper I explore the changes that occurred in the performances of 10-year-old children when they practised two popular interactive tasks in pairs. Both the learners' feedback and the recorded data suggest that this type of systematic repetition/practice is beneficial for children's language learning and boosts their confidence in using English.*

Background and rationale

A: Have you got frog in the second floor?

B: No. I have got one dog.

A pair of 10-year-old Hungarian children are confidently tackling a 'Spot the differences' task. This is the third time they have done this type of task in a three-week period and, although they have received no special coaching in how to do the task, their improvement is dramatic.

In this paper I report on one aspect of a larger study in which I explored task-based interactions with younger learners. The common feature of the majority of studies in the task-based literature is that they focus on the performance of sophisticated adult learners of English whose English is of fairly high level. In my study, I was motivated to find out whether younger learners at much lower levels of competence could also benefit and learn from using tasks, in particular from **task repetition**.

The focus in this paper is on the effects of a special type of task repetition. Several studies reported in the literature on tasks have described the beneficial effects of task repetition (Bygate, 1996, 2001, Lynch and Maclean, 2000, 2001). However, in term of what repetition means, all the above studies differed. In Bygate's (2001) study subjects repeated the tasks 10 weeks after the first attempt and they did not know they were going to repeat them. Bygate (1996, 2001) used monologue-like tasks such as retelling a story. In Lynch and Maclean (2000, 2001), the repetition was more immediate. It happened within the same session and the task was interactive. Speakers had to talk about a poster they had designed and answer questions directed to them by various visitors to the poster. Each time, therefore, the interactions were slightly different but still revolved around the same poster and the same topic.

In my study, I used yet another type of repetition. The children carried out the tasks three times altogether and each time there was a gap of three to four days, or sometimes more, between recordings. Each 'repetition' involved doing a similar, but not identical task. The children knew they were going to be recorded on repeated occasions but they did not know exactly when.

Context: a state primary school in Hungary

I recorded altogether 10 pairs of 10-year-old children carrying out two popular interactive tasks. In Hungary, similarly to many other countries in Europe and Asia, children are not likely to use English outside the classroom. At the time of the study the children had been learning English for two years but their level of English was still rather low. They were used to a formal style of textbook-based teaching with plenty of emphasis on rote learning, grammar and translation. As far as the speaking activities were concerned, they often drilled and then acted out memorized dialogues in front of the class. Fluency-focused activities, which would have required learners to speak without preparation, were not used at all because the teacher felt the children were not ready.

I decided to make the recordings outside the classroom for two main reasons. First of all, I was not the children's class teacher at the time and I could not interfere with their regular English classes. However, I was familiar with their curriculum as I had previously taught in similar schools in the same town. Secondly, and perhaps more importantly, I was interested to find out what the children could do without any help or interference from the teacher in a class. I selected two classic **information gap tasks**: 'Spot the differences' and 'Follow the route on the map' (see sample pictures in Appendix 1). The first task was a **two-way task** (both children could see their own pictures and exchange information about them) and the second one was a **one-way task**, in that one child needed to convey the route information to the other child. Both tasks were new to the children in that they had never come across these or similar tasks in their regular English lessons. I wanted to find out whether children at this age, at a fairly low level of proficiency, could cope in L2 at all with these highly demanding interactive tasks and whether the repetition of the tasks (with very similar but not exactly the same materials) would lead to any changes in their performances without any intervention from the teacher. The children had never previously used fluency tasks in English so I knew I was taking a big risk.

Method

Designing and recording the tasks

I decided not to use published materials but instead, drew my own pictures for the tasks (see Appendix 1). This was so I could control the content of each picture and I could design the different versions of each task carefully, following the same principles each time. I created sets of A and B visuals for both tasks. Each 'Spot the differences' task included a picture of a house with five rooms in it where people were doing various things such as sleeping, eating, talking, cooking, etc. In each task there were six differences between visuals A and B. In the case of the 'Follow the route on the map' task, there was a scene of a forest with people doing various things and only one version (A) had a route drawn on the map. In each task the children were given one picture (either A or B) that their partner could not see and together they had to complete the task (to locate the six differences or to draw the route).

Instructions for the tasks

All the children were gathered together and a sample set of pictures for each task was put on the board. All discussion was conducted in L1 (Hungarian). I told the children that these were two games for learning English that I was trying out and I was excited to find out whether they worked or not.

Spot the Differences task

DEMONSTRATION: The children were encouraged to identify the differences together and as they shouted them out, I circled them on the board.

INSTRUCTIONS: This game should be played in pairs. You should find the differences together but without looking at each other's pictures. You will be looking for similar differences to the ones you can see on the board. Both of you should talk. You should help each other. When you say 'finished' I will stop the recording.

Follow the route on the map task

DEMONSTRATION: The children were told that someone had put a spell on the forest and there was only one safe route to get the little monster back to his den. They looked at the sample forest and sample route on the board.

INSTRUCTIONS: In this game, again, you will work in pairs and you cannot look at each other's pictures. One person gets the picture with the route on it and he or she should help the other pupil to draw the same route but both of you should talk. You should help each other. When you say 'finished' I will stop the recording.

For each repetition of the task, the children were given a different version of the house scene and the forest scene while the basic design of the task still followed the same principles. This way I ensured that each version of the task was 'new' in that they could not use or remember differences or routes from the previous versions. The expected language content necessary to solve the tasks was based on the units already covered in the course-book the children were following at the time.

The children could select a classmate to work with and these pairs stayed together for the whole time of the study. I invited the children to do the first version of both tasks in the mother tongue to familiarize themselves with these tasks. Other than this opportunity to experience the tasks in L1, they did not receive further training or instructions about how best to approach these tasks. This was an important decision because I wanted to find out how the pairs would cope if left to their own resources. After the Hungarian recording, I invited each pair (without any previous warning) to a quiet room in the school and I recorded them interacting in English. These recordings were repeated with new sets of the same tasks three times within a period of three weeks.

Findings: the benefits of task repetition revealed

When the English recordings were about to start, I was quite worried that the tasks might be too difficult for them after all and that they might say nothing or very little. However, my initial hunch was right because the tasks worked very well. The children enjoyed interacting with a friend and all their performances changed dramatically with each recording. To illustrate the most typical changes that occurred, I will describe some differences between their first and last performances.

One of the most noticeable changes of the performances was that children increased their pace on the tasks. Pace comprises several elements. First of all, the amount of silence was measured in their first and last performances. Then, the total number of words delivered by each pair per minute was also considered. Both of these measures showed dramatic changes in the children's performance.

For example, in their first recording Pair 6 produced 34 turns each and it took them 15 and a half minutes to complete the task. Three and a half minutes of this time were spent in silence. In their last recording this particular pair used less language in total, about 20 turns each. This time, however, it took them a mere five minutes to complete the task and out of their total time only 30 seconds was spent in silence. At the same time their speech rate doubled. In the first recording they produced an average of 30 words per minute, while in the last recording about 63 words per minute. The scores in both games were relatively high, in the first recording they found five differences and in the last one four differences.

The following two extracts show what was produced within the first minute of each recording:

[/ = pause of about 3 seconds; *Italics* = language produced in L1 and translated]

Pair 6: English recording 1

A: Have you got three blue bir bird? ////
B: Yes, //// Hm, in the bathroom, bathroom have you got a fish?
A: Hm, ////// *where*?
B: Yes, I have got two fish. //
A: In the kitchen have you got a mouse?

Pair 6: English recording 3

A: Have you got frog in the second floor? /
B: No. I have got one dog.
A: *I mean the bathroom*. Have you got cat in the first floor?
B: Yes, I have. Have you got two apples in the kitchen?
A: Yes, I have. Have you got one dog in the first floor and have you got one dog in the second floor?
B: Yes, I have. //
A: Have you got pig in the first floor?

B: Yes, I have. Have you got two spiders in the second floor?
A: No, I haven't got. I have got one spider // Have you got two men in the first floor?
B: Yes, I have.
A: Have you got one woman in the second floor?

Here is another example that shows similar changes on the 'Follow the route on the map' task. Pair 2 produced 17 turns altogether on the first map task. This took them six minutes in total. Out of the six minutes almost two minutes were spent in silence. By the last time they finished the interaction in just five minutes and produced more than twice as much language, altogether 46 turns. At the same time they spent only 20 seconds in silence. Their rate of speech increased from just 13 words per minute to 25 words per minute. Again, it can be concluded that their overall pace on the task increased quite dramatically.

This is what they produced in the first minute of their first and last recording of the map task.

Pair 2: English recording 1

Cs: Go // go straight on //.

Zs: Yes.

Cs: Tree //// a girl (gesturing up).

Zs: Yes.

Cs: //// a boy.

Zs: Tree or girl? ////

Pair 2: English recording 3

Cs: Hm, / two animal (gesture; between).

Zs: Yes.

Cs: One animal, one animal (gesturing between) go straight on.

Zs: Yes.

Cs: Hm, / elephant go straight on, elephant go straight on (gesturing line).

Zs: Yes.

Cs: Boy, two fish.

Zs: // What? Boy? Boy?

Cs: Two fish /

Zs: *A fish.*

Cs: fishing, fishing (gesturing fishing).

Zs: Fishing.

Another area of change I noticed was grammatical accuracy. I analysed each pair's language use in their first and last recordings. For example, the use of the present progressive tense was one area I looked at in each pair's performance. All the pairs used this structure in both tasks.

For example, in the spot the differences task Pair 1 used 'there is/there are' as their basic structure. However, in the first recording one of the speakers (A) used an 'extended' version of this structure: 'there is somebody doing something'. Being the more competent speaker, he produced four examples of this structure in the first recording at which point B attempted it as well. His attempt was incorrect: 'There is a ground floor, read, reading a boy.' Nonetheless, the message was understood and the conversation proceeded. Speaker A produced another correct example, and then two contributions later, B attempted it again, this time his utterance was well-formed: 'There is a boy eating in the second floor in the kitchen'. In the third recording of the same task they both used the pattern but this time both correctly. Speaker A even managed to combine 'have got + ing noun' and there is + ing noun' in the same sentence.

B: The boy is reading in the ground floor.

A: I have not got a boy reading but there is a girl sleeping on the ground floor.

B: Yes. And there is a girl eating ice-cream in the first floor.

Another important area where changes were obvious was children's ability to interact with their partner to avoid ambiguities in communication. For example, in the 'Spot the differences' task it is important to acknowledge each other's utterances because remaining silent can lead to ambiguities.

Consider these two extracts from Pair 8. In the first recording there is no acknowledgement at all of the utterances.

Pair 8: English recording 1

B: A *kitchen* is kitchen. Never *mind*. Near my *fridge* there are milk, cheese and *bread*.
A: *In English*.
B: Bread.
A: My / room is a man / There is a man and he has got a guitar in his hand.
B: In my right room there is a man on the bed and he's *and he is reading a book*.

By their last recording this is how they changed:

A: The bathroom is, um, two two fish are jumping into the bath.
B: In my bathroom, um, there is a frog.
A: Yes. My bedroom is one dog.
B: Yes, in my bedroom there is a spider.
A: No, two spider.

In this extract both speakers recognize the importance of acknowledging each other's utterances, either by maintaining the topic (In my bathroom ... in my bathroom) or more directly by simply saying 'Yes'.

I noticed many other types of changes. For example, by the third recording in English some children became more talkative in the role of the listener, some used more systematic search strategies to find the differences, others used less L1, still others monitored their performances more carefully. The rate of change was different for various pairs and individuals but everybody's performance improved.

Other ways to analyse the same data

I found that the data was very rich and the transcriptions of task performances could have been explored taking many other points of focus. When teachers record similar task performances, they might like to explore some of these aspects of the performances, too:

- Meaning negotiation devices used by pairs (see Lee Chapter 9, Essig, Chapter 16)
- Communication strategies used by speakers
- Evidence of co-operation between pairs (eg co-constructed utterances)
- Code-switching between L1 and L2 (eg Eldridge, 1997)
- Task solutions (number of differences and number of correct routes by each pair)

- Strategies used to monitor task performances (eg phrases about getting the task done)

Learner Feedback

I interviewed all the children in pairs, in Hungarian, after the recordings. They all reported that they felt they improved their performance from recording 1 to 3 on both tasks. Every single pair described their last performance on both tasks as something that went faster, more smoothly, more continuously and with less hesitation. Here are some examples of what they said (translated from Hungarian) about improving their general pace:

Pair 1:

At the beginning of the one before we were quiet for a long time and then one of us started it, and then there were more long silences, but here we began it much better. We didn't wait at all. We went on with the next sentence.

Pair 5:

Here in the last one we are talking more continuously. We knew it better. In the second one we finished more quickly.

Pair 7:

I think it went better than the first one. We were talking more continuously. And it was less bitty.

Pair 8:

It went more quickly. We didn't stop all the time.

Learners reported yet other benefits. Pairs who worked together got to know each other better, they learnt from each other and they enjoyed working with the same partner. This contributed to lowering their anxiety levels. Many of them mentioned that they would not have liked to change partners, and it gave them a sense of security to work with the same partner.

Pair 5:

I think it was good that we could be with whoever we wanted to be with, so I did not have to be with a boy. We could not have worked together so well with someone else each time. And Monika and I are getting on really well and we are good friends. And this was better than having to work with a boy.

Pair 9:

> *It was good to be with Eszti because I did not know how well it went for other children. I could predict how she was going to react. I was happy because we are friends anyway. It would have been more difficult with someone else.*

They also commented on the real-life value of the tasks, i.e. the opportunity to practise spontaneous interaction with a peer.

Pair 10:

> *I enjoyed them and I would like to participate again. Because our English would develop by doing these games.*

Many children thought the tasks in the study were useful for their language learning. In particular, they felt that the map was useful in that they would be able to give directions better in the future. Children felt that they would be more confident in the future about asking and giving directions in English.

Pair 2:

> *If I go to London, I would know how to make myself understood.*
> *I could give directions better or if I am given directions I would know better where to go. We know things like right, left and next street better.*

Pair 7:

> *It happened to me before that on the train that an Englishman asked us, my mum and I about how to get to Vienna. My mum does not speak any English and I could not explain. I think I could do it now.*

Reflection and evaluation

Overall, my data suggest that children at this age and this proficiency level can work together on interactive tasks even without special training or intervention on the part of the teacher. I would argue that this type of repetition is valuable because it can tell the teacher what the children can do themselves and the teacher may see where interventions might be most useful.

Task design for children

Unlike Carless's (2001) study, which looked at the practical issues of implementing tasks in a primary classroom, my study focused on the children themselves by taking them out of the classroom. However, the findings, I feel, have important implications for teachers with regard to what has been discovered about the tasks and the children's language use.

This study explored only two tasks with just 10 pairs of children. It would be interesting to find out whether teachers in other contexts would find similar results in their explorations. However, some useful observations can still be made on the basis of this limited data. One of these concerns the levels of difficulty in these two tasks. Even though they were both interactive gap tasks, the 'Follow the Route on the Map' task seemed significantly more difficult for children. First of all, the two tasks required different turn taking patterns. The 'Spot the Differences' task required a 'question and answer' type of turn taking while the other task required a more continuous type of discourse produced mainly by one speaker. The 'question and answer' turn taking was more flexible and more natural for children to engage in. The map task required the use of 'connected' language where it was necessary to link several points of reference to describe a route. In connected, sustained discourse the speaker has more of a processing burden because he/she has to concentrate on various aspects of the speech at the same time. Secondly, in 'Spot the Differences' children were supported by an in-built 'step-by-step' progression towards task outcome. This meant that when a pair were searching for the six differences, if they made a mistake, they still had plenty of chance to find the rest of the differences and do well. In the map task, once the route deviated from the original, it was unlikely that the pair could do well or could rectify their solution. These are two crucial differences in two apparently similar information gap tasks, which influenced the level of difficulty experienced by the children.

Based on my experience, I would encourage teachers to introduce information gap tasks at lower levels of language competence but it is important to explore the inherent design features of a task which can raise or lower the level of difficulty (see Robinson, 2001). Asking the children to carry out the tasks first in their L1 seems a good way to judge whether the tasks are likely to work in L2. There are important differences between what various age groups can do in L1 and thus in L2 (Lloyd, 1991).

Naturally, tasks which would put high cognitive or interactive burdens on children in their L1, should be avoided in L2. As long as children are comfortable with a task in L1 and have the necessary vocabulary in L2, teachers might like to try new tasks. However, younger children, especially those below the age of seven, will find these types of tasks too demanding because they require that speakers take into account their partner's messages and respond to them according to the partners' needs. The need for such high levels of awareness about the partners' concerns makes these tasks too demanding for younger children.

Further ideas for tasks for children

I suggest that as long as teachers build support into information gap tasks, they could achieve similar benefits with other tasks of this type (such as 'Describe and draw', 'Reconstruct a picture together' or 'Describe and order pictures together') as well. These tasks could be introduced, used and practised with this age group in a similar way as described in this paper either inside or outside the classroom. The teacher can set up friendship pairs and the children can practise with different sets of the same task. Systematic repetition can develop children's confidence in using the language at a low level of proficiency and can help them improve various aspects of their language use.

Appendix 1

11

Collaborative Tasks for Cross-cultural Communication

David Coulson

Summary *Tasks that promote a collaborative communication strategy may help learners produce more accurate and fluent language in conversation with foreigners. To develop my Japanese learners' awareness of this strategy, I designed a syllabus with a range of one-way tasks in which they practised making repairs to each other's communication breakdowns. Use of this strategy allowed increasing accuracy, fluency and discourse equality across two intercultural parties.*

Context and rationale

Cross-cultural conversations: identifying the problem

My learners were first-year, lower-intermediate students (aged 18–19) studying British and American culture at a two-year women's college in Japan. Their motivation to learn English was apparent from their writing which generally showed great concern for formal accuracy. However, they did not have strong reading habits and had many gaps in their vocabulary knowledge. Most learners had never been overseas, and many were hesitant in speaking. One aim of this course was to improve their conversational abilities when talking in international groups. I had 25 students in each class and the atmosphere was generally enthusiastic. My insight for this study originally occurred at my previous college with learners at a similar lower-intermediate level. As a course requirement, they talked to international students on campus in small groups. However, they regularly reported having problems holding the floor. In Japanese culture, it is considered rude to interrupt. So when the more fluent foreigners took over the conversation, not allowing the students time to express what they wanted to say or repair breakdowns, my students could not get back into the conversation. To investigate this, I asked them to record their conversations. When analysing this data, I found that the most successful groups used collaborative strategies to help each other express their meanings more accurately and maintain their speaking turns. This was reminiscent of the way learners sometimes confer before answering my questions in class to confirm their answers.

Building on this finding, I designed a series of one-way group-work tasks for my speaking classes at my new college, starting with 'Describe and Draw' tasks based on pictures. I had two related aims in mind. First, I wanted to make my learners realize that it is possible for them, working jointly, to produce more accurate, fluent language, and thereby acquire greater competence. Second, I hoped to develop awareness of collaborative interaction as a strategy in conversation leading to more balanced interaction with English speakers. 'Equal power' discourse, where 'all participants ... have equal rights to speak' (Markee, 2000: 68), or maintaining one's own in conversation with native, or non-native English speakers, is likely to be more conducive to further language acquisition.

Background: English Days and Team-Talking

Twice every year my department organizes a party on campus to which local native and non-native English speakers are invited. This is known as 'English Day' and, as well as being an interesting intercultural occasion, its main purpose is to provide our students with chances for various kinds of interaction such as interviews, informal presentations on cultural topics and free conversation. The small number of guests means that learners have to talk in groups.

Recordings of previous English Day interactions, with students talking in groups of six to seven, typically showed that most students passively observed while one member of the group attempted to make her point, but often without great accuracy or fluency. This frequently resulted in the foreign guests dominating whole conversations. With such unequal discourse, neither confidence-building nor language learning opportunities are available for most learners. So my first change to English Day was to reduce the number of learners in groups to a more intimate three, a dynamic in which collaboration could more readily appear.

My aim was to encourage my learners in class to develop what I dubbed **'Team-Talking'** – a collaborative peer strategy, leading to team-centred repair of an incomplete utterance. One form such repair action might take is spontaneously intervening on behalf of a partner to assist or clarify her utterance which she is having difficulty in self-repairing. Often, this assistance results in more accurate or fluent clauses. The speaker who initiated the troublesome utterance is often able to finish it, after the collaborative input from the other team members has given her a chance to reformulate her response. This is because Team-Talking interaction does not appear to threaten the face of the speaker whose utterance needs repairing. This speaker is also apparently aided by having disengaged momentarily from the direct, and perhaps stressful, burden of the language production.

As part of my communicative syllabus in preparation for English Day, I used the series of one-way tasks mentioned above in order to introduce and accustom my learners to the Team-Talking strategy. Developing awareness that active participation and collaboration in conversation are helpful at their level was central to this process. A parallel concern was to examine how well this task focus would allow my learners to communicate more equally in the high pressure of English Day where students would need to sustain whole conversations in English with strangers.

Method

Investigating learners' interaction

The first stage of the investigation was to collect some data of learners' interaction to see how much they could already co-operate with each other. I invited groups of three to interview me, in a format similar to English Day. I recorded and transcribed these interactions. I have found that analyses of careful transcriptions of conversation can reveal the degree of control of learners' production and even moments of language learning in progress (Markee, 2000: 133–7; Poupore, Chapter 19 this volume), especially on a syntactic and lexical level. I will illustrate in the example below, and in others later, how learners who engage in the Team-Talking strategy can repair the breakdowns of their peer.

Perhaps due to nervousness, many learners did not co-operate with each other in the interview as much as I had expected. But sometimes, as in the next example, the learners oriented remarkably well to each other, interacting in a highly collaborative manner, which I took as the basis for introducing the strategy. The group started talking about harmful preservatives, an unfamiliar topic for which Learner 1 probably had no pre-fabricated language, eg set phrases, as is clear from line 01 below when she falters.

(Da = *David*, L = *learner*, [ ] = *overlap*, / = *short pause*, /// = *longer pause*

01L1	Sorry, I don't know that word (*to L2* 'yakuhin' *medicine*) It was, bad ... medicine
02L1	Sorry. Do you know?
03Da	I understand what you mean
04L1	Banana goes bad very soon, so
05Da	Oh really, oh yes
06L1	The medicine made the banana // keep good]
07L2	[maintain
08L1	Maintain // its ///
09L2	Banana is fruit so that long // long maintain is difficult, but]
10L1	[the medicine made
11L1	the banana maintain its taste.

At 02, Learner 1 tried a confirmation strategy with me, which was successful since I answered that I understood. However, such a confirmation alone contributes nothing to improving linguistic structure. Fortunately, Learner 1 was not satisfied with her own output and continued the explanation, attempting the passable utterance 'keep good' at 06. It is the interventions by Learner 2 at 07 and 09 which are crucial. In response to the mini-pause by Learner 1 before 'keep good' at 06, Learner 2 intervenes with 'maintain' at 07 which starts Learner 1 on a restructuring path. Learner 2 again assists her partner at 09, which provides the necessary stimulus and time for Learner 1 to process the input before retaking control of her topic and producing the accurate, and unfaltering, clause at lines 10–11. This interaction, then, highlights the potential for Learner 2 to provide exactly the kind of input her partner, Learner 1, needed to reformulate in an accurate, fluent manner.

Learner strategies and 'Team-Talking'

Skehan (1996: 22) argues that using communication strategies in tasks may get meanings across but does not necessarily encourage learners to focus on form. For example, Learner 1 resorted to seeing if I had already understood her incomplete message. Skehan also criticizes research in this area (1998: 25) for failing to explain how learners might use strategies not only to avoid breakdowns but also as a means to strengthen their command of language. Team-Talking (TT), at least partially, would seem to answer this concern. In line 4, Learner 1 persevered with the phrase 'Banana goes bad very soon', and indeed, with the collaboration of her friend, was able to create an accurate phrase one might not have thought possible by looking at the top of the exchange. With learners mutually supporting each other in this way, a potential for accurate restructuring certainly appears available.

Unlike the successful interaction above, some learners fell into remarkably long silences of nearly one minute in their interview before collaboration started. In regular conversation, it is hard to imagine any interlocutor being so patient. These silences seem to be caused by a processing overload of the speaker's speech, and exacerbated by a nervous 'white-out', which seems difficult for many learners to recover from alone. Since collaborative input from peers seems to reanimate the language production process, my pedagogic aim was to accelerate learners' mutual assistance in completing speaking tasks. It seemed likely that the process evident in transcriptions like the one above could be simulated and developed so that more groups would readily assist each other, and this might also result in improved linguistic ability, and greater discourse equality in conversation. Storch (2002: 121) refers to the collaborative phenomenon as 'collective scaffolding', and uses a Vygotskyan perspective to describe how socially co-constructed meaning is not only cognitively essential, but also how it creates substantial second language development. See Shehadeh, Chapter 1 and Poupore, Chapter 19 for more on this.

Integrating Team-Talking tasks into the syllabus

My first-year classes met once a week for 90 minutes. My syllabus strands included:

- a four-skills course book on multi-cultural communication.
- a requirement to read 12 pre-intermediate graded readers.
- a requirement to write and rehearse a group presentation for English Day about any aspect of life in Japan.

In each strand, I wanted to promote the use of the TT strategy and so I integrated the one-way group tasks, starting with the easier ones. In the relatively short class time available, my aim was to give learners a means to more promptly express their utterance before being interrupted and irretrievably losing the floor.

To introduce TT, I started with one-way picture descriptions. The purpose was for two or three partners to describe the picture sufficiently well so that their partners could draw as exact a picture as possible. I used simple but quirky images, some from on-line newspapers or magazines. For example, the first image was of a cat resting snugly in a saucepan on top of an oven hob. The second was a couple and a priest flying strapped to the top wing of three biplanes, performing a wedding ceremony. The third was of a cheerful magician who can saw himself and his wife in half. The benefit of using such images is that almost all learners can describe them to complete the task at a satisfactory level. But conveying the quirky details requires slightly complex language which, I hoped, would be developed through TT interaction, especially since the describing partners would almost certainly recognize what the speaker was trying to express.

Pairs of learners were given one minute to prepare their thoughts on the image, but not enough to allow memorization of language. This was to take advantage of Foster's interesting, and surprising, finding that 'unguided planning' in tasks leads to *greater* accuracy than 'guided planning' (Willis & Willis, 1996: 133). Before the description task, I used pre-tasks (Willis, 1996a: 42) that helped learners to explore the topic for themselves, thus preparing them for the grammar and vocabulary they might need. In the case of the unusual wedding picture, for example, the group had to make a list of their ideal wedding ceremonies and locations and report their findings to the class.

By the third round of tasks (one per week), the learners were becoming increasingly aware of the TT strategy and were using it to solve various kinds of hitches. Evidence of this happening can be seen in this sample of TT interaction from the third image in the series (the cheerful magician) in which L3 and L4, the describing team, co-operated to solve L3's breakdown – *'he feels laughing'* – in describing the magician's cheerful demeanour at 02. Their co-operation eventually allows L3 to repair her own language, producing the accurate *'he seems very happy' at 09.*

(L3, L4 picture-description team; L5,L6 drawing team)

01L4	It is illusion.
02L3	but it feel ... he feels laughing
03L5	(*laughter*) laughing?
04L4	His reaction is (*1 sec*) warm
05L6	warm]
06L5	[wife] [wife, wife
07L3	[waaam]
08L4	umm no, laugh], [laugh
09L3	[laugh] (*1 sec*) he seems very happy.
10L4	ah yes laugh
11L5	(*laughter*) like you. I understand

With L4 dealing with L5 and L6's confusion, L3 is given a few moments to reflect on her output. When the negotiation returns to the word 'laugh' at 08, L3 is able to produce her intended meaning at 09 with 'he seems very happy', accurately and fluently. It should be clear that this is very much a co-constructed effort. When I asked these learners their own opinions, L3, especially, reported that she had more confidence to talk as a result of the previous lessons in which I had been teaching the strategy of TT with English Day specifically in mind.

However, it took my learners a while to get used to the TT strategy. To help them do this, I introduced, as materials for post-task exercises, transcriptions of interactions where the learners had co-operated effectively and managed to draw the picture accurately. The study of these transcriptions demonstrated to the groups how they could have done better, and helped to convince them to adopt the strategy. I also used transcriptions of recorded interactions from the previous year's English Days. By asking learners to comment on the stronger and weaker aspects of the group's interaction, learners became more conscious of the strategy and willing to use it.

Expanding the variety of tasks

As learner confidence grew, I increased the degree of precision required by the picture descriptions. From a Japanese newspaper web-site, which runs an international cartoon competition, I found a collection of simple, colourful yet universally meaningful cartoons which mostly lent themselves well to my task requirements. An example appears below.

These images required learners to express slightly more precise meanings in the main task, so I invited them to start using the TT strategy in the pre-task discussions too. As the pre-task for describing one of the cartoons with an environmental theme, for example, I asked learners in groups of four to describe any local environmental issues they knew, and to rank them according to importance. Then they reported the first item on their list to another group. The only condition was that the member whose idea was being reported should remain quiet and let her friends talk for her. Finally, each group leader reported their idea to the whole class, ideally with improved accuracy and fluency for having rehearsed the language with collaborative input from peers. Such staging of activities naturally prepares learners for more collaborative interaction in the main cartoon-description task. The learners who acted as listeners regularly drew very accurate pictures.

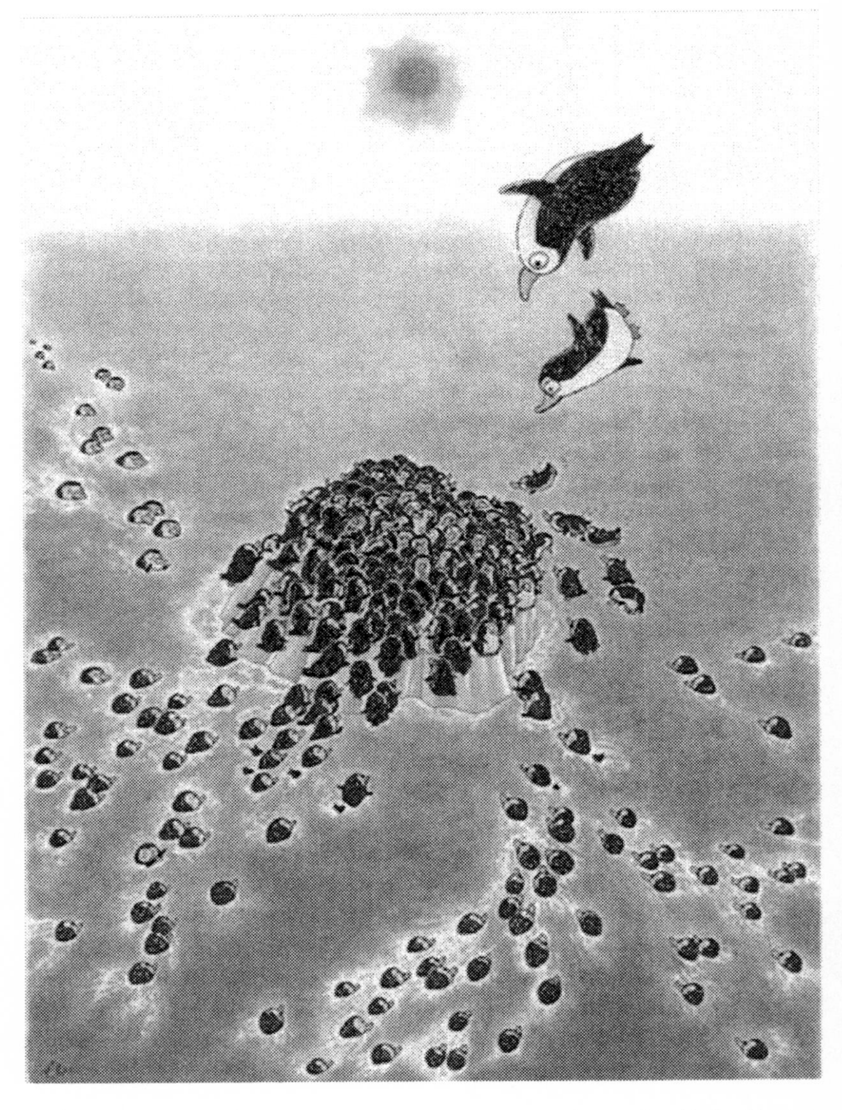

Figure 1 Cartoon 'The Last Iceberg' by Joji Bigo from the *Daily Yomiuri*, January 3, 2003. The artwork won the Gold Prize at the Yomiuri International Cartoon Contest, 2002

Rehearsing for English Day

One of the English Day activities is to make a presentation to their guest about, for example, an aspect of Japanese culture, such as hot springs. In class, the groups repeatedly rehearsed giving this presentation to each other. A process of shaping and clarifying their ideas and language through TT was evident as the groups increasingly moved away from rote memorization of their presentation text in response to a lack of understanding from successive rounds of listening students. Such rehearsal was directly useful for English Day in that by collaboratively dealing with the unexpected misunderstandings, observations and questions at this stage, they would be better prepared linguistically and strategically to deal with the pressure of interacting with their foreign guest.

Summarizing graded readers

In preparation for the speech writing and practice, I set book description tasks. Since reading graded material is an essential aspect of language development, each week, as homework, I had my class read one graded reader well within their ability. Working in groups of three, each learner told the outline of her story. The three books were then rotated and in the second week, the two who had read the same title collaborated to describe in more detail one aspect of that story to the third person. When learners had read all three books, each group decided their favourite, and then went around the class giving a summary and describing memorable episodes. This again provided similar chances for the group to develop their collaborative explanations. Groups then started on the next set of three books.

Findings

Performance on two English Days

In this section, I will show two transcripts, one each from English Day 1 (ED1) and English Day 2 (ED2), showing the change in ability of the same group of learners to express their utterance more promptly and accurately through TT. In ED1, the first time the strategy was being used outside the classroom, the result was rather disappointing. My learners were nervous in advance of the day, especially since they have so few chances to meet foreigners, and this may have partly accounted for the dissatisfaction with their own performance that many felt. However, after reflecting on the reality of cross-cultural communication in class, I advised them to continue practising collaboration in tasks. Since each group had recorded their conversation, I asked them to transcribe their interactions. Since many of the conversations were indeed rather one-sided, this exercise helped them to see where they could have spoken more promptly to support each other. In the following several weeks until ED2, I also continued with my task syllabus, focusing on developing the ability of groups to quickly attend to breakdowns in other members' language. By ED2, it was noticeable that many groups were enjoying stronger, fairer interaction and thereby holding the floor.

In the first extract from ED1, a flustered Learner 10 was unable to explain, in her own terms, despite an attempted repair from Learner 11 at line 7, why she failed to enter the university of her choice. Due to an inability to explain accurately or fluently, and despite the initial attempt at collaboration (lines 07–11), the group lost the floor to the chatty guest.

(*Gu = guest*)

01**Gu**	Why didn't you enter Niigata from the first I mean after graduating from the
02**Gu**	Sanjo High School, why didn't you?
03**All**	Ohhh, ahhhh
04**L10**	It's very
05**L11/L12**	Ouch, ouch, ouch,] ouch (laughter)
06**L10**	[I I had . exami exa]
07**L11**	[fail failed to .]eh
08**Gu**	[ah you have failed
09**Gu**	the examination ah yeah]
10**L10**	[two times
11**L?**	two times (laughter)
12**Gu**	Don't worry, don't worry, it was very difficult I know that] [but I think
13**L10**	[yes . yes]
14**Gu**	you can enter from the third grade it is quite good so but to the problem is
	(The guest continues talking for 31 seconds)]
15**L12**	[so she want to . wanted to want to be a
16**L12**	psychologist, so please her (1 sec) expla (4 secs) (*Japanese: I don't know*) so please her reason

Eventually, L12 had no choice but to interrupt the guest's monologue at 15 and ask her to listen to L10. The group reported feeling very uneasy in this interaction, since they had had to resort to a bald interruption to take back the floor.

After an intervening period of several weeks during which I asked learners to transcribe and reflect on their interactions, and further practise classroom tasks to develop their TT strategy, I was happy to find this group's performance in ED2 showed greater consciousness of collaborative interaction. This enabled them to maintain greater composure and work harder at explaining and asserting themselves more accurately and fluently. The following sequence was the pivotal moment in a conversation to find out how their German guest had learned English. Unfortunately, the guest could not understand what they were trying to say, necessitating the group to clarify their output.

01L10	what do you think about why /// how
02L11	what dya think eh
03L10	she's / conversation ability / up
04Gu	Ability?]
05L10	[to become up // to became more higher
06Gu	umm / we what do you exactly mean with became higher what do you mean
07L10	ah what do you mean] ahh
08Gu	[the ability] [and]
09L11	[yes], [what what do you need]
10L10	[ah yes/to
11L12	[to develop
12L12	to develop ability
13Gu	Umm umm I see

Of particular interest here was how Learner 11's intervention at 02 relieved Learner 10 from the constraints of her syntactic breakdown at line 01, allowing her the chance to reformulate the utterance (albeit unsuccessfully at 03). All the while, Learner 12 was paying attention to this problem of accuracy and was able to modify the lexical elements into a verbal phrase 'to develop ability' at 12. The success of this group repair effort enabled the interview to continue with minimum embarrassment. In this sense, although there is a lengthy diversion, this actually served to reduce tension and promote the interaction, again demonstrating the value of using the TT strategy.

Reflection and evaluation

It was through the introduction, strategy practice, reflection and further practice of various classroom tasks that many of my learners were able to enjoy stronger, fairer interaction, especially in the second English Day. Unfortunately, since my learners do not have many chances to talk to foreigners, I cannot say whether regular use of the TT communication strategy definitely leads to sustained improvement. Teachers whose lower-intermediate learners have more regular access to using the language outside the classroom might like to investigate this issue. However, in my small-scale study, the classroom practice of the TT strategy greatly enhanced the ability of many groups to repair the breakdowns of their peer, maintain the floor and produce increasingly accurate and fluent language as a result. The result was a greater degree of discourse equality in cross-cultural communication, and a motivating sense of being part of the English-speaking world.

I hope that my learners who experience balanced, productive interactions with English native-speakers or higher proficiency foreigners, through the supportive TT strategy, will draw a sense of achievement and confidence from the experience which will help them to better enjoy interactions in English by themselves in future.

For myself, I have found that analysing transcriptions of learners' interaction is a marvellously revealing way of discovering how they actually use language, and to me this has proved invaluable as a way to develop my classroom teaching.

Part C

Exploring Task Language: Lexical Phrases and Patterns

Whereas the chapters in Part B explored learners' interaction, the chapters in Part C focus on the actual language forms used naturally and spontaneously by fluent or native speakers when doing specific tasks, and then look at how learners may benefit from studying the transcripts and recordings of fluent speakers doing similar tasks to those they have done.

The first two papers both focus on **multi-word items** or '**chunks**', and in particular on '**lexical phrases**', chunks associated with specific language functions such as 'asking for repetition' or 'agreeing'. These chunks may be '**polywords**' or **fixed phrases** like *As a matter of fact, Of course, At the end of the day, See what I mean?*, or partially fixed phrases like *See you later/tomorrow*, **sentence stems** like *Do you mind if I ..., What I mean is ...*, or even whole sentences, like *What time is it?* They can be **frames**, like *as ... as, not only ... but also*, and there are numerous lexical patterns: *easy/difficult to, agreement/relationship between, reasons why* (examples from Willis, 2003: 144). They perform many functions including **social** and **pragmatic functions**: *Hi. How are you?* **discourse organizers**: *By the way, The thing is*, and **vague language**: *something like that, that sort of thing, and so on ...*

When speaking we do not have the time or the cognitive resources to build up our message word by word, paying constant attention to grammar. Instead we draw from our huge stock of prefabricated chunks that are stored in memory as ready-made 'units of meaning'. Pawley and Syder (1983) suggested it is the use of such chunks that leads to native-like fluency.

Learners who have had a lot of exposure to English often acquire these chunks naturally. Task-based interactions can also give learners opportunities to hear and use them in context. But what about learners who have not had much exposure? Learners who have been taught grammar and vocabulary as separate entities are less likely to be aware of the importance of lexical phrases and often compose what they want to express one word at a time. This generally results in slow and rather unnatural speech. Both Hobbs and Baigent make a strong case for raising learners' awareness of such phrases through a task-based approach.

James Hobbs in Chapter 12 looks in particular at lexical phrases that serve an **interactive function**, like '*Let's start*' and '*That's interesting*' or '*Well, what I think is …*' He recorded and transcribed six native-speakers doing seven tasks to find out what interactive phrases they naturally used. These recordings produced a mini research corpus of around 10,000 words, yielding examples of lexical phrases that were typical of normal English task interactions. With this data, he was then able to classify the lexical phrases into categories (eg agenda markers, feedback, closing phrases) and produce materials for his learners so that when they did the text-book interview tasks and heard the recordings, (following a TBL cycle) they became aware of the various functions of interactive phrases. Hobbs gives excellent advice on making and using selected task recordings, and offers suggestions for language-focused activities. He also makes the valid point that we do not have to use native speakers for recording tasks; fluent non-native speakers of English may be more suitable, as they are closer to the learners' world and thus more accessible; they may also illustrate language that is more typical of fluent international English than native speakers might.

Maggie Baigent in Chapter 13 takes a far broader angle on lexical chunks. She recorded her advanced learners doing tasks that, when recorded by native-speakers, had yielded a rich array of lexical chunks of many types. She tried to get learners and other teachers to identify in their own transcripts the phrases they had spoken as 'chunks', ie without composing them word by word. But this was not easy – many people are simply not consciously aware of using chunks. Finally, she identified them herself, classified them (discourse signalling chunks, topic related chunks and vague language were just three of her categories), and made interesting comparisons between the use of chunks in native and non-native transcripts, and across task types. She then looked at what makes learners appear more fluent – how far was it due to the use of chunks – and got conflicting results according to the measures used. She gives many practical suggestions for teaching chunks at pre- and post-task stages. One question she asks is 'how far would such chunks be predictable by teachers?'

This is one of the questions answered by David Cox in Chapter 14. He wanted to investigate whether it was possible for teachers to predict the language that learners might need in order to do 'open' tasks, ie tasks where learners can talk about their own experiences, exchange personal opinions, as opposed to closed tasks like 'Find ten differences', or 'Explain the route on the map', where the language and themes and agenda are predictable in advance. He recorded 23 pairs of native-speakers doing five tasks adapted from a textbook, and asked 20 teachers to try to predict the phrases and structures they would use.

Cox ends his chapter with a discussion of how a bank of spoken texts such as task transcripts and associated written texts can be built up in order to give learners rich experience of language in use. This bank could form a 'pedagogic corpus' (Willis, 2003) from which illustrations of grammar and lexical patterns can be assembled for students and highlighted in language-focused exercises or consciousness-raising activities. Thus we can see how data from tasks and texts can form the basis for a language syllabus.

What links all the papers in Part B and Part C is the concern that teachers have for natural interaction patterns and spontaneous language use: exploring what really happens in naturally occurring task interactions, not what we might predict or pre-select for learners to use. The richness of task interactions is revealed by the data included in the chapters. Students in these teachers' classes seemed to like working with 'real' data. If materials are well designed, learners are not overwhelmed by this richness, but learn a lot from it.

All three teachers, Hobbs, Baigent and Cox offer good practical ideas and advice for readers wanting to explore the language of tasks and implement similar processes.

12

Interactive Lexical Phrases in Pair Interview Tasks

James Hobbs

Summary *I wanted to improve my students' performance in pair interview tasks as they used a lot of mother tongue and sounded quite stilted. In order to identify lexical phrases they could use to make their interactions flow more smoothly, I made recordings of native speakers performing tasks from the coursebook. I then designed materials to direct students' attention to these phrases by using the task recordings in class within a TBL framework.*

Context: pair interview tasks

Many teachers use pair interview tasks in order to get their students talking about common conversational topics and/or to prepare their students for oral examinations.

The interview tasks I used in my class of 16 lower-intermediate Japanese undergraduates at a private Japanese university were adapted from activities in *Face to Face* (Fuller and Fuller, 1999). Two examples follow here.

Task 1. Topic: character and personality (adapted from *Face to Face*, p. 84)

> *With a partner practice asking and answering the following questions. Write short answers.*
> 1. What word best describes your character?
> 2. Who do you think understands your character better: your friends or your parents? Why do you think so?
> 3. What would you like to change about your personality?
> 4. What kind of people do you like to hang around with?

5. Whose character do you like more: your mother's or your father's? Why?
6. What kind of boss would you like to work for?
7. What qualities do you look for in a boyfriend/ girlfriend?

Task 2. Topic: shopping (adapted from *Face to Face*, p. 34)

With a partner practice asking and answering the following questions. Write short answers.

1. What's your favourite store, and why do you like to shop there?
2. If you had 20,000 yen to go shopping, how would you spend your money?
3. If you only had 5,000 yen to buy your boyfriend/girlfriend a present, what would you buy?
4. Do you think it's a waste of money to buy CDs? Why or why not?
5. If you saw a person shoplifting, what would you do?
6. In what foreign city would you like to spend a few days shopping? Say why.
7. What souvenirs do you like to receive when people come back from trips abroad?

As they stand, the activities above are not really tasks in the sense generally used in this volume, as it is unclear what, if anything, learners will do with the information they obtain – no specific goal is given. To provide a sense of purpose and outcome, I gave the following instructions:

> *Work in pairs taking turns to ask the interview questions. Then determine your partner's most interesting answer and prepare to present it to the class.*

As a variation, I sometimes assigned each student one or two questions and asked them to collect answers from all their classmates. They could then either select the most interesting answer to tell the class about, or turn the results into a brief survey report.

Thus, while the textbook, like most, was not written specifically for use in a TBL setting, these activities were easily adapted to a TBL framework; a pre-task activity focused on topic-specific vocabulary, the task cycle included preparation of an oral report of the information obtained, and a focus on form came at the end of the lesson.

Background and rationale

Problems with pair interview tasks

When I listened in to my learners doing these tasks, I noticed they used a lot of Japanese, and their interactions did not run smoothly. Consider this sample of actual classroom data:

S1: Have you ever travelled abroad?
S2: No I haven't.
S1: Where do you want to go?
S2: I // I want to go to America.
S1: America. *pizza, ne.* (For pizza, right?)
S2: *Chigau yo sore itaria.* (No, that's Italy)
S1: *So ka na.* (Really?)
S2: *Ja ikimasu* (Right, my turn) Have you ever used / used the / the Internet?

There are several reasons why such interaction may be typical in a class of learners sharing a common L1.

Learner interpretations of task requirements

If instructions are to 'ask and answer questions', many students will do exactly that, and little else. They will readily revert to the L1 to clarify something or ask for help (*How do you spell that?*) to elicit repetition (*Sorry?*) to comment on an answer (*That's interesting*), and so on, as such moves are not seen as part of the task. In particular, the use of the L1 in these cases often seems to reflect a mistaken belief that a breakdown in communication amounts to a failure to perform the task correctly. This situation is not helped by students' continual exposure to textbook dialogues in which nobody is interrupted, nobody is misunderstood, repetition is rarely requested, speakers rarely pause, and virtually every utterance is a whole sentence. As Carter (1998: 47) notes, such dialogues bear little resemblance to typical native speaker conversations, yet learners often believe that this is what is expected of them.

Mental processing constraints

Interactive lexical phrases such as those illustrated above are typically used to grease the wheels of real-time communication, as we don't have time to compose each one from scratch. Even if learners understand task requirements, many simply don't have access to a large enough pool of appropriate interactive phrases to use when needed. This may result in rigid *question–answer–question–answer* exchanges, or students may slip unconsciously into L1 mode to give feedback, request repetition, and so on. In the latter case, a teacher can draw learners' attention to this by having them transcribe recordings of their own performance on tasks.

Classroom roles

Structuring interaction with simple target-language utterances such as '*Let's start*', '*Right, my turn*', or '*Really?*' may seem like a straightforward proposition, but for many learners this entails a fundamental reappraisal of their role in the classroom. A monolingual group of learners raised on a diet of teacher-centred instruction may have had little experience of using the target language to initiate an exchange or respond to an opinion, and it may be difficult to shake the belief that such moves in the classroom are made by the teacher and only the teacher.

I found that even gifted, motivated learners sometimes resorted to their native language for interaction that was not directly within the question–answer–question–answer framework suggested by the task instructions. So having established that the role of interactive phrases in task performance was something that needed to be brought to the attention of learners, my first task was to create an appropriate syllabus strand.

Method

Creating a research corpus to identify syllabus items

I needed to find out

- What interactive moves will students need to make in order to successfully complete the tasks under consideration?
- What language forms realize these moves in informal, unplanned native speaker discourse?

Our first instinct may be to sit down with a pen and paper and jot down a list of what *we think* are the typical phrases that a fluent English speaker would use while performing a particular task. Perhaps leafing through a few textbooks might provide some additional ideas. But if lessons are to be based on samples of language dreamed up by teachers or textbook writers, how can we guarantee that this is a true reflection of the language that will be encountered outside the classroom? In other words, how can we ensure that the language we present to our learners is indeed *typical international* English, and not simply *grammatically correct* English?

Obviously, most teachers have neither the resources nor the time to conduct large-scale investigations into naturally occurring language usage. However, a practical alternative that provides useful insights without requiring an excessive investment of time or resources is to record fluent speakers performing the actual tasks to be used in the classroom. In my case, I solicited the cooperation of six native speakers, and made a total of seven recordings. The recordings were then transcribed (see Appendix), a process that required 1–2 hours per recording and yielded a corpus of some 10,500 words. This is not enough data to justify statements of the form 'Native speakers say *X*' or 'Native speakers don't say *Y*', but at the same time it seems fair to argue that actual phrases used in the discourse of native speakers performing tasks are more reliable units for syllabus design than language pulled out of a hat by a teacher or a textbook writer.

Making usable recordings

If recorded interaction is also to serve as listening material in class, the teacher may face something of a dilemma, especially for learners not used to natural speech. In some cases, the features that distinguish authentic conversations from typical textbook dialogues are precisely those that make it extremely difficult to present such data as part of a structured classroom activity. The problem lies not only in the speed of native speaker talk but also in the abundance of pauses, false starts, and utterances that are not complete sentences. Such conversations may also feature a large amount of overlapping speech, idiomatic language, and vague language (*'you know'*, *'sort of'*, *'and all that'*), and often lack the clear structure and direction typical of textbook dialogues. Such problems are compounded if learners only get to listen to the dialogue as a sound recording, stripped of all the visual clues that aid comprehension. If these are particular concerns, there are several practical steps that a teacher might take with a view to obtaining more usable data:

- Before recording, remind speakers to concentrate on completing the task, and not allow themselves to get sidetracked with other matters. One way to keep speakers 'on-task' is to set a time limit.
- If possible, record speakers who are strangers, or at least not close friends. Conversations between strangers tend to be slower-paced, with fewer interruptions. It has also been suggested (Jane Willis, personal communication) that pairing an older speaker with a

younger speaker often yields more manageable data. In my own case local access to native speakers was limited. One recording involved a husband and wife and, while yielding a rich source of lexical phrases, was far too fast, complex, and disjointed to present directly to a group of lower-intermediate learners.

- Avoid recording two speakers with similar-sounding voices. It will be difficult to focus on the finer nuances of interaction if students have difficulty simply telling one speaker from the other.
- To provide visual clues as an aid to listening, consider using video instead of simple sound recordings.
- Make sure that you are familiar with the recording equipment you use, and that it is up to the job. There is little classroom potential for a recording on which speakers' faint voices are barely audible above the hiss of the tape.

Turning recorded data into a language syllabus

The process of compiling an extra syllabus strand focusing on interactive lexical phrases began with transcribing the recordings and analysing them for such phrases. Consider the following example:

1. NS1: Alright, are you ready to go?
2. NS2: Yeah, I'm ready.
3. NS1: Alright, let's start with number one then ... what word best describes your character?
4. NS2: Best describes my character? ... ummm ...
5. NS1: That's a hard one.
6. NS2: It's not easy ... I think I am ... umm ... energetic.
7. NS1: OK. I'd agree.
8. NS2: And what about you?
9. NS1: Complex.
10. NS2: Complex?
11. NS1: Complex.

The first speaker takes the role of interviewer, and in her utterances it is easy to notice an opening ('*Are you ready to go?*'), a question marker ('let's start with number one'), and feedback ('*OK. I'd agree*'). With NS2, meanwhile, we find partial repetition of the question used as a stalling device ('*Best describes my character? ...*'), further stalling before an answer is given ('*It's not easy ... / ... umm ...*'), a move to return the question to the questioner (*'And what about you?'*), and repetition of the answer as feedback (*'Complex?'*). These were noted, and then compared with other recordings of native speakers performing this and other opinion exchange tasks.

By analysing all the transcripts in this way it was possible to make a comprehensive list of the interactive phrases used, and to group them into distinct categories common to all the recordings. While the number of interactive lexical phrases increased with each transcript, the same categories of lexical phrases re-occurred in transcripts, irrespective of the task or speakers, and the categories of interactive lexical phrases were essentially the same in all the recordings.

- Openings (eg 'Are you ready then?', 'You ready to go?').
- Pause fillers and vague language (eg 'That's a hard one', 'You know', 'or something').
- Opinion markers ('I think ...', 'As far as I can see ...', 'If you ask me ...').
- Feedback ('Really?', 'That's interesting', 'Right').
- Agenda markers ('Moving on', 'OK, next question').
- Returning the question ('What about you?', 'How about you?').
- Closing ('Alright, I'm going to stop there', 'Let's stop there').

Within some categories it was possible to make further sub-divisions. For example, the category of pause fillers and vague language was sub-divided as follows:

- Stalling devices – phrases ('Well ...', 'Umm ...', 'That's a hard one').
- Stalling devices – repeating the question ('Best describes my character?').
- Vagueness conveyors and other fluency devices, as in the following extract:

  Whenever I see rap/ *you know*, when I see it on a/ *like* on a video on TV *or something* it's just somebody pointing their finger at you and yelling. *I mean*, is that what rap music is all about?

With a small corpus, we can easily notice such features through manual analysis. However, concordance software such as Wordsmith (PC) or Conc (Macintosh) enables us to isolate all the occurrences of a particular word or phrase. For example, having noticed that *you know* appeared several times as a fluency device, I wanted to discover how frequently it appeared this way, as opposed to appearing as the subject and verb in a declarative or interrogative clause. In one conversation alone, the computer revealed seven occurrences of *you know* used as a fluency device, as in the following two examples:

... I mean, **you know**, people have the hair they were born with ...

... someone from, **you know**, maybe a non-Japanese ...

In contrast, there were only two occurrences of *you know* that were not fluency devices, and both appeared in the same line:

I mean, do **you know** the guy? Do **you know** Rowan Atkinson?

Fine-tuning the syllabus – the role of experience and intuition

While I noted earlier that we should be sceptical of the extent to which our intuition can inform us about what constitutes typical international English, we should also avoid becoming slaves to our data by rejecting the possibility of drawing learners' attention to any language not found in the recordings. As one author argues, 'while it is true that one needs to guard against excessive subjectivity, this overlooks the value of personal experience and intuition as important aids to effective course design' (Waters, 1997: 84). It is important to bring to our learners' attention the possible variations in phrases encountered in the data. For instance, an example of an opinion signalled by '*As far as I can see ...*' brings to mind a fairly closed set of alternatives based on the lexical chunk '*As far as ...*':

As far as [I can see/I'm aware/I understand/I know/I'm concerned] ...

We can investigate the frequency and function of such phrases, and find still more phrases, by searching larger corpora of spoken English, many of which can be accessed free of charge via the Internet (eg the COBUILD Corpus Concordance Sampler, as used by Sheehan, Chapter 4). Certainly, we should not become so preoccupied with our own data that we miss opportunities to help students expand their stock of phrases by adapting the phrases they encounter. In other words, instruction should focus students' attention not on the rote memorization of fixed phrases, but on experimenting and keeping a look out for potential variations of a particular phrase.

Presenting findings to learners: designing materials

The TBL framework proposed by Willis (1996a,b) and Shehadeh (Chapter 1) consists of three stages:

1. Pre-task: introduction to the topic and the task.
2. The task cycle: performance of the task in pairs, followed by the planning and 'public' presentation of an oral (or written) report of findings.
3. Post-task: analysis and practice of language forms relevant to the task.

While it may be tempting to present interactive lexical phrases to learners by beginning each lesson with a focus on the 'interactive strategy of the day', this would be at odds with the principles of task-based learning. If the task cycle is preceded by an explicit focus on interactive lexical phrases, the focus of the task cycle is no longer on the goal itself, but on the language used to reach the goal. In other words, the task cycle becomes simply a stage for the display of language forms presented earlier in the lesson. This is exactly what task-based learning is *not* about; in fact this would have far more in common with traditional present–practice–produce methodology, which rests on the belief that teachers can determine what language their students acquire and when they acquire it – an assumption which is now largely discredited.

Seeking to adapt lessons to the TBL framework, I experimented with using NS recordings at the pre- and post-task stages.

Pre-task: focus on meaning

The pre-task stage is used to clarify the objectives of the task, and to highlight useful topic-specific vocabulary. As part of this, students listened to a recording (or more often a part of a recording) of two native speakers performing the task they were about to perform. The focus at this stage was on the information conveyed, not on the language forms used to convey it, nor on the structure of the interaction. In order to maximize exposure to relevant vocabulary, and to avoid presenting learners with too great a challenge, I usually gave students a list of multiple-choice questions. A typical question was:

Kathryn says that she is ...

(a) easygoing
(b) mysterious

(c) complex
(d) energetic

Students seemed to welcome the opportunity to listen to 'real' conversations between 'real' people, and seemed particularly interested in hearing speakers they already knew (several of the recordings involved other teachers working at the same institution). However, it was often difficult to find a section of a recording in which key information was not separated by long stretches of less relevant details.

Post-task: focus on interactive lexical phrases

For the post-task stage I designed activities to focus conscious attention on the interactive lexical phrases in the recordings, first by listening, then by reading the transcript. The following example is part of a language focus activity based on an interview task about shopping:

Transcript

K: Right. So ... talking about music. Do you think it's a waste of money to buy CDs?
S: Do I think it's a waste of money to buy CDs?
K: Yeah.
S: Well, if you have somebody who can copy them for you I think it's great. I mean that/it's not/alright, what was I going to say? I think if you have somebody who can copy them for you, yes, it's a waste, but ... the quality's never the same and I don't know anybody who can copy a CD. You can copy a tape. No I don't think it's a waste of money.
K: OK.
S: How about you?
K: I don't either. I like CDs.

Questions

A: Listen and answer the questions.

1. What does Kathryn say to introduce the topic of music? (Answer: Talking about music.)
2. What is Susan's first reaction to the question? (Answer: She repeats the question.)
3. What does Susan say to ask Kathryn's opinion? (Answer: How about you?)

B: Listen again. Which of these words/phrass do you hear? Who says them?

Yeah	Well
Really?	I mean
I see	You know
Let me think	OK

Reflection and evaluation

With this group of learners I did not implement these procedures in a sustained, systematic manner that would allow for a thorough evaluation of their effectiveness. Nevertheless, I was encouraged by what I observed. Students were enthusiastic about using 'real' language data, and also seemed to recognize and appreciate the effort I had made to create materials. At the end of the course it came as no surprise that performance on tasks remained far less fluent than that of native speakers, and many students continued to rely heavily on particular phrases ('OK, next' and 'How about you?' were especially popular). However, I was satisfied that interaction between students had become much more like 'conversation', and that I had planted the seeds of future language development.

Further ideas for language focus activities and use of task recordings

The example above is just one example of what can be done, not a model formula to be adapted to each and every recording. The list of possible language focus activities is long, and includes

- **Cloze** listening: students listen to the tape and fill in missing words/phrases in the transcript.
- Prediction: students choose words/phrases to fill gaps in the transcript, and then listen to check answers.
- Frequency counts: students listen/read and count how many times a speaker uses a particular phrase (eg 'Really?', 'OK, next').
- Listening/reading for specific functions: eg students listen/read and try to identify phrases signaling a question shift.
- Key words in lexical phrases: students listen/read and find phrases containing a particular key word (eg 'ready', 'like', 'something').

All these five procedures can be used for highlighting almost any language feature, not just lexical phrases. More ideas for exploring language can be found in Willis, 2003.

The procedures described could be used to research and teach interactive lexical phrases for use in many kinds of tasks used in many different teaching contexts. Besides promoting greater fluency in the communicative contexts associated with particular tasks, this may also stimulate language development by encouraging a general focus on collaborative communication (see Coulson, Chapter 11). As shown by Baigent (Chapter 13), different tasks will generate different sets of 'task-specific chunks', including interactive lexical phrases. Some tasks may involve more requests for clarification, others may require frequent negotiation of turn-taking, and so on, but the basic principle remains the same; to determine the interactive lexical phrases appropriate to a particular set of tasks, begin by recording fluent speakers (they don't have to be native speakers) actually performing those tasks.

The transcripts of task recordings can also be used as sources of other language features; much will depend on the particular teaching situation. We might begin by focusing on the functions that are easiest to identify, or that seem the most useful. We could return later to examine the same material for other functions or notions, such as expressions of location or time or quantity. Indeed, it may be asking too much to expect students to process all the relevant language from a transcript in one session, while students may lose interest if they spend several sessions looking at the same transcript. Conversely, it may be a source of motivation and encouragement if students return to earlier transcripts and find that what was previously incomprehensible now seems quite comprehensible, even predictable.

Finally, it is also worth noting that many possibilities lie between the two extremes of wholly authentic native-speaker data and wholly concocted data. Especially with lower-level learners, teachers may be justifiably concerned that native speaker recordings will be simply too fast and too complex for learners to process. One possible solution could be to use recordings of higher-level non-native speakers. Another might be to simply omit sections that seemed rather hard to catch, or just to select a few simpler sections of data and prepare learners well for them. Alternatively, we could adopt the approach mentioned (though not necessarily recommended) by Carter (1998: 52). He discusses the possibility of 'modelling data on authentic patterns' by rewriting, or even re-recording a native speaker dialogue, keeping the interactive lexical phrases as close as possible to the original, but removing sections where speakers drift off topic, or sections of difficult idiomatic language, and so on. Purists may protest that this introduces unacceptable distortions in the data, but teachers would have a powerful defence if this led to an improvement in performance on tasks; this is, after all, why the use of fluent-speaker recordings is being advocated in the first place.

Conclusion

If interactive lexical phrases are the real building blocks of conversation, we must wonder why the teaching of spoken English still often revolves around the teaching of formal grammar rules. Indeed, writers such as Nattinger and DeCarrico (1992) and Lewis (1993, 1997) claim that lexical phrases should replace grammar rules as the basic units of language syllabus design. That is, learners should spend less time mastering grammar rules to explore the *possible* sentences of a language, and more time studying examples of fluent speakers' discourse to discover which utterances are *common* in a given context.

Appendix

Transcript for task 1, question 5

K: All right, ooh, this is on to/ like ... social morality ... If you saw a person shoplifting. what would you do?
S: Slap their hand. Yeah. What would I do, if they were shoplifting?
K: Yeah.
S: I think I would go and tell ... either the clerk or the information centre in the store / just tell them I / I believe someone's taking something, but I don't / I don't know / I mean you need to / you know / that's what I should do. What would you do?
K: I'd like to think I would do the same.
S: You'd like to think so. This is /
K: [I would/ I think I'd have to be / This is the thing because I feel as a foreigner in Japan I would have to be certain /
S: [Yeah
K: [that's what I saw ... before I went in and accused someone.
S: If it was a kid versus an adult would you feel easier about doing it?
K: If it was a kid?
S: Yeah.
K: Yeah.
S: So would I.

Transcript for task 2, questions 2 & 3

M: OK. Who do you think understands your character better ... your friends or your parents?
S: My husband. Oh that wasn't the possible answer ... ummm ... well my father's dead ... I really can't answer that question, how about yourself?

M: Hmmm ... I like to think my friends understand me better than my parents because I spent all my teenage years telling my parents YOU DON'T UNDERSTAND ME.
S: (laughter) Now you tell all your friends you don't understand ME. OK ...
M: OK, so what would you like to change about your personality?
S: My personality or somebody related to me?
M: [your pe/
S: [my personality? Ummm ... I giggle too much. It would be really good if I could stop that.
M: I see. Well, how can we stop that?
S: (laughter)

13
Multi-word Chunks in Oral Tasks

Maggie Baigent

Summary *In this chapter I describe an investigation that I made into advanced learners' use of multi-word chunks in four tasks, and the effect of different task types on the chunks produced. I examine errors, omissions, and the effect of chunks on overall fluency, and conclude with some implications and suggestions for the TBL classroom.*

Context and rationale

I conducted this research while teaching advanced level learners at the British Council English Teaching Centre in Bologna, Italy. All my students had Italian as their first language and were keen to improve their spoken English. While it is easy to observe the motivating effect and general communicative outcome of using oral tasks in the classroom – my learners clearly enjoyed such tasks – it is much less easy to observe the actual language used, particularly in larger classes. However, I felt that my students were often handicapped in their oral production by a lack of multi-word chunks, with the result that even at fairly advanced levels they have difficulty in producing very natural-sounding English.

Background

Multi-word chunks

It is now fairly generally accepted that much native speaker language output is not created by putting together 'grammar' structures and 'words' but comes in ready-made **multi-word chunks** of language (also known as multi-word units/items, and lexical phrases – see the introduction to Part C and Hobbs, Chapter 12), which are stored in our memories and produced as such when we speak or write, thus facilitating fluency (see Pawley and Syder, 1983).

In English, these chunks include more familiar items like phrasal verbs and compound nouns, but also fixed or semi-fixed expressions like:

- discourse organizers (by the way)
- functional phrases (Good morning)
- idiomatic expressions (fall in love)
- sentence stems (if only)
- vague language (sort of)
- verbal expressions (it's not worth)

and any number of collocations. **Collocation** – the tendency of words to co-occur in naturally produced language – is a particularly tricky area. Many collocations are idiomatic or non-literal to some degree: *hard work*, for example, would probably be noted by teachers and learners as a 'useful phrase', but many other 'useful phrases' may simply not be noticed as their meaning is obvious from their component parts – *tiring/easy/physical work*. Nevertheless, these adjectives all collocate with the same noun and these transparent collocations too should have a place in any consideration of multi-word chunks. There is an excellent discussion of the nature of collocation in Chapter 7 of Michael Lewis's book, *Teaching Collocation* (2000).

Method

Setting up the experiment

I hoped that analysing some recordings of tasks made by learners outside the classroom might help our understanding of the use of multi-word chunks in typical classroom tasks. I hoped too that it might reveal something of learners' own perception of chunks, and provide some evidence on which to base decisions about future classroom practice.

I was particularly interested in investigating:

- how far the specific tasks generated particular chunks, whether lexical or discourse organizing
- differences between native speakers' and learners' use of chunks
- errors occurring in the learners' chunks
- the effect of chunks on fluency
- learners' own awareness of the chunks they use

Two pairs of advanced learners (preparing for the University of Cambridge Certificate of Proficiency in English, Common European Framework level C2) carried out and recorded four oral tasks. All had Italian as their L1 and none had had much exposure to English outside a formal learning environment. A pair of native speakers recorded the same tasks for comparison.

These were all typical classroom tasks: two were of a more interactional nature sharing and comparing experiences and feelings (on the topics of travel and storms); the others were problem-solving tasks (discussing which seasons short poems referred to, and deciding whether a collection of statements were true or false: see Appendix 1). These were taken from the Collins COBUILD Level 3 course book, an early (1989) attempt by Jane and Dave Willis to create a course based on oral tasks and a lexical, rather than grammatical, syllabus.

These particular tasks were chosen because the transcripts of native speakers doing them contained a high density of chunks and because the nature of the tasks seemed to some extent to prescribe the language needed for their implementation. They were also well within the language range of the learners (this was an intermediate course book) as I felt this would reduce the cognitive load and elicit a sample of language which was as spontaneous as possible.

Identifying and classifying the chunks

Having made the recordings and transcribed them, the next decision was how to identify and classify the chunks used in the tasks.

Identification was not straightforward. Because one of my interests was to explore learners' own awareness of chunks, I asked each speaker to read through their transcription and mark anything which they believed they knew and had produced as a single chunk. To help, I gave them an extract with examples of chunks underlined and the following instructions:

Here is an extract from a recording of two people doing one of the tasks you did:

RS: So, how d'you feel about storms?

EL: Well, they're fine as long as – I don't really like being caught in the middle of them. I mean, as long as you're at home or even in a train. I like storms when you're in a train.

RS: Mhm.

EL: I was just, erm, going up north in a bus to Durham last week and er, it was absolutely pitch black outside and really pelting down. And that was quite fun. But if you're actually out in it, I find that – I don't like getting wet.

RS: Right. Yeah. I actually like storms. I love them except for the lightning, because I know it can be dangerous.

The bits underlined are 'chunks' of two or more words that go together to make up a commonly-used expression in English.

Can you now look at the transcription of your recording and underline any similar chunks which you think you know and used as a single bit of language? (They might be idiomatic expressions, phrasal verbs, conversational phrases like 'I mean', or any sort of collocation – words that just 'go together'.)

If you think you used something as a chunk but you're not sure, underline it and put a question mark by it.

I also asked the two native speakers, colleagues of mine, to mark up their own *and* the learners' transcripts. I hoped that recognition by at least one other person would help me to identify chunks in the transcripts, but in the end I found that I had to rely largely on my own intuition and experience gained from reading about chunks.

Another difficulty was, not surprisingly, deciding whether to include common but not fixed collocations – eg *tropical storm* seems clear but *terrific storm*? And what about common verbal forms, especially those which seemed to be task-specific, eg *I'd like to*? In fact, there often is no clear dividing line between our use of prefabricated chunks and a creative use of language, or between 'grammar' and 'vocabulary' as pointed out by many people, including Lewis (1993, 1997). Often, chunks form parts of 'frames' with a slot in the middle and/or at the end in which any word (of a similar class) can go, for example *I don't really like being caught*, where any verb with an *-ing* form can fit, or *it can be* where any adjective could follow (see Willis, 2003).

I then classified the chunks on the basis of patterns that emerged from the NS recordings, which suggested the following categories:

- General discourse markers (I mean; not only)
- Task-type related discourse markers (What about the next one?)
- Topic-specific chunks (pitch black)
- Vague language expressions (and so on)
- Other chunks

'Vague language' is the term used by Joanna Channell (1994) to cover the kind of imprecise language we use all the time, sometimes because we cannot be more specific (*a kind of* bluey-green) but often because we feel it would be pedantic or too direct to be more precise (I spent a *load of* money at the weekend; he *tends to* be *a bit* fussy). I was surprised at the amount of vague language used by both native speakers and learners so I felt this could usefully serve as a category on its own, not least for eventual teaching purposes.

Both native speakers and learners used chunks from all categories in all tasks. Variations seemed more connected to the amount of talking time and to individual preferences than to a clear native/non-native speaker difference. Examples of chunks produced in Task 1: *Tell each other what other places or countries you've been to and how/why you were there* are given below.

Table 1 Examples of chunks produced in Task 1 by category

	Native speakers	Non-native speakers
General discourse markers	I mean (×3) it depends	for example of course (×4) I must admit the nice thing is
Task-type related discourse markers	me too what about you how come as well	different from (×2) as well exactly the same and you
Topic-specific chunks	travelling around (×3) at the time on a separate occasion do a (Portuguese) course had a passion for decided to go (×2) anywhere else stereotype image	a different world (×4) (three/two) summers ago in summer (×2) the first time at that time last year
Vague language expressions	six or seven a few a little bit lots of tend to	a lot (×2) and so on things like this quite a lot a bit
Other chunks	not even just for fun	if you have time young people a friend of mine (six/ten) years old high school

Table 1 Continued

	Native speakers	Non-native speakers
		post a letter something to eat at the end of except for strange sensation

Findings

Relationship between tasks and chunks

Not surprisingly, each task generated its own task-specific chunks, both lexical and discourse related. For example, Task 2 (discussing storms) produced many purely topic specific lexical chunks such as *tropical storm; fork lightning*. Task 3, on the other hand, (speculating about the seasons portrayed in short poems) produced an enormous number of task-type related discourse organizers eg *the first one; because of; what about.*

However, many of the chunks that fell into these two categories only became task-specific in that particular context. For example,in Task 1 (comparing travel experiences) there were a large number of time expressions: *at the time; on a separate occasion; in summer*. Or in Task 2: *keep me awake; frightening/horrible experience.*

In addition, the learners – who, incidentally, tended to spend longer on the tasks than the native speakers – produced a far greater number of *non*-task-related chunks.

So, while the type of task and topic did generate a certain amount of related language, much of this would be difficult to predict in advance to any great extent, beyond the most obvious lexical chunks: *thunder and lightning* in Task 2; *in summer/winter* in Task 3. This is partly for the reason mentioned above, and partly due to the different experiences of the individuals doing the task. For example, in talking about storms, one of the native speakers told of a storm in the Amazon, generating chunks like *in the jungle; sharp drop; tropical storm*. One of the pairs of learners talked about their experience of storms while driving, so produced chunks like *in the car; on the road*. Even in Tasks 3 and 4, which had a more clearly-defined structure, there was a tendency for the learners to bring in their own experiences.

Errors in learner-produced chunks

In general, it was interesting to see quite how many correct chunks of language were produced by the learners, including many which are unlikely ever to have been 'taught' to them, e.g. *something like that; but anyway*.

However, there were errors, although none that caused an obvious breakdown in communication. Moon (1998) divides learner errors with chunks into three categories: formal, pragmatic and stylistic. Errors in the *form* of a chunk may be, for example, a wrong choice of lexis, a literal translation of an L1 idiom or other type of L1 interference, or caused by a misunderstanding of the exact make-up or limitations of the particular chunk (e.g. **she fell in his love* for *she fell in love with him*). We may consider pragmatic and stylistic errors together as chunks that are correct in form, but inappropriate in the context in which they are used.

In this study, the learners generally maintained a fairly neutral style and there were no real instances of chunks which were incorrect for stylistic reasons. There were occasional errors of a pragmatic nature: *I must say* sounds inappropriate in the utterance *I've visited er ... few countries, I must say*; another learner used *it tastes good* to refer to a national cuisine rather than a specific item of food.

The majority of errors, however, were formal, both lexical and syntactic. Examples of syntactic errors were: **fashion world* (for *the fashion world/the world of fashion*); **every kind of people*. Lexical errors included errors of collocation: the **strength of nature*; **made something wrong* and fixed phrases imperfectly produced: **in this point of view*; **I hope no*. There were other expressions where only the context and some of the constituents gave a clue to the speaker's meaning: **put up your dresses* (for *put on your clothes*) and **open day* for *broad daylight*.

L1 influence was evident in many of the errors: **let's go for exclusion* (by process of elimination); **I can't do anything* (I can't help it), for example, are word for word translations of the corresponding Italian expressions. Generally, however, the number of errors made was small compared with the number of chunks used successfully, with the percentage of erroneous chunks ranging from 7.1 per cent to 16.6 per cent of the total.

Missing chunks

Comparing the transcripts with the native speakers' I noticed two categories of 'missed opportunities', which suggest gaps in the learners' repertoire of multi-word chunks. First, the native speakers tended to produce more precise, often topic-specific lexis, including fixed collocations, e.g. *had a passion for; stereotype image; travelling around*. The learners, on the other hand, relied heavily on more general expressions, e.g. *strange sensation/feeling/situation/things*.

Secondly, I was struck by the almost total lack of sentence-length or complete meaning units in the learners' chunks. Those produced by my colleagues in these tasks were idiomatic to a greater or lesser degree e.g. *just for fun; it's a long story;* and usually had a precise pragmatic role – evaluative, showing solidarity or humour, etc. The native speakers also made more use of elliptical expressions in the construction of their conversation: *me too; how come?; neither am I.* By comparison, the learners tended to use longer, and more literal equivalents in both these types of situation, e.g. *When did you go there? it's not pleasant; it is the opposite for me.*

Chunks and fluency

I asked two colleagues experienced in teaching/examining for the Cambridge Proficiency examination to listen independently to the recordings and award each learner a mark for fluency, according to the marking scale used for this exam.

The teachers were in close agreement, and using their combined marks, we get a ranking from most to least fluent of:

1st Learner D
2nd Learner A
3rd Learner C
4th Learner B

This corresponds exactly to their ranking in terms of the density of chunks produced over the four tasks (8.32, 6.38, 4.61 and 4.14 chunks per minute of speaking time respectively). In such a small-scale study this can only be seen as indicative, but it does seem to support Pawley and Syder's (1983) suggestion that speaking in chunks is one of the keys to greater fluency.

Measuring **density** in terms of chunks per minute seemed fair for these learners who speak roughly at the same rate, and could be argued as being fair in timed oral tests where learners have, say, a limit of three minutes to talk. However, a fairer measure, which would not penalise people who naturally speak more slowly needed to be found.

So I tried the '**gap measure**' (Fielding, 1996), which involves working out the average number of words *between* chunks. This gave results of: Learner A – 7.21; B – 7.39; C – 7.14; D – 7.46 ie a ranking of:

1st Learner C
2nd Learner A

3rd Learner B
4th Learner D

Clearly, there is little correlation between the two sets of results in this case. However, a couple of comments are in order. First, Fielding used this system for *written* English. It is perhaps less suited to measuring chunk density in spoken interaction as it penalizes the frequent false starts of spoken language. For example, the learner judged the most fluent in this case tended to use a different fluency strategy – repeating and restarting short phrases to hold the floor, while pursuing his overall message sometimes over a number of turns, as this extract shows.

D: *Well, me I am not scared too by ... by that thing, mm but um ... they're strange because they, they makes you, they put you into a strange situation ... you realise the, the strength of nature when you =*
C: *uhuh*
D: *= you are in these things but then, then you, you realise how, how many things man has made to ... to keep er himself so sh- himself sure=*
C: *mm*
D: *= and to keep himself away from this troubles*

Perhaps a way around this could be to 'tidy up' the false starts and repetitions to reveal the essential language produced – a similar process to that used by a writer before presenting a text for public view (or indeed a speaker in a more formal oral presentation).

However, one striking result of calculating chunk density using a 'gap measure' was the huge difference between the native speaker and learner output: the native speakers had average gaps of 4.28 and 4.82 words respectively, whereas the advanced learners' average gaps ranged between 7.14 to 7.46. Allowing for a difference between intermediate and advanced learners, this general finding is in line with the findings of Foster (2001) who found that native speakers used twice as many chunks as intermediate learners in unplanned conditions. It also strongly supports Pawley and Syder's (1983) suggestion that chunks are a feature of *native speaker* fluency.

Reflection and suggestions for classroom practice

A task-based approach to teaching/learning requires attention to fluency, accuracy and complexity of language (e.g. Willis, D., 1996a).

My study seems to support the view that the use of multi-word chunks helps fluency. However, Skehan (1996a: 22–3) warns of the danger of using tasks which allow learners to rely too heavily on their repertoire of 'prefabricated phrases and established routines' at the expense of experimenting with language of greater complexity. While I agree that learners should be given the opportunity and the incentive to stretch themselves linguistically, I do not think the two things need be mutually exclusive.

I think what is needed is an approach that recognises the vital role that lexis, and particular lexical phrases, play in shaping the language we use, a 'lexical approach' as advocated particularly by Michael Lewis (1993, 1997). The fact is that native speaker language seems to be *predominantly* made up of prefabricated phrases, a view also supported by corpus research, e.g. Sinclair (1991).

Unfortunately, there is still little awareness of this in many teaching and learning contexts. In this study, it was interesting to see the results when the participants were asked to identify chunks in their transcripts. One learner and one teacher showed a reasonable awareness but worryingly, one of my colleagues – a well-qualified and experienced teacher – failed to identify any chunks at all in three of the learner transcripts, where I had 34, 74 and 71 respectively.

On the other hand, the errors made by these advanced learners in even very basic chunks (**at house*; **put up your dresses*) suggest that there is a gap left here by traditional grammar and vocabulary teaching which needs to be filled.

A lexical approach to language and learning complements rather than contradicts a task-based approach. It simply means that our attention to accuracy and complexity should focus just as much on multi-word chunks as it does on more purely grammatical constructions. Some examples of opportunities to do this follow.

Pre-task activities

Pre-task activities should probably aim to anticipate as many purely *lexical* chunks as possible related to the topic, particularly collocation of various kinds, e.g.:

- eliciting adjectives which collocate with topic-related nouns
- matching verb–noun collocations
- identifying collocations in a text

and see Lewis (2000) for many more ideas from practicing teachers.

Foster (1996) suggests that planning time before the task can improve learner performance in the task in terms of accuracy and complexity of language produced. Essig (Chapter 16) found that with planning time, his learners produced a wider variety of more precise lexis. I think there could be a good case for some discreet teacher intervention when there is an individual pre-task planning stage:

- responding to individual learner queries
- monitoring for 'missed opportunities'

This would also partially solve the difficulty of anticipating individual vocabulary needs, as described above in relation to the 'storms' task.

During the task

While any form of rigid prescription of language at the task stage runs counter to a purist task-based approach, Skehan (1996a) does suggest that we may wish to 'manipulate' the task in some way. One way to avoid teacher prescription but still put pressure on learners to extend the range of language they use is to ask them to individually select for example two new chunks and resolve to use them as they carry out the task.

Post-task activities

There are numerous post-task opportunities for focusing on multi-word chunks, for example

- A reporting stage (oral or written) could be a good time to focus particularly on discourse-structuring chunks or sentence stems.
- Consciousness-raising activities of the type proposed by Willis and Willis (1996) involve observing words in context. A particular focus at this point could be on sentence-length chunks, particularly more idiomatic ones, and elliptical expressions, which the learners in this experiment did not seem to have acquired naturally. These could be based on either native speaker transcripts or recordings of more advanced learners such as those used by Gairns and Redman (2002), the latter arguably providing a more appropriate model for English as an international language (see Graddol, 1997).
- A reporting stage can be followed up by a class error-correction slot to focus on the accuracy of chunks produced, and/or work on missed opportunities (e.g. *it was raining very much* could be rephrased as *it was pouring with rain*).

- Revising/recycling is essential if new items are to become part of a learner's active repertoire. Informal testing activities which challenge learners to remember (e.g. complete/correct the chunk; how do you say ...?; choose the best chunk; etc.) offer another opportunity for 'fine-tuning' ie a focus on accuracy and a useful memory jog. If learners are to carry out a similar task or one on a related topic, this type of recycling activity can become part of the pre-task introduction, 'a chance to recall things they know' (Willis, 1998b: 2).

Subsequent findings

With the learners in this study I was only able to give some individual feedback on their performance. Since then, however, I have used all the approaches suggested here with learners of different levels and have observed that:

- learners tend to use planning time to focus on lexical rather than grammatical accuracy
- a 'second attempt' in the form of a reporting stage or repetition of a task produces greater precision of multi-word chunks (see also Essig's findings in Chapter 16)
- once chunks are identified as such, learners readily perceive them as an aid to expressing ideas more precisely and more fluently

These will be areas of further exploration in my own classroom research and would also be worth looking at in other contexts.

Appendix 1

Note: tasks adapted from the Collins Cobuild English Course Level 3

Task 1

Tell each other what other places or countries you've been to and how/why you were there.

Task 2

Tell each other how you feel about thunder and lightning and storms in general.

Task 3

Read these poems and discuss which season you think each piece refers to and why.

The rains start to come
The plants raise their heads

Fresh flowers appear, elegant smells
A new life has begun
Karamo Sonko, 18, The Gambia

As the days grow longer
The animals play
And as the colors of the rainbow spread,
The leaves of the trees turn into soft colors.
Then the leaves play with each other.
The sun looks down and
Thinks nature is
A good way for the world to be.
Grant Tennille, 5, USA

It always seems surprising when you wake
up in the morning and find everything is
white with snow. Then, when the sun comes
out, the snow sparkles like lots of crystals.
R. Hunt, 13, United Kingdom

Listen to the grass blade growing,
This music is hidden
And heard all day long.
Listen to the black-bird singing,
The song is the same
And new every time.
Listen to the rain drop falling,
Its sound is a moment
In our short lifetime.
Listen to the soft wind blowing,
He's singing a song
For all of mankind.
Lucia Atanasiu, 16, Romania[1]

Task 4

CROCODILE QUIZ

Discuss whether you think these statements are true or false. Try to agree on your answers.

a Most species of crocodile are man-eaters.
b Over 2,000 people a year are killed by the Estuarine crocodile.
c In Egypt, along the banks of the River Nile, crocodiles kill up to 1,000 people every year.
d Crocodiles will eat refuse as well as living creatures.
e There are giant crocodiles/alligators living in the sewers in some South American cities.
f Crocodiles can grow up to 11 metres in length.

g Many crocodiles and alligators live over 100 years.
h So many crocodiles have been hunted and killed by man that 16 species are now extinct.

Now read the article overleaf and check your answers together.

(Note: the last part of the task was not recorded.)

Note

1 Extracts from *Cry for our Beautiful World,* used with permission of Helen Exley Giftbooks.

14

Can We Predict Language Items for Open Tasks?

David Cox

Summary *I wanted to find out if teachers of EFL would be able to predict structures and phrases that would naturally occur when people from different English-speaking countries carried out five 'open' (experience-sharing/opinion-giving) tasks. The results were interesting as they call into question the practice of setting tasks at the end of a three-stage PPP cycle to allow students to put into use the language item that has previously been taught and practised.*

Rationale

Along with other teachers, I had often wondered whether it is possible to select or devise tasks which will naturally generate specific language items. Willis (1996a) suggests that experienced teachers may be able to predict the language of a **closed task**, such as one in which pairs try to find a specified number of differences between two pictures, but, she claims, with open tasks it is 'virtually impossible'. I designed this investigation to try to find out if, in fact, teachers can successfully predict language items generated by **open tasks**.

Method

Devising the tasks

I selected five tasks from Nunan's *Atlas* series (1995a). I chose *Atlas* because my students, at a private language school in Japan, found its tasks to be both interesting and engaging. Some were labelled as tasks in the book and others were activities from language focus sections. In the teacher's book, Nunan explains that these sections 'analyse specific grammatical and functional points that have been presented in the preceding task chain' (Nunan, 1995b). A secondary element to the investigation was, therefore, to find out whether participants doing the task recordings would use the particular language items under focus in the corresponding language focus section in *Atlas*.

I adapted the instructions in order to give the tasks a more precise outcome (for more details on this see Appendix 1). Then I piloted the instructions with some colleagues to eradicate any ambiguities. The revised task instructions follow here. You might like, as you read them, to see whether you can predict any phrases or structures that might occur.

Task 1. List the three most interesting cities or places in your country and why people should visit them.

City/Place	Why is it interesting?
....	....
....	....
....	....

Discuss your ideas briefly and then say which of your partner's places you would most like to visit.

Task 2. What advice would you give to the person who wrote this letter? Discuss your ideas and then agree on the two best suggestions.

Dear Angie,

My husband and I are worried about our daughter. She refuses to do anything we tell her to do and is very rude to us. Also, she has become very friendly with a girl we don't like. We don't trust her anymore because she is always lying to us. Are we pushing her away from us? We don't know what to do, and we're worried that she is going to get into trouble.

Worried Parents

Task 3. Discuss what you think life will be like in fifty years. List three aspects that you agree on.

Task 4. Find out about your partner's favourite spare time interests when he/she was a child. What, if anything did you find you had in common?

Task 5. Talk about an embarrassing incident that has happened to you. Decide whose incident was most embarrassing.

Recording the tasks

I sent the task instructions and recording instructions (below), along with a blank audio cassette, to 20 friends and relatives in Australia, Canada, Ireland, the UK, and the USA.

I asked the recipients to record two pairs of native speakers carrying out the five tasks. Participants were asked to be natural, and they were told that the purpose of the recordings was to give my students the opportunity to listen to authentic conversations, instead of the usual scripted dialogues that they were accustomed to hearing in their lessons. (Some of the recordings have since been used for this purpose.) Before speakers began each task, they were given a two-minute silent thinking period to consider what they might say during the task. This was in accordance with the work of Foster (1996), who found that learners of English, when given time to plan what they might say, produced more complex language and paused less often. Participants were then asked to follow the task instructions carefully, and to try to keep their discussion within a two-minute time limit.

I asked the participants to try to complete the recordings within two months. Around 25 pairs of people recorded the tasks. Understandably, not everyone was able to spare the time to set up the recordings, and there were also a couple of technical problems. However, after two months, recordings for analysis were available in the following numbers (each recording having two speakers interacting).

Table 1 Task recordings made by native speakers of English

	Recordings	Speakers	Duration (mins.)	Word Count
Task 1	23	46	50	8,090
Task 2	24	48	49	8,050
Task 3	25	50	58	9,449
Task 4	25	50	53	8,553
Task 5	25	50	59	9,502

This makes a total of 269 minutes of data (43,644 words), which shows that the participants spoke at an average rate of approximately 160 words a minute while doing the tasks. So two minutes of recorded data gave a transcript of somewhere around 320 words. It is quite useful to compare these figures with the length of an average reading text that learners are used to, and also with the number of words that learners produce in one minute's worth of task recording. (Pinter, Chapter 10, used this speech rate measure with her young learners.)

Making the predictions

The teachers who made the predictions of language items were all employees of GEOS Language System, one of the largest English language schools in Japan. Most of the teachers had joined the company with little prior experience of language teaching, and were trained in planning lessons that followed a Presentation, Practice, Production format. (See Introduction and Shehadeh Chapter 1.)

I faxed a questionnaire, together with a covering letter, to 50 branches of GEOS. The instructions at the top of the questionnaire invited teachers to predict any structures and phrases that native speakers might use in carrying out the five discussion tasks which followed.

To avoid influencing teachers' predictions, I gave no examples of language items. I used the term 'phrase' loosely to refer to a chunk of language ranging in length from a single 'polyword' (Nattinger and DeCarrico, 1992) such as *nevertheless* to a sentence-length utterance, such as *That's the most embarrassing thing I've ever heard*. The term 'structure' I intended to cover items such as relative clauses, conditional clauses, 'comparatives', 'superlatives', and 'the tenses' (eg 'simple past', 'present continuous', 'future perfect'). However, in case the distinction between phrase and structure was not clear, I asked teachers to write their language predictions under one general heading, 'Predictions', rather than under specific headings, 'Phrase' or 'Structure'.

In the covering letter I gave brief details of the purpose of the study, and how the results might benefit teachers and learners. I told teachers that there was no need to supply their names along with their predictions. Twenty teachers responded.

Analysing the data

I transcribed the task recordings and stored the resulting data in five separate computer files – one for each task. Then I used a concordancing program to analyse the data in each file. I used the program first to search for language items matching teachers' predictions, and then to find the most common language items that had not been predicted by teachers. Transcribing and analysing the data were very interesting, but also very time-consuming! As it turned out, my analysis of the data showed that I could easily have identified typical language by analysing as few as five recordings for each task. See Appendix 2 for samples of the recorded data.

Findings

Tables 2 to 11 below provide a summary of the main findings from the investigation. In each table, structures are written in upper case and phrases in lower case. The first column of figures gives the number of teachers (out of a maximum of 20) who predicted each structure or phrase. Secondly, 'Occs in data' denotes the number of occurrences of each item in the recorded data. Finally, '% Spkrs' gives the number of speakers (as a percentage) who used each structure or phrase.

Task 1 Three interesting cities or places

The figures in Tables 2 and 3 show that teachers were, generally, unable to make accurate predictions. Perhaps the most interesting finding was that 'forceful' phrases with modal verbs, such as *you should, you must, you have to,* and *you've got to* were not used by speakers in carrying out Task 1. This is particularly notable because *should* was the target item in the *Atlas* language focus for Task 1. Instead of using these 'forceful' phrases, speakers used more tentative phrases such as *I would say ...,* and ... *is a place I would recommend.* For other such phrases, see transcript of Task 1 in Appendix 2.

Table 2 Language predicted by native speakers for Task 1

Structure/phrase	No. of prdtns Max 20	Occs in data	% Spkrs	Example in recorded data
SIMPLE PAST	2	51	50	*A friend and I went to London ...*
PRESENT PERFECT	1	19	48	*I've been to a casino in Niagara ...*
COMPARATIVES	1	25	37	*... it's almost as good as the Lake District.*
the best place/city	6	0	0	
you should/must/ have to	6	0	0	

Table 3 Language not predicted by native speakers for Task 1

Structure/phrase	Occs in data	% Spkrs	Example in recorded data
RELATIVE CLAUSES with *which*	39	50	*... Ayer's Rock, which is in the centre of Australia.*
you can	30	43	*... and you can visit the White House.*
it's got	17	20	*... it's got such a relaxed, holiday feel about it.*
is a (very) *adjective* place	15	33	*It's a very historical place.*
Vague language: sort of	12	15	*..., erm and it's more sort of unspoilt.*

Task 2 Problem page letter

The figures in Tables 4 and 5 show that teachers were a little more successful in their predictions for Task 2 than they were for Task 1. However, while a large proportion (18/20) of teachers correctly predicted that a modal verb phrase of some sort would appear in the data, predictions of individual phrases were not so accurate. Of further note was the total absence of the following (predicted) standard advice-giving phrases: *How about—?, I recommend—, Why don't you—?, Have you tried—?, Have you thought of/about—?*

Table 4 Language predicted by native speakers for Task 2

Structure/phrase	No. of prdtns Max 20	Occs in data	% Spkrs	Example in recorded data
IMPERATIVES	4	42	35	*... don't forget that they are young adults.*
CONDITIONALS	8	61	52	*... if they push her too much she'll just rebel.*
(modal verb phrases)	18	126	100	*... you've got to start trusting them ...*
How about ...? I recommend (etc.)	9	0	0	
... try and/to ...	1	28	40	*... they shouldn't really just try and tell her ...*

Table 5 Language not predicted by native speakers for Task 2

phrase	Occs in data	% Spkrs	Example in recorded data
be a (good) idea to/if	5	6	*... it might be an idea to discuss it with them.*
be (very) important to + INF	5	10	*... it's very important to stay clear-headed.*
be good (for X) to	3	6	*... it might also be good to have a meeting*
The (adj) thing (to do) (modal) be	6	13	*... the thing to do is to stay calm ...*
'filler' you know	27	35	*a lot of being parents is like, you know, riding the storm*

Task 3 Life in fifty years

The figures in Tables 6 and 7 demonstrate the degree to which English speakers rely on *will* (and to a lesser extent *going to*) to make predictions. Also of interest was the occurrence of the *Atlas* language focus item *will/won't be able to*, which was not predicted by any teachers.

Table 6 Language predicted by native speakers for Task 3

Structure/phrase	No. of prdtns Max 20	Occs in data	% Spkrs	Example in recorded data
SIMPLE FUTURE (will)	14	249	98	*I think people will travel even more ...*
FUTURE CONTINUOUS	1	13	12	*... technology will be running our businesses ...*
FUTURE PERFECT	4	6	10	*... alcohol will have become socially unacceptable.*
going to	4	68	60	*... people are going to be living longer.*

Table 7 Language not predicted by native speakers for Task 3

phrase	Occs in data	% Spkrs	Example in recorded data
will/won't be able to	6	10	*... they'll be able to prevent teeth going rotten.*
___ years ago	10	14	*Well, fifty years ago, if you'd said, 'Ha! We'll be ...'*
'filler' you know	26	24	*... it's absolutely amazing, you know, like ...*
'filler' I mean	17	24	*Yeah I mean there was no such thing as fax machines ...*

Task 4 Childhood interests

The figures in Tables 8 and 9 show that teachers were, on the whole, a little more successful in predicting language generated by this task than they were with the previous tasks. Again, however, many phrases predicted by teachers did not occur in the task recordings.

Table 8 Language predicted by native speakers for task 4

Structure/phrase	**No. of prdtns Max 20**	**Occs in data**	**% Spkrs**	**Example in recorded data**
used to (past habit)	13	141	76	*... and I used to love climbing trees as well.*
would (past habit)	2	38	46	*He and I would ride round and round ...*
SIMPLE PAST	20	600+	100	*I liked to build things with scraps of things.*
PAST CONTINUOUS	1	10	20	*I was always drawing.*

Table 9 Language not predicted by native speakers for task 4

phrase	**Occs in data**	**% Spkrs**	**Example in recorded data**
all + time expression	10	20	*... all day long.*
neg + activity + or anything like that	3	6	*I never used to play with dolls or anything like that.*

Task 5 Embarrassing incidents

As Table 10 shows, the past perfect tense was used by nearly half the speakers. This might seem to be quite a high frequency, and that the past perfect is, therefore, well worth practising with students. Conversely, however, there is a danger in giving students lots of practice with a structure which they then think is very common, but which, in fact, was used by only a minority of participants in this study.

Table 10 Language predicted by native speakers for task 5

Structure	**No. of prdtns Max 20**	**Occs in data**	**% Spkrs**	**Example in recorded data**
PAST PERFECT	1	41	44	*... some clown had sewn the ticket half way.*
SIMPLE PAST	17	500+	100	*... I got in quickly, jumped in, slammed the ...*
PAST CONTINUOUS	3	56	64	*I was coming from a meeting in Hong Kong.*

Table 11 Language not predicted by native speakers for task 5

phrase	Occs in data	% Spkrs	Example in recorded data
subj+ didn't know + WH-	7	14	*I didn't quite know where to put my face.*

Reflection and conclusion

The discovery that a great many predicted language items did not appear in the recorded data calls into question the appropriacy of expecting learners to use language items (like *should*) in contexts where fluent speakers would not naturally use them. Interactions like the following are very unlikely to happen in the English speaking world outside the classroom.

A: *I like scuba-diving.*
B: *You should visit the Great Barrier Reef in Australia – it's amazing! I like shopping.*
A: *Oh, you should go to the new shopping centre.*

If learners feel it necessary to use *should* all the time (for example at the Production stage of a PPP cycle where *should* has been presented), they are confined to one wording and are missing out on experimenting with other ways of expressing a whole range of similar meanings. Learners may wish to express their opinion less forcefully than *should* suggests, so phrases like *I would say* or *I would recommend* or *Well, what you could do is* would be much more appropriate. In a PPP lesson learners are being unnaturally constrained when they should be experiencing the richness of meaning potential and practising normal conversation skills.

These findings add weight to the case for a task-based framework. While doing a speaking task in such a framework, students (like the speakers who took part in this investigation) are free to use whatever language items they like, unhindered by any perceived pressure from the teacher to use certain structures or phrases. The good sense in giving students this freedom is highlighted by the fact that, for each task, the speakers in the study employed a wide variety of language items. After being given this important freedom of approach to a task, learners would then benefit from a focus on form (see Doughty and Williams,

1998 for the importance of this) and from being made aware of a wide variety of useful items. This form focus could be implemented post-task, either when planning a public report of the task findings to present to the class (Willis, J. 1996a, 1996b) or through language focus activities, like those in Nunan's *Atlas* series (1995a).

Further suggestions for form-focused language study

A careful read through the task transcripts in Appendix 2 allows a great many foci for language to study to be identified, in addition to those listed in the tables earlier. Here are a few examples of consciousness-raising activities, some of which focus on functions, some on lexical phrases and some on grammar.

For Task 1, ask learners to identify ways of making suggestions, ways of giving reasons and to find phrases which evaluate suggestions. Focus on the word *would* and ask learners to find six phrases with *would*, classify them and practice saying them. (Ask if any of the *woulds* appear with an *if* clause.) Ask learners to identify clauses beginning with *which* and *where* (there are four) and then write sentences on the same pattern about places they would recommend.

For Task 2, ask learners to find expressions giving advice, and then to classify them along a cline of quite tentative to more definite. They could also identify examples of vague language, discourse related phrases (eg *first thing, in other words*), interpersonal phrases like *You know?*, sentences or clauses with the word *If* and patterns with verbs+*ing*.

You could collect further examples of these particular features from other texts or transcripts that your learners have met earlier. These texts and transcripts become a collection of useful language data that Willis (2003: 163) calls a **pedagogic corpus**:

> Grammarians and lexicographers work with a corpus of language, a set of texts, to enable them to describe the grammar and the vocabulary of the language. In the same way, learners process a set of texts to enable them to develop their own vocabulary and to work out their own grammar of the language.

Students can constantly refer back to familiar texts and investigate whatever grammatical or lexical features are highlighted for language study in their course book. If you have to cover a structural syllabus, and have a large enough pedagogic corpus, you will probably find that all the useful items are illustrated somewhere, and there will be much more useful language besides – for example lexical phrases and chunks as identified by others in this volume. This is one way that tasks can be used as the basis for a syllabus. A course can be sequenced according to topics, each with tasks and texts, which can be used alongside a checklist of grammatical and lexical items. These can be ticked off each time they have been focused on, recycled and tested. There is no guarantee that they will have been learnt, but at least it offers some accountability, and a far richer diet of language.

For teachers preparing students for exams with an emphasis on grammar, this approach of exploiting a pedagogic corpus for samples of target language features can be supplemented with examination style exercises, eg cloze tests and multiple-choice items, using natural examples from the texts themselves. As Sheehan implies (Chapter 4) students working with natural language data learn how to learn through becoming text investigators. Another advantage is that students will be exposed to a far wider range of vocabulary, collocations and lexical phrases – also useful for examinations.

If you are in a similar situation to Loumpourdi (Chapter 2) obliged to teach a grammar course following a set syllabus, then you may well need to restrict yourself to using 'closed' tasks. Although the language in closed tasks tends to be more predictable, there will always be alternative ways of expressing similar meanings. Broadly speaking, as the present study suggests, some tasks will almost certainly generate certain features: for example *will* was used by 98 per cent of speakers to predict the future, modal verb phrases were used by 100 per cent of speakers to suggest what someone worried about a family member should do, and all speakers used the simple past forms to talk about past habits and embarrassing incidents. But just as anecdote tellers switch from simple past to what is known as the dramatic present, alternative forms will also appear, like, in the prediction task *I can see beer being very very expensive indeed.*

I have included in Appendix 2 some sample transcripts for the tasks I used in my study, so you could try out some of these tasks with your students. After doing each task you could encourage your students to analyse the discussion that the speakers produced identifying the kinds of features listed above. The students could practise and make a note of any phrases or patterns they think they will find useful in their own spoken English.

If you need to focus on other items on your syllabus you could design some closed tasks, record some friends doing them, then find out whether they used the language items in question. If they did, great! If not, you might still decide to use the task if it generates other items that your students need to know, and alternative ways of expressing those general meanings. For advice on making task recordings see Hobbs, Chapter 12.

Finally, any data that you collect by recording your own tasks can be used not only for teaching but also for further research into different areas. And, of course, it can be used by other people. Ketko (2000), for example, used the transcripts of my recordings to analyse multi-word chunks in spoken data which she then compared with data from her learners doing the same tasks, in a process similar to that used by Baigent in Chapter 13. As Pinter (Chapter 10) commented, once the data is assembled, all kinds of avenues open themselves up for exploration.

Appendix 1 Details of adaptations to original tasks

Task 1 Three interesting cities or places

I took Task 1 from a task chain in *Atlas 2* (Nunan, 1995a: 67). The theme of the task chain was travel, and the language item under analysis in the language focus section that followed it was the modal *should*. I adapted the task to give it a more definite outcome.

Task 2 Problem page letter

Task 2 was also designed by adapting a task in *Atlas 2* (p. 106). The theme of the task chain was giving advice to people with personal problems, and the language items under analysis in the subsequent language focus section were the modals *have to, should and could*. As with Task 1, I made the *Atlas* Task instructions more explicit so that participants would know when the task was completed.

Task 3 Life in fifty years

I designed Task 3 by adapting the first line of a dialogue in a language focus section in *Atlas 3* (p. 28). The focus of this section was the modals *will/won't be able to*.

Task 4 Childhood interests

Task 4 was designed by adapting an activity in a language focus section in *Atlas 3*. The language item under focus in this section was *used to*.

Task 5 The most embarrassing incident

I designed Task 5 by adapting an activity in another language focus section in *Atlas 3* (p. 54). The language item under focus in this section was the past perfect tense.

Appendix 2 Samples of recorded data

Note: Backchannel responses (see Leedham, Chapter 8) are in parentheses.

Task 1 Three interesting cities or places (Heather and Debbie)

H: I would say, my choice is, is the first one's the obvious being London, the capital city; and the next choice for me is Poole – my home town – because I know it so well, and erm there's a lot of history there as well. And then Bath, which is always a popular place with visitors, 'cos erm you've got the Pump House and the Roman influence and the gorgeous building in The Circus.

D: Okay, mine would have to be the same as yours for the first one – London, being the capital city with all the famous buildings to visit and obviously the history of the city of London. My second choice is Cambridge, which is my closest erm large town to where I live, which has the famous universities. And, thirdly, Stratford-upon-Avon, erm, as a visitor to the UK I think it's very important for a visitor to follow the history of William Shakespeare, where he was born.

H: Mm, I agree. Depending on how much time the person has to visit, I think you really need to have at least, I would say about four days as a minimum to see London.

D: Oh definitely. A week if you can spare it, but I guess most people can't.

H: Mm, most people don't have as much holiday time as the British, unfortunately.

D: No, with the two places I've chosen though, er if you're visiting London, erm it's easy to access the other two – they're only an hour outside of London.

H: That's, that's a good way of doing it, having a base.

D: Yes.

H: Bath's quite easy, you can go on a day trip there, and Poole's only, again, a couple of hours, but that's nice if you're visiting England in the summer, so that you've at least got a bit of a beach to see and the gorgeous countryside going into the Purbecks.

D: Of the places erm that you've chosen, I would probably like to I'd like to visit them all, but my favourite would probably be Poole. I'm not particularly a city person and Poole is very beautiful on the harbour, but, as you say, it really needs to be summer.

H: Yeah, and Stratford-upon-Avon, if anyone does have the chance to go and visit there it would be nice to spend an evening there or be able to spend it over night, and go and see one of Shakespeare's plays, cos you can often get reasonable tickets at the last minute. The theatre, that would be lovely.

D: You can have an afternoon tea. And wander along by erm by the canal, there's a pretty walk.

Task 2 Problem-page letter (Nadine and Audrey)

N: Well I think, first thing, that you don't want to lose the daughter, so you would try and make quite sure that rude as she was and awful as she was, you wouldn't erm alienate her completely. You've got to somehow keep hold of her because you can't do anything unless she's there with you.

A: Of course you could, if she was prepared to, invite this friend round for a meal or something, or even go out perhaps in the car somewhere, somewhere that they perhaps like to go, perhaps the beach or something.

N: Yeah.

A: In other words you've really go to try and keep the doors open (yeah and maybe ...) for discussion.

N: Maybe if the daughter saw that the friend didn't fit in because she was so awful (yes), it might make the daughter aware of (yes she might ...) different values or something.

A: ... think well after all Mum and Dad aren't as bad as I thought, if she could see you interacting (yeah) with this other girl it might help, I don't know, it's a very difficult (it is) question.

N: But I, I think that I would talk about the lying, I think I would try and discuss what it's like to be lied at, (yes) and how she would like (yeah) to have people lying to her.

A: Yes, quite.

N: And really (yes) pulling that out into the (yes) open, (yes) rather than just pretending you were half-believing it or, you know I wouldn't shout at her (no) but I'd discuss (yes) the telling of truth (yes) and how it affected ... (perhaps)

A: Perhaps if you said to her, 'Can you imagine what it would be like living at home if we lied to you? You'd never know where you were going.' (Yes) You know?

N: Yes, yes, yes. 'Or if Dad and I lied all the time (yes), we'd just (yes) you'd never know what, what you were (yes), where you were.'

A: Yeah I, I think you've got to discuss it (umm), but I suppose it's probably difficult when she's already rude and not listening and ...

N: Yeah yeah, no I liked your point of inviting this girl round to your house, I think. (Mm) So it is a difficult question (yeah) I know and I'm sure it's something that, (but I think) thousands of people (I think) have (yes) have that problem.

A: Yeah I'm sure they do, but I think you've got to bring it up and I think you've got to not argue.

Task 3 Life in fifty years (Rich and Claire)

R: Well, it'll be 2050 by then, near enough. I think there'll be much more emphasis on part-time work, rather than four or five days a week work. Everything in life will be much more computerised even than it is now, and, erm, I can see beer being very very expensive indeed.

C: Erm, I think that people'll work from home far more than they do today, transport will be quicker, more public and greener, and entertainment will be far more insular ...

R: How do you mean?

C: You know, people amusing themselves on their own, virtual reality, that sort of thing.

R: Oh right. Like the home computer and Nintendo gone mad.

C: Yes.

R: And there'll still be football, though.

C: Yes (yeah, okay). And what was that other thing you were thinking of? There'll be more ... ?

R: There'll be space exploration, obviously. We'll have space exploration, it's what the future's all about.

C: So which three aspects do we agree on?

R: Part-time work from home (yes), home workers, that kind of thing, massive computerisation, and, erm, things will be more expensive because of inflation.

C: Definitely.

R: Okay.

Task 4 Childhood interests (Sheri and Scott)

Sh: So what kinds of things did you like to do when you were a kid, Scott?

Sc: Er, what did I like to do? I loved to erm, 'a kid' meaning how old though?

Sh: I don't know, like when you were six or seven.

Sc: Six ... I loved playing soccer, (yeah). Soccer was a favourite pastime for myself. I played a lot of soccer. How about you, Sheri?

Sh: Er, let's see, I liked to build things with scraps of things, I was a very creative child. I liked boxes – boxes were my favourite toy because I could make stuff out of them.

Sc: Mhm

Sh: And I wasn't really into sports.

Sc: No? I see.

Sh: No, but were you into anything else? Because we have to find something in common.

Sc: Erm, I did like building tree – I built several tree-houses, (oh yeah?) and so I was that imaginatively, (actually) extremely creative ...

Sh: My brother and I used to build tree-houses (yeah?) too, so ...

Sc: I loved building tree-houses (yeah?), I would er make forts and I would fight all the evil invaders that would come into my fort.

Sh: Yeah? So did my brother and I!

Task 5 Embarrassing incidents (David and Mark)

D: This took place in, probably the 1970s when stores weren't quite so sophisticated as they are today. I was in the clothing department of a very busy department store and decided to try a pair of trousers on, and the shop assistant referred me to the changing room, and I went in. They had the sort of louvre doors, the sort of saloon room door, saloon bar door, you know, on hinges, you know the sort, and I went in, took my trousers off, and I put my left leg in the trousers and I went to put my right leg in the trousers I'd picked up in the store, and some clown had sewn the price ticket half way-they'd actually stapled the price ticket half way up the trouser leg, and I went to put my foot through and of course couldn't. I tripped backwards through these doors, went cata-cata-cata straight out onto the shop floor (<laugh>), with one leg in the trousers, one leg half way up the other trousers, jumping around, fell flat on my back, right in front of all the shoppers, on a Saturday morning!

M: <Laugh> That's pretty good. I don't know if I can top that, but the only thing I can think of that's even mentionable on tape is in Japan, in a good old onsen, which is a hot spring. It's happened to many, many people, in the days before I could read any Japanese characters, least of all the ones that said 'man' and the ones that said 'woman'.

D: <Laugh> I think I'm ahead of you here!

M: Yes, I think you probably are! Just, well, stripping off naked, as you do, and going into the bath with all the beautiful 80-year-old women, that's about it <laugh>. I won't elaborate. So whose do you think was the most embarrassing? I'd have to say yours was.

D: Yeah, I think probably, um ... Given that, um ... Well you can imagine the scene, can't you? This man wearing a pair of white underpants dancing around on one leg ...

M: Oh! White underpants? That's it, that's the winner!

Part D

Investigating Variables: Task Conditions and Task Types

There are many alternative ways of designing and implementing tasks. But how do we select which ways are best for our particular learners? In order to make sensible choices, we need to know what is likely to happen when tasks are set up and implemented under different conditions. The teachers in the five chapters in Part D describe how they explored the differences in learners' interactions when they changed the way that they designed or set up a task, or followed up a task.

The first three papers explore the use of tasks within the context of a broader task cycle. In Chapter 15, Craig Johnston recorded mature adult learners doing tasks and found that quite often, the language they used in the privacy of their pairs to achieve the task goals successfully was very simple and stilted, sometimes nothing but a few words or phrases put together. He was afraid that their language would **fossilize**, in other words remain forever at that low level. So he experimented by giving learners time after a decision-making task to plan how to tell the whole class what they had decided together during the task, and then he recorded their more public reports. To examine precisely what differences occurred in the language at Task and Report phases, Craig used four different kinds of measure, assessing syntactical accuracy, lexical accuracy, syntactical complexity and lexical variety. He illustrates clearly what each measure involves (so that you could use the same measures) and comes up with some interesting results.

In Chapter 16, William Essig, convinced of the relevance of storytelling to our every day lives, explores the different effects that result from telling a story spontaneously (without time to plan or rehearse). But he also looks at what happens to learners' language when they are asked to re-tell their story to someone else later on, having had time to plan how they will re-tell it using dictionaries and other resources. He also compares private and public contexts. He made all his story recordings in one lesson, then, having come up with eight hypotheses, he tested each one by looking closely at the recorded data. Not all his hypotheses were borne out, which shows how useful it is to investigate rather than simply assume things are true. And his students really enjoyed telling and re-telling their stories.

While Johnston and Essig both explored the effects of *post-task* activities, Antigone Djapoura, in Chapter 17, looked at the *pre-task* stage of a task-based cycle. She investigated whether allowing her learners' pre-task planning time affected their task-performance, and in what ways. Like Essig, she sets out a number of hypotheses which she then goes on to test. Her research design is similar to that used by Foster and Skehan (1996) and she compares her results with the findings of that study. This is an excellent example of what is often called a *replication study*. The value of a replication study, as she herself says, is that 'looking for patterns in results across these two studies gives us the opportunity to make more powerful generalizations'.

The final two chapters in Part D look at variables in task design, rather than the effects of different phases in the task-cycle.

Greg Birch in Chapter 18 is worried (like Craig Johnston) that task-based interactions might promote fluency rather than accuracy and thus lead to fossilization. He sees the need to try to attain a balanced focus and wonders whether different task types systematically offer different learning opportunities. He uses the work of Skehan (1998) on assessing task difficulty and examining task characteristics in order to predict whether learners doing particular types of task are more likely to focus their attention primarily on fluency, accuracy or complexity of language. He selected two one-way information gap tasks suitable for his 16-year-old students, and recorded three classes of 40 students doing both tasks. He predicted, on the basis of Skehan's work, that both tasks (but for different reasons) would push learners to a reasonably accurate and fluent interaction, but would not push them to use complex constructions. Was he right? Read it and see.

In Chapter 19, Glen Poupore compares learner interaction arising from two different types of task: problem-solving/prediction tasks, where all learners have the same information but need to reach some kind of joint decision, and jigsaw tasks, where each learner has some information that the others don't have but need. However, in order to make this comparison, and to find out which type of task is more likely to lead to learners' language development, he needs some way of measuring and defining what he feels is 'quality interaction'. Assuming, as

Long (1988) and others have since done, that when learners negotiate meaning (eg ask for clarification) they are likely to learn more, Poupore explores his data to discover what other aspects his learners negotiate and uncovers how far these negotiations push learners to a higher quality of interaction.

Both Birch and Poupore discover that some kinds of task may be better than others for achieving different kinds of interaction and learning opportunities. It is now up to us as readers to continue the explorations, so that we can gain a larger and clearer picture of which types of task are likely to achieve what.

15

Fighting Fossilization: Language at the Task Versus Report Stages

Craig Johnston

Summary *I wanted to test the claim that a public report stage in the task cycle can help learners monitor the quality of their language output. To do this, I used four different measures (syntactical and lexical accuracy, syntactical complexity and lexical variety) to investigate the differences between task-stage and report-stage language. I found some marked differences, suggesting that a report stage is indeed valuable.*

Context and rationale

Students at the conversation school where I work in Japan place a high - priority on talk time and meaning-focused language use. Communicative tasks serve very well in this environment, however the quality of language employed by students in completing tasks is sometimes a concern. To take an extreme example, here is an excerpt from an exchange between two low-intermediate students who are trying to decide on a seating plan for well known guests at a dinner party:

(Note: Koizumi is Japan's Prime Minister at the time of writing. Soseki and Tokugawa are well known historical figures in Japan. More details on the context of this excerpt will follow).

Kumiko Koizumi here?

Hiroko: Koizumi

Kumiko: That's good idea

Hiroko: Soseki ...

Kumiko: Ah, Tokugawa

Hiroko: next to Tokugawa ruler same ruler I ...

Kumiko: OK, so our final agreement
Hiroko: Partner? (*inaudible Japanese*)
Kumiko: No, uh
Hiroko: Final?

Despite the obvious problems, Kumiko and Hiroko understood each other and went on to complete the task successfully but using very minimal language. This highlights an area of concern in task-based learning, as noted by Seedhouse (1999). With success defined by task completion, often under a time constraint, students may focus disproportionately on fluency (ie expressing their meanings quickly, using gestures and even their L1 to do this) at the expense of accuracy and complexity (Skehan 1996a: 22). This in turn may lead to '**fossilization**', ie the stagnation of L2 development.

One response to this challenge is to employ a post-task 'report stage' during which the learners report to other groups, or possibly the whole class, on the outcomes they achieved during the task (Willis, J. 1996a: 54–60). The report stage, by taking advantage of the natural desire to present a higher quality product when one knows the product will go on public display, seeks to reassert a focus on accuracy and complexity (*ibid*: 55; see also Essig, this volume). This shift in focus is supported by a planning stage which precedes the report, allowing students to organize their thoughts, select appropriate language, and consult resources such as a dictionary. Intuitively it seems that the planning and report stages should help, but I wanted to find out if empirical data would support this and, if so, to what extent and in what ways? Does the difference in quality warrant the extra time spent? This paper describes an investigation that I carried out in search of answers, or beginnings of answers, to these questions.

Method

The students and the task

I carried out this study with a group of three students. A larger group would have yielded more data, however the small size of the office space, paired with the need for clear recordings, necessitated a small group. The participants, Hiroko, Kumiko and Asuka, are all middle aged women, studying English primarily for pleasure and the opportunity to meet with foreigners. The task instructions were as follows:

Imagine that the following people are coming to your house for a dinner party.

- *Junichiro Koizumi (Japan's Prime Minister at the time of writing)*
- *Makiko Tanaka (controversial former Foreign Minister, recently fired by Prime Minister Koizumi)*
- *Ieyasu Tokugawa (iron-fisted shogun of Japan, early seventeenth century)*
- *Buddha*
- *Soseki Natsume (one of Japan's most celebrated writers, late eighteenth and early nineteenth centuries)*
- *Sanma Akashiya (universally loved funnyman, appearing on numerous TV shows)*

Your mission is to create a seating arrangement, around a circular table, which will allow them to enjoy interesting conversations with their neighbors, hopefully avoiding arguments.

Step 1: By yourself, decide on an arrangement.
Step 2: Explain your arrangement and your reasoning to your partner. Then listen to your partner's explanation of her arrangement and write it down.
Step 3: With your partner, create a final arrangement that you both agree is best.

Procedures

Grouping of students and report preparation

With only three students, I had to partner with one of them. The alternative, a single group of three, would have made the report redundant; why report on what you did if your audience did it with you? After the task had been completed they were asked to prepare a report for homework describing how they and their partner solved the problem. The following week everyone was paired with a new partner, to whom they presented their report. At both stages the two pairs worked in separate rooms to enable clear recordings.

Measurement

I used the transcribed task discussions and reports to measure syntactical (ie grammatical) accuracy and complexity as well as lexical (ie vocabulary) variety and accuracy. These concepts, and their relevance, will be discussed in more detail as they arise, below.

Findings

The results are presented below in three sections, the first dealing with accuracy, both syntactical and lexical, the second with syntactical complexity and the third with lexical variety.

Before discussing the results, I should point out that Asuka's report was cut short by a question from Hiroko. This launched the two into a spontaneous discussion and effectively terminated Asuka's report. For this reason, analysis of Asuka's report was not carried out beyond Hiroko's question, making it roughly half as long as those of Hiroko and Kumiko. Some interesting results were observed nonetheless.

Accuracy

Syntactical accuracy

Syntactical accuracy was measured by comparing the number of error-free clauses with the total number of clauses (Foster, 1996: 133). For example, Kumiko's (report stage) statement that 'He's a famous novelist and he seem to be gentle' scores 50 per cent on this accuracy test:

He's a famous novelist	and	he seem to be gentle.
Error-free		Error (seems)

Since only one of the two clauses is error free, the score is 50 per cent. The levels of syntactical accuracy for all three students, at both task and report stages, are shown in Table 1 below.

Table 1 Syntactical accuracy

Student	Percentage of error-free clauses at the task stage	Percentage of error-free clauses at the report stage
Asuka	(6/33) 18.2%	(6/20) 30 %
Hiroko	(2/39) 5.1%	(5/34) 14.7%
Kumiko	(15/47) 31.9%	(6/32) 18.8%

(Figures in parentheses indicate the number of error-free clauses and the total number of clauses, respectively.)

Surprisingly, Kumiko's accuracy actually dropped. In a later interview, Kumiko indicated that she had been too busy to put much time into her report. This may account for the drop. It may also be the case that, as the most proficient English speaker in this small, friendly class, Kumiko felt very little to be at stake in presenting her report, and so may not have approached its preparation with the same care as Hiroko and Asuka. Both Asuka and Hiroko produced decidedly more accurate language in their reports, Asuka posting a 65 per cent gain and Hiroko almost tripling her percentage of error-free clauses. Given the low level of accuracy in their task language, these are important results, suggesting that the planning/report stage may indeed help boost accuracy and play a part in combating fossilization.

Lexical accuracy *(or Lexical selection)*

Accuracy, as defined above, does not help us evaluate lexical choices and so I will use the term ***lexical selection*** instead; 'improved lexical selection' meaning 'a more native speaker-like choice of words'. Using lexical selection as a measure of accuracy, we find that the above results actually understate the gains. Consider the following comparison of Hiroko's task and report language:

Task	Report
Soseki is a novel writer so Koizumi Prime Minister is ... very like reading books so next to the Soseki.	Koizumi's right hand side seat is Soseki. Koizumi likes reading a book so they get along well with each other.

I think most readers will agree that the report version represents more native-like use of the language and yet, by the above test of syntactical accuracy, it actually scores lower than the task version. (Both have three clauses but only the task version has a grammatically error-free one: *Soseki is a novel writer*. In context, *they get along well with each* other

Table 2 Changes in lexical selection

Speaker	Language used during task stage	Language used during report stage
Kumiko	Koizumi and Tanaka must be sit at separate table. (Grammatically and semantically flawed; separate tables were not an option.)	... keep Koizumi and Tanaka and Tokugawa apart from each other.
Kumiko	Sanma-san is very good, uh, has a nice character.	He (Sanma) has a sense of humor and friendly.
Kumiko	Soseki is a famous nov, novel ...	He (Soseki) is a famous novelist.
Hiroko	Quiet, quiet person is Tokugawa, Soseki, Buddha. And talkative is Koizumi, Tanaka, Sanma.	I separated to every second seat a talkative person and a calm person sit.

requires the insertion of 'would' to be considered error-free.) What then makes the report version the preferred one? I would suggest that it is the improved lexical selection represented by the phrase, *'A' gets along well with 'B'*. Note that the 'correctness' of this phrase cannot be explained by grammatical rules; it is a 'chunk', a single unit of vocabulary (Bolinger 1975). Table 2 presents other examples of differences in lexical selection. In each case, the gains achieved spring not from grammatical accuracy but from superior choices of words.

The improved lexical selection seen in the reports is another important result, further supporting the inclusion of planning and report stages in the task cycle.

Syntactical complexity

Complexity 'concerns the elaboration or ambition of the language which is produced (Skehan, 1996a: 22)'. A review of the transcriptions showed that report language was markedly more ambitious. For example, task stage language was typified by simple utterances such as those in this four-turn excerpt:

Hiroko	Now is Koizumi and Tanaka is this ...
Kumiko	Don't, don't get along with each other.
Hiroko	Each other, so ... Tokugawa
Kumiko	Tanaka-san here

Even when taking longer turns at the task stage, the students' language remained very simple as in the following example. (Putting aside the many syntactical errors, notice that Hiroko has relied heavily on the simple conjunctions *and* and *so*.)

> My, my, ah, I thought Buddha is only sitting and very quiet, so Sanma between and Tanaka Makiko sitting Buddha, and Soseki is novel writer so Koizumi prime minister is ... very like reading books so next to the Soseki.

The one example of more complex language use occurs at the beginning when *'I thought Buddha is only sitting ...'* sets up the dominant clause, *I thought*, and the dependent clause, *Buddha is only sitting ...* This in fact was the only example of complex clause relations in Hiroko's entire task performance. Compare this with the opening lines of Hiroko's report:

> Our final arrangement, the party. I separate, I separated to every second seat a talkative person and a calm person sit. Koizumi Prime

> Minister left hand side seat is Tokugawa, because they are statesman and ruler and Koizumi ask to Tokugawa how to continue political view of Koizumi.

Though still imperfect, we immediately recognize a striking improvement in the quality of language use. This is achieved partially through improved lexical selection and more accurate use of syntax. But it also shows more elaborate and ambitious use of grammatical structures and this will be my focus here.

First, we see that the report contains the subordinating conjunction 'because', creating a dominant/subordinate clause structure used not once in Hiroko's task performance. Second, Hiroko has correctly used '*ask (someone) how + to-infinitive*', a relatively complex structure, well beyond the ambition of anything produced during the task stage. These are important points because they show that, through her report, Hiroko is either experimenting with or practising language abilities which might atrophy or not emerge at all if her speaking opportunities were limited to the production of spontaneous task language. (See Shehadeh's explanation of 'the output hypothesis perspective' in Chapter 1.)

Kumiko showed a very slight decrease in quantity of complex structures but made gains in quality, achieving more sound constructions during the report. Compare '*Hiroko's idea of the seating arrangement was [[to keep Koizumi, Tanaka and Sanma apart each other]]*' (report) with '*when they talk each other, Koizumi feels very comfortable and calm [[to hear what Buddha is saying]]*' (task).

Asuka made the most noticeable gains of the three with almost half of her report stage clauses being bound to others in complex relationships, up from less than one-in-five during the task stage. Her opening lines quickly produced two structures not attempted at the task stage: first, the relative clause (in square brackets) '*We had same opinion [[that Tanaka sit next to Sanma]]*', and soon after, the embedded clause '*We talked about [[where does Buddha sit]].*' These examples show that, like Hiroko, Asuka flexed linguistic muscles at the report stage which she had not used during the task stage. This provides further support in favour of the planning and report stages.

Lexical variety

More varied lexis contributes not only to the quality of the text, but also allows the student to keep her mental lexicon active; this is important because failure to use an item may lead to its becoming irretrievable.

If indeed the report stage leads to greater lexical variety this would be another reason to support its use. As a general measure of lexical variety, the type-token ratios of the six different texts were calculated and are shown in Table 3. (*Type* refers to the number of *different* words used, while *token* refers simply to the total number of words.) A higher result indicates less repetition of the same words and a proportionally greater variety of lexical items in use.

Table 3 Type/token ratios as a measure of lexical variety

Speaker and text	(types/tokens)	Proportion
Asuka – task	(76/214)	0.36
Asuka – report	(54/115)	0.47
Hiroko – task	(67/186)	0.36
Hiroko – report	(116/263)	0.44
Kumiko – task	(94/295)	0.32
Kumiko – report	(96/209)	0.46

Here we see a fairly consistent result indicating a clear trend towards increased lexical variety. To get a clearer picture of the changes in lexical variety, the number of different nouns (excluding those which refer to the six characters in the task), verbs, adjectives, adverbs, determiners and conjunctions were counted for each text. (Because the adverbs category in English is so diverse, I have limited the scope of the term to adverbs of manner such as 'well' and 'easily'.) The results are shown in Table 4, below.

Table 4 Number of different words used for various word classes

Speaker and Text	Nouns	Verb	Adjs	Advs	Determiners (eg *a, the/this, that, these, those/my, her/etc.*)	Conjunctions
Asuka – task	5	9	8	1	3	4
Asuka – report	8	10	2	1	4	3
Hiroko – task	12	8	8	2	2	3
Hiroko – report	23	21	12	3	5	6
Kumiko – task	8	13	10	1	5	3
Kumiko – report	14	16	12	4	7	2

The data in Table 4 confirm a marked increase in lexical variety. For Kumiko and Hiroko, whose reports were delivered in full, the increase in lexical variety manifested itself in all word classes except Kumiko's use of conjunctions. Both of them almost doubled the number of different nouns used, and Hiroko more than doubled her variety of verbs and determiners. Asuka, despite her abbreviated report, managed gains in her variety of nouns, verbs and determiners. Given that her report was only half the length of her task, this appears to be an impressive result.

A number of factors are likely to have contributed to the increase in lexical variety.

- Both Hiroko and Asuka used a dictionary during the planning stage.
- Planning time provides the student with deeper access to their own mental lexicon. (See Foster 1996: 134)
- During the task stage, Hiroko, for example, appeared to rely heavily on visual communication, supplementing this with utterances such as 'Tanaka-san here', and 'then Sanma'. During the report, however, she had to communicate her ideas without visual support and turned to phrases such as 'Koizumi's right hand side seat is Soseki Natsume'.
- At the report stage, students described not only their solutions, but also the processes whereby the solutions were reached. Asuka, for example, used the mental process verb 'decide' in her report (eg 'so we decide [sic] that Ieyasu seat is next to Koizumi'). Such words are less likely during the task stage when she and I were still in the process of making those decisions.
- A final factor, quite evident in the language generated by Hiroko and Kumiko, is that during the task stage they focused on getting the job done. In their reports, however, they expanded on feelings and reasons and other content not even mentioned during the task. Hiroko, in her report, comments that Makiko Tanaka would ignore the people seated on her right and left, opting instead to 'talk over their heads' to the more humorous Sanma. Perhaps this was on her mind during the task stage but she couldn't express it, or perhaps it came to her later. In either case, it contributed to the increased lexical variety (and interest) of her report.

Reflection and evaluation

Student reactions

I spoke briefly with the three at the conclusion of this investigation in order to obtain feedback. Kumiko, as mentioned, was unable to spend much time preparing her report and so did not particularly enjoy the planning stage. She did, however, enjoy presenting her report and listening to the others. Hiroko and Asuka gave quite positive reactions and said that they had enjoyed having the opportunity to use a dictionary and polish their grammar. They noted, however, that they found each other's reports a little difficult to understand; the more ambitious syntax and lexis which make the report stage valuable from a language production standpoint may also create comprehension difficulties for the listeners. Viewed in a positive light, there may be rich opportunities here for language learning. (See 'the interaction hypothesis perspective' and 'the socio-cultural perspective' in Shehadeh, Chapter 1.)

Conclusions

With the exception of Kumiko's decreased grammatical accuracy at the report stage, all four measures of performance used in this study indicate that the planning/report stage may have a beneficial impact on accuracy, complexity and variety. How far this intervention, in isolation, goes towards refining interlanguage and combating fossilization remains unclear. This study was very small, and therefore cannot produce any conclusive findings, but it does suggest that that the planning and report stages enabled the production of superior language for these three students, and can therefore be recommended as part of a strategy to prevent fossilization. In addition, and perhaps equally important, it sets out a method by which others can investigate this phenomenon on a larger scale.

16

Storytelling: Effects of Planning, Repetition and Context

William Essig

Summary *This chapter reports the results of a small-scale research project in a womens' college in Japan in which I explored the effects of planning time and a change of context (private vs. public display) on the repetition of oral narratives by my students. Analysis of the transcripts suggest that planning time and a change of context to public display have beneficial effects on both the fluency and accuracy of the students' retellings of their stories.*

Background and rationale

Before the Internet, before television, before printing presses, even before hieroglyphics, there was the telling of stories which played an important role in people's lives. Ever since humankind began to communicate orally, there have been stories to be told. The stories we tell help to define who we are in the eyes of others. Our stories represent our histories. As we share our stories over and over again, we often polish and elaborate those tales to make them more interesting, fascinating, heartwarming or touching. In other words, the repetition of storytelling enables each story to become more attractive. Additionally, our desire to create a good narrative results in our planning what we are going to say before we actually verbalize it to others. Another aspect of storytelling is the social context in which the storytelling takes place. This also has an impact on what we say and how we tell the story.

Since storytelling can be such an integral part of everyday life, it seems only natural that our students should have or would like to have opportunities to share their own experiences with their friends and classmates as well. However, due to the lack of sufficient communication skills in English, simply telling a story could be a difficult task for many of our students. What sort of Task-Based Learning (TBL) methods could we apply in order to help improve our students' oral narrative skills? What would be the effects of planning time and a change of context – from 'private' story telling in pairs to more public story-telling to the whole class – on the repetition of oral narratives? These were the questions I sought to answer when I embarked on this project.

Eight possible outcomes

My general hypothesis was that the second narrative, both in public and private contexts, would be more developed than the first, unplanned narrative. Specifically, I proposed the following eight hypotheses:

1. Task repetition would result in a greater number of clauses produced by students during task completion.
2. There would be fewer pauses in the retelling of the narrative.
3. An obvious increase in fluency (see Appendix 2) would occur in the second narrative.
4. Planning time before repeating the task would allow the students to incorporate a wider variety of lexis.
5. The second narrative would have greater lexical density (see Appendix 3).

These five possible outcomes were concerned with both public and private presentations. Concerning the differences between public and private narratives, I proposed the following:

6. Public display would be more accurate than private narratives.
7. Public presentations would have more lexical density.
8. Public presentations would have a higher degree of fluency.

Method

Context and procedures

For my project, I selected at random eight students from my junior college in Japan, women of 18–20 years old whose English ranged from high elementary to low intermediate levels. The students were enrolled in a 12-session voluntary course titled 'Speech Communication'. The purpose of this course was two-fold: first, to help the students to develop the ability to speak for extended periods of time, and second, to learn how to make a formal oral presentation in front of an audience.

I divided my eight students randomly into two groups, Group A and Group B. Both groups produced an oral narrative twice. Group A told their stories first in the privacy of their group and then in front of the whole class. Group B, however, told both of their stories in private.

The actual research took place during the sixth lesson of the course. This was done for two reasons. First, I wanted the students to become accustomed to a task-based framework dealing with extended speech. Second, I hoped to lessen the inhibiting effects of using a tape recorder. For the first five lessons of the course, most private and all public performances were recorded. I emphasized to the students that the recordings would in no way affect their final grades. By the sixth lesson, the students had lost almost of their hesitancy and fear over the use of tape recorders during class. Although my research took place in Japan, these procedures would be applicable to other countries as well.

The actual procedures for the experiment were as follows:

1. Put the students randomly into two groups.
2. Ask the students to relax for a minute or so and to think of an unusual, happy, exciting, frightening, or memorable experience which they would like to share with the members of their group.
3. Students decide who goes first, second, third, and fourth.
4. Instruct the listeners to pay careful attention to the story and to be prepared to ask questions about content, details, and misunderstandings once the story was completed.
5. The first speaker in each group tells her story.
6. At the end of the story, the students begin the question/answer period (four-minute time limit).
7. Steps 5 and 6 repeated for the other three students.
8. At the conclusion of all four narratives, tell the students they have fifteen minutes to make notes, use their dictionaries, ask each other or teacher for assistance as preparation for retelling their stories. Also, tell the students that Group A's second narratives will be told in public and Group B will do it in private.
9. After 15 minutes, instruct the students to stop making notes.
10. The four students from Group A tell their individual stories to the whole class as a public performance without using their notes.
11. Once Step 10 is completed, the students in Group B tell retell their stories in the privacy of their four-member group. While they are performing their tasks, teacher talks to Group A about their narratives.
12. Thank all the students for sharing their interesting stories and collect the cassette tapes, making sure they are labelled correctly.

By the end of the lesson, at the conclusion of the experiment, I had 16 taped narratives for analysis.

Findings

Comparison of first and second narratives for group A (private–public)

I transcribed and analysed the recordings, looking at each hypothesis in turn. Hypothesis 1 stated that students would produce a greater number of clauses in the second telling of their stories. The average number of clauses, however, actually decreased for three of the students. Despite the fact that Hypothesis 1 was not supported by three out of four subjects, an interesting result did occur. Instead of trying to make their second narratives longer or more detailed, the analysis of the transcripts revealed a 'tightening up' of the narratives by the students. Compare the following excerpts from Student A (see Appendix 1 for the complete transcript).

/ indicates a pause of one second

> Student A2 (First): *Then the train got to Kyoto Station and we got off the train/and so the train left/the train was leaving the strange man was /// looking/on the train eh from the train //// the man didn't get off the train so the man was on the train / and then the train was leaving he was looking at us*

> Student A2 (Second): *Then the train got to Kyoto Station and I got off the train / but / after I got off the train when the train was leaving / the man was still looking at me so strangely*

Hypothesis 2 predicted that there would be fewer pauses in the retelling of the stories. Hypothesis 3 stated the second narrative would be more fluent (see definition in Appendix 2). Two of the students showed a dramatic decrease in the number of pauses they used in their second narratives. The other two students had a minimal decrease. Nevertheless, all four students showed improvement in this area. They also had less silent time in their retellings. The students' retellings showed mixed support for Hypothesis 2. The results of the analysis would seem to support Hypothesis 3 (see Appendix 2). All four members of Group A showed a noticeable increase in their rates of speech. Student A3's increase in the number of repetitions was most likely caused by her desire to include new lexical items in her second narrative:

> Narrative 1: *I opened the door / and there were three men standing there and doing something*

Narrative 2: *Then I opened the door quickly/and I supposed to go downstairs but there are there were three men standing there and/relieving by relieving themselves/I was so surprised*

Hypothesis 4 predicted that planning time would enable the students to incorporate a wider variety of vocabulary in their second narratives. It was supported by the results of the analysis. Below are some examples of the most noteworthy changes and additions made by the students: Hypothesis 5 predicted that the second narrative would be lexically denser than the first one (see definition in Appendix 3). This hypothesis cannot be supported by the data. The changes in the mean numbers of nouns, verbs, adjectives, and adverbs between the two narratives were minimal and mixed. Perhaps their goal was to produce a story that was clearer and more concise than for their first attempt. One noteworthy result not predicted by the five hypotheses was the increase in the number of error-free clauses in the two narratives.

Even though three of the five hypotheses received either a lack of support or mixed support, the results of the analysis of the two narratives for the four members of Group A revealed substantial improvement in the oral production of their stories in the areas of fluency and accuracy. Overall, the speakers used fewer pauses and repetitions, their speech rate was faster and they produced more error-free clauses.

Table 1 Major lexical changes Group A

First Narrative	Second Narrative
go to my home	*return home*
I rush into a mistake train	*I dashed into the wrong train*
—	*reached the station*
—	*my mother is surprised*
—	*he announced a lost child*
I got off my class	*I left my school*
doing something	*relieving themselves*
—	*they turned around*
had a bad mistake	*made a big mistake*
—	*I couldn't say anything*
—	*few minutes later*
big	*Huge*
experienced (slot machine)	*did (slot machine)*
wedding	*wedding ceremony*
—	*make a toast*
—	*very hot*
—	*like desert*

Comparison of first and second narratives-group B (private–private)

There was a slight decrease in the mean number of clauses in the second narratives. (For the complete transcripts of Student B2's two narratives see Appendix 3.) Individually, three out of the four students spoke fewer clauses in their retellings. These three members of Group B, like their Group A counterparts, seemingly attempted to make their second narratives more compact and concise than their first ones. Consider the following excerpts to make comparisons:

> Student B3 (First): *at that time a man /// a black man ran ran // toward so we beside we didn't notice / a man*
>
> Student B3 (Second): *than a black man walked toward us be we didn't um but we didn't notice him*
>
> Student B4 (First): *um I went there with my family / an a uh that was / ah ah my father visited there on business but eh I and my / eh family except father was / eh um on vacation*
>
> Student B4 (Second): *eh I went there with my family and that / that was my father's business //// my father went business but we went there on vacation*
>
> Student B1 was the only member of her group who produced more clauses in her second narrative than in her first one. I gather this increase was primarily caused by adding extra information to her retelling. The '*akahoko*' referred to here is a kind of Japanese sweet.
>
> Student B1 (First): *I said to my mother / strange people gave me my present / ah it is 'akahoko' oh ///*
>
> Student B1 (Second): *mother asked me what's this I say strange people give me gave me //// I said to my mother / what do you think about this 'akahoko' my mother say I don't know /// but I want to eat this me I say me too*

The embellishment of her narrative through the addition of dialogue added enough extra clauses to give substantial support to Hypothesis 1. The other three students, however, produced fewer clauses in the second narratives. For this group as a whole, therefore, Hypothesis 1 was not adequately supported by the results.

Hypotheses 2 and 3 were concerned with fluency. All four students showed a dramatic decrease in the number of pauses produced in their second narratives. Hypothesis 2 predicted that this decrease would occur, and the results support this hypothesis. Two illustrative examples of this decrease are given below:

> Student B3 (First): *we wanted to // convenience store 7–11 so we so 7–11/was /// in front of hotels*
>
> Student B3 (Second): *my friend and I want to go to a convenience store 7–11 and this convenience store uh in front of my hotel*
>
> Student B1 (First): *one day /// I / take / train by myself I'm sitting on the/seat /// one old woman come to / my seat*
>
> Student B1 (Second): *I usually take train by myself from my school to my house when I will go back to my house / one day when I was sitting on seat strange old woman say like this I have many souvenirs*

Three of the four students of this group showed a noticeable improvement in the other fluency measures in the second narratives, therefore, Hypothesis 3 can be justified when the overall results of the fluency measures are considered (see Appendix 2).

Hypothesis 4 stated that planning time would allow students to incorporate a wider variety of lexis into their second narratives. This hypothesis was validated by three of the four members of Group B. Table 2 is a summary of the principal lexical changes produced by the students. Since Student B4 made many exceptional lexical changes and additions by adding two new parts to her second story, I would like to separate her positive modifications from the other three students.

Table 2 Major lexical changes Group B (Students 1–3)

First Narrative	**Second Narrative**
—	*usually*
present	*souvenirs*
please give me you my present	*please accept*
—	*I'm in trouble*
come to my house	*come back to my house*
I went to my house	*I arrived my home*
I belong to	*I used to belong to*
—	*awaited our our turn*
—	*on the backstage*
—	*Superstition*
hand	*Palm*
an interesting period	*so embarrassed and so scary story*
we walked street	*we crossed the street*

Table 3 Major Lexical Changes Student B4

First Narrative	Second Narrative
—	*spring holiday*
—	*company*
—	*incorporating*
visited	*looked around*
—	*often listen to the music*
—	*stereo*
loud sound	—
big sound	—
—	*Redwoods*
—	*beautiful*
—	*went shopping*

Conversely, Hypothesis 5, which predicted greater lexical density in the second narratives, was not at all supported by the analysis of the transcripts. This could very well be a further indication that the students from both groups were concerned more with better fluency and accuracy rather than with expanding or lengthening their narratives.

Public and private display: post-task comparisons

Group B produced both sets of narratives within the privacy of their four-member group. Group A, however, presented their second narratives in front of the whole class as public performances.

Hypothesis 6 predicted that public display would be more accurate than private presentations. When measured by the number of error-free clauses, both groups showed substantial improvement. These results not only support Hypothesis 6 but may also indicate that the public display of narratives may cause students to pay more careful attention to the accuracy of their utterances which is a crucial element of a TBL framework.

According to Hypothesis 7, the public display of narratives should have a greater degree of lexically density than the narratives presented in private. The public display group certainly showed an increase in lexical density. The private display group, however, actually showed a slight decrease in lexical density. The crucial factor, though, was that in both narratives, it was the private presentation group who had a higher level of lexical density than the public group did. The private group also produced a greater number of total content words in their second narratives than the public display group produced. Hypothesis 7, then, cannot be supported by the results of the analysis.

Finally, Hypothesis 8 predicted that public performances would be more fluent than their private display counterparts and this proved correct. The public display group had fewer pauses, fewer repetitions and a faster speech rate than the private display group.

Reflection and evaluation

This research project had two purposes. The first was to discover what, if any, changes in output might occur during the repetition of a storytelling task when the students are given the opportunity to spend some time to plan the task-repetition. The results of the research showed that substantial changes did occur in many elements of the task-repetition. Both groups of students were able to produce second narratives that were more fluent and accurate than their first attempts. The secondary aim was to discover what differences there could be between second narratives told in private and in public. The results confirmed the hypothesis that task-repetitions performed in public are likely to be more accurate than those performed in private. Additionally, the data indicated that public performances were more fluent than private performances.

Although the research shows that task-repetition and public performances led to a general improvement in the output of the students, it is not possible to declare with certainty if these positive changes could have been actual or coincidental due to the small scale of my study. For this, a larger scale research project is needed to test these same eight hypotheses.

Further research

What I discovered from doing this research has helped me to realize that there are many more questions about planning time, task-repetition and context that need to be considered (see Johnston, Birch and Djapoura in this volume). The following questions are all possible areas for further research:

- Does the amount of planning time make a difference? (Foster, 1996; Mehnert, 1998)
- How do the results change when a task is repeated twice or more times rather than just once? (Lynch and Maclean, 2001)
- What are the effects of different intervals of time between repetitions?

- Does task-repetition affect the retention of new words and structures?
- How do students feel about task-repetition?
- Can task-repetition/public display help introverted students to become more outgoing?
- What are the possible effects of the teacher's, or other students', input during planning time?
- Can transcripts of a student's output help her to improve her performance?
- Can a student listening to her own first attempt at a task help the student to improve her second attempt?

Doubtless, there are numerous other questions that can be raised about these exciting research areas.

I have included in Appendix 4 a list of storytelling tasks that I have used successfully. Any of these could be used to experiment with the use of planning time, retelling the story after a break and switching from private to public context.

Conclusion

Throughout this chapter, I have focussed on the linguistic changes that occurred. In conclusion, I would like to point out another factor that plays an important role in using narratives in the classroom: enjoyment. The students who took part in this project had a wonderful time, sharing stories as both tellers and listeners. I have also found this to be true with other students. I have seen the widening of their eyes and the positive change in their voices when they are given the opportunity to express something real, meaningful, and true through their stories. True, the classroom is a place for learning, but it is also a place for sharing. And I can think of no better way to share who we are than through the stories we tell.

Appendix 1

Complete transcripts of Student A2's two narratives

First Narrative Private

umm // a few days ago I was on my way home / and I was on a train with my boyfriend /// umm I didn't have / eh I didn't have anything to do so I was reading comics when I was reading it a man was looking at me / then he / was reading my comics too / and sometimes he looked at me and he smiled at me strangely I was scared so I hid behind my boyfriend / then the strange man looked / looked at me over my boyfriend's shoulder like / here is my boyfriend sort of and then // like like (laughter) then I was really scared so I always hid from him then the train got to Kyoto Station and we got off the train / and so the train left / the train was leaving the strange man was // looking / on the train eh from the train //// the man didn't get off the train so the man was on the train and after we got off the train / and then the train was leaving he was looking at us //// for a while / I was scared that's it (2:55)

Second Narrative Public

A few days ago I was on a train I was on my way home / and I had nothing to do so I was reading magazine on the train / and at that time I was with my boyfriend then I was reading magazines there was a man he was smiling at me so strangely and I was little bit scared but I was interested in magazines so I was reading again // sometimes the man was trying to read my magazine / and he was approaching me little by little / uh so I was hid behind my boyfriend / but the man / was trying to look at me over my boyfriend's shoulder / with strange strange smiling / the train go to Kyoto Station and I got off the train / but / after I got off the train when the train was leaving / the man was still looking at me so strangely it was my scary time that's it (1:52)

Appendix 2

Table 1 Group A Fluency Measures

Measure (Narrative 1/ Narrative2)	Student A1	Student A2	Student A3	Student A4
Number of pauses	19/17	20/11	13/10	24/13
Length of pauses (seconds)	24/23	33/11	16/10	33/20
Number of repetitions	8/5	5/0	5/6	8/4
Words per minute	50.6/71	57/81.9	71.6/84.4	39/52

Table 2 Group B Fluency Measures

Measure (Narrative 1/ Narrative2)	Student B1	Student B2	Student B3	Student B4
Number of pauses	34/26	30/26	24/10	48/33
Length of pauses (seconds)	6/43	35/25	37/11	78/43
Number of repetitions	5/2	18/8	11/7	8/15
Words per minute	46.5/57.5	42.9/51.4	65.6/79.2	3.6/42.5

Note: *Fluency* is defined here as a Combination of the number and total length of pauses, the number of repetitions, and rate of speech in words per minute.,

Appendix 3

Complete transcripts of Student B2's narratives and an analysis of lexical density

First Narrative Private

I'd like to tell about my junior high school (?) club club in junior high school // when I was junior high school student I belonged to I belonged to ah brass band club and I played clarinet / I like it very much / and I / I practiced it very hard every day and // when the competition held / was held I have to I had to play alone in front of the ground and before the / before we played / I was very tense and I I wrote / I wrote the Chinese character 'hito' on the hand three time and I swallowed / but my heart is beating still beating / and / eh / eh I played and we started to play / the music but my my // my / head is **white white white white** and **just** (?) I was I um / I didn't **think** about anything anything but / we and I / when I / when I **played solo** / I I could **play** all **things** but I didn't **remember** /// uh I didn't **remember** and / after I I was **very good** it's **good** it was **good** and I'm **happy** but I didn't / eh / **remember** them I **think** it's / um / **interesting things** because I did I did that I did it but I couldn't didn't **remember** (3:10)

Second Narrative Private

This is my strange story / in the junior high school student I used to belong to / brass band club / I played clarinet I practiced it hard every day one day I was said I was said my club leader please / please play / a solo / in the in the competition / so I practiced it harder / it um the competition came and we awaited awaited our our turn on the backstage I was getting tense / and I did / one superstition I // wrote I wrote Chinese character 'hito' on palm on my palm I swallowed on my palm three times and I **swallowed** it but I **still** / was **tense** / and / we **began** we **began** to **play** / the **music** / but my **head** is **white** / and / after we **played** we **played** I was **said** my **friends** you are **good** your **solo** is **good** but um I didn't **remember** anything I **just remember** I **just remember** I **stalked** in **front** of **band** and I **played** but // **almost** all / of that I didn't **remember** I **think** it's **strange** (2:48)

Note: *Lexical density* is a measure of the complexity of a given text. It is represented as the percentage of lexical words (nouns, verbs, adjectives and adverbs, as opposed to grammar/discourse words like *and, that, of*) in the text. As an example, I have calculated the lexical density of the last five lines of these two narratives. Repetitions were counted. Lexical words are in **bold**.

	Total words	Lexical words	Lexical density(%)
First	82	22	26.82
Second	72	29	40.27

Appendix 4

Storytelling tasks for classroom use

1. *Circle Fairy Tales.* Students (3–5 per group) sit in a circle taking turns telling a fairy tale one sentence at a time. Dictionaries may be used. Change the order and tell the story again. Form new groups. Each student tells her story alone and listens to other students tell their stories.
2. *Chain Stories.* Similar to 1 above, but students create an original story based on the first sentence supplied by the teacher, for example, 'Susan was walking along the street when she saw a box.'
3. *Picture Stories.* Use pictures/cartoons from magazines or newspapers as the basis for telling stories.
4. *Tell Us About ...* Students ask each other to describe experiences, such as, tell us about a trip you took. Other events include high school, last summer, yesterday, your last vacation, last weekend.
5. *The Last Time ...* Students ask each other, 'When was the last time you?' Students can make a list of activities on the board or in groups. Example activities include went shopping, baked a cake, cooked dinner, played sports, were absent from school.
6. *Have You Ever ...* Like 5 above. Possible experiences may include flown in an airplane, been hospitalized, had an accident, kept a pet, met a famous person, been to another country. For story tasks 4, 5 and 6, the list of possible activities/experiences is limited only by the imagination of the teacher and the students.
7. *When Did You Feel ...* Students tell stories based on emotions such as sad, happy, excited, frightened, worried, disappointed.
8. *Lights, Camera, Action.* Students tell the plot of a favorite movie or television drama.
9. *Impersonations.* Students tell a real or imaginary story from the viewpoint of one of the characters.

All of these storytelling tasks can be used following the 3-step procedure outlined in this chapter; tell the story, plan the retelling, tell a better story in private or in public.

17
The Effect of Pre-task Planning Time on Task-based Performance

Antigone Djapoura

Summary *My primary aim in this small-scale study is to investigate whether allowing learners pre-task planning time affects their task-performance. I also examine the effects of pre-task language instruction.*

Background and rationale

The question of how we measure language proficiency or success in language learning seems to be problematic. It may be that what is being measured in some classrooms is not the ability to use a language, but the ability to manipulate language forms (Lightbown and Spada 1999). Although most language schools around the world which use a Presentation methodology (often labelled PPP – see Introduction) claim to be 'communicative', success is usually not measured according to one's ability for 'language use', but according to one's 'knowledge about language' and ability in 'language manipulation' (Willis 1990). This certainly seems true of many English classrooms in Greece.

A solution may be to adopt task-based learning, but this has been criticized for encouraging learners to concentrate on fluency at the expense of accuracy (see Moser in Chapter 7 and Johnston in Chapter 15). I feel, however, that this criticism is groundless since, in addition to the language focus stage which follows the task cycle, there are a number of other techniques that can be employed to ensure a balance between accuracy and fluency even during the task cycle. The task-based framework is based on the assumption that pre-task planning time allows some attention to form, together with the report phase for which learners will naturally want to polish up their language for their 'public' performance, as we have just seen in Chapters 15 and 16.

Skehan (1998) shows that a number of studies of speech production suggest that planning before a production task may have one of two effects. It may lead to greater accuracy stemming, presumably, from a greater attention to form. It may, on the other hand, lead not to an increase in accuracy, but to a more complex and ambitious encoding of language used. Motivated by these findings I decided to collect data from my own students and examine the effect of pre-task planning time on the quality of their language (ie how accurate, complex and fluent it is) during task performance, thus finding out whether planning time is actually an effective means of achieving a balance between accuracy and fluency.

Four hypotheses

My general hypothesis was that given pre-task planning time, learners would produce better quality language. Specifically, four basic hypotheses are examined:

1. Under planned conditions, there will be greater **fluency** in language; that is there will be fewer repetitions, fewer reformulations, fewer replacements, fewer false starts, fewer pauses and less silence.
2. Under planned conditions there will be greater **accuracy** in language; that is there will be a higher proportion of error-free clauses in their task interactions.
3. Under planned conditions there will be greater **complexity** of language; that is there will be a greater number of subordinate clauses.
4. The effects predicted in Hypotheses 1–3 will all be greater when planning is guided in some way by the teacher or the materials.

The above hypotheses are derived from Foster and Skehan's (1996) study, *The influence of planning and task-type on second language performance* which was used as a basis for my study.

Context and method

I teach in a private Language Institute of about 1000 students, in a rural area south of Nicosia, Cyprus. My class was made up of twelve pre-intermediate Greek-speaking students studying English as a foreign language. They are all between 14 and 15 years old and have been studying English for five years, three hours per week. They are all extremely motivated students who are really enthusiastic about using tasks in the classroom and who see the whole procedure as an enjoyable game rather than a 'lesson'. I decided to gather my data on one day at the end of their academic year during normal class time.

The tasks

I realized that I needed to select tasks that would provide a reasonable level of challenge for my students, but not be too difficult for them. Tasks which have heavy cognitive load (difficult content) and demand great cognitive effort on the part of the subjects would allow less attention to be devoted to form (Skehan 1998). I chose three task types: *Problem Solving, Ordering and Sorting, Comparing.* The actual tasks consisted of a logic problem, a list of jobs to be ordered and ranked, and two pictures for a Spot the Difference game (see Table 1 and Appendix 1). I thought that it would be more interesting to use three different task types rather than just one, because in this way we can see whether in all task types the effects of planning are the same or whether a certain task type produces different results (although this is an issue which is not extensively dealt with here).

The task types I used are also different from those used in Foster and Skehan (1996). The reason for this decision is that if the task types used in the two studies were the same, then in the case of similar findings one could argue that this is a result of task type, rather than a result of planning time.

I wanted to explore what would happen if:

(a) Learners did the task straight away with no time to plan it;
(b) I gave them ten minutes to plan the task without any guidance;
(c) I gave them direct language instruction (guidance) before they did the task.

Therefore the planning condition was operationalized as ***guided*** and ***unguided***. Task 1 is set out in Table 1, as an example of the details of the actual instructions that each group of students received to help them plan.

Research design

I divided the whole class into three groups of four. I had selected this particular class because the individuals in these groups were thought to be at about the same level of English language proficiency. I used three audio-cassette recorders placed in the middle of each group. The students are familiar with the use of cassette recorders since they are often used as part of teaching methodologies in class.

Table 1 Task 1 description and instructions for the three different groups

Problem Solving Task Logic Puzzle – *Crossing the River* *An old lady wants to cross the river with a wolf, a goat and a cabbage. She only has a small boat and can only take one thing at a time with her. Suggest how she can do it, so as the three things will be carried to the other side safely.*	
Non-Planners	Students start doing the task as soon as they read the instructions, without having any planning time.
Unguided Planners	You have ten minutes to prepare for this task. You can make notes during the ten minutes, but you won't be allowed to use them during the task. Be sure you can explain the decisions that you make to your partner.
Guided Planners	You have ten minutes to prepare for this task. You can make notes during the ten minutes, but you won't be allowed to use them during the task. These are things you can do to help you prepare: Think what problems the old lady could have. Think about the importance of the order in which the three things have to be carried (*Firstly ... then ... finally ...*). Think what grammar you need to do the task (ie hypothetical statements, '*if she takes ..., it will be ...*') Think what vocabulary you need to do the task. Think how to avoid difficulties and solve problems with grammar and vocabulary.

I presented the basic instructions for each task to the class at the same time. However some groups were told that they had to start doing the task immediately, whereas the other groups were told that they had ten minutes to plan what they want to say. The guided planners' group also received a sheet with the extra instructions. I was monitoring to ensure that all the groups did what they were supposed to do. In order to achieve some kind of consistency all groups had to do all tasks, carrying out their tasks under the three different conditions outlined above. Table 2, below, shows the procedure followed. By rotating the groups in this way the chances of getting false results as a consequence of differences in task difficulty, or difference in students' ability, or students getting used to working under one condition, are minimized. By the end of the lesson, I had nine sets of data for analysis.

Table 2 Task conditions for each group in tasks 1 to 3

	Group A	Group B	Group C
Task 1	No planning time	Planning time	Planning time + Instruction
Task 2	Planning time	Planning time + Instruction	No planning time
Task 3	Planning time + Instruction	No planning time	Planning time

Data analysis

I wanted to test all four hypotheses, so I used a variety of methods for data analysis. The dependent variables were of three types: accuracy, complexity and fluency. The measures I used were the same as the ones used by Foster and Skehan (1996), from which the following explanations are taken (*ibid*: 310).

Accuracy: was measured by the percentage of error free clauses; that is a clause in which there is no error in syntax, morphology or word order. This is exactly the same as the measure used by Johnston in Chapter 15. The following piece of data has six error free clauses:
(/ represents a pause of approximately one second)

> *... She can only take one thing with her //// when she cross the river ... /7/ If the old lady takes the cabbage ////, the goat will stay with the wolf ... //// and will eat it ////. Let's start from the beginning ////. If the old lady take the wolf with her /7/, then the goat will eat the cabbage //// ...*

Complexity: was measured as the total number of clauses divided by the total number of c-units (communication units). A c-unit is defined as an utterance which provides referential or pragmatic meaning. A clause is either a simple independent finite clause or a dependent finite or nonfinite clause. The following example shows the procedure. In this excerpt there are 12 clauses and 6 c-units (the c-units are numbered):

> *(1) '... Yes, but I don't agree // (2) because I have a cousin // who works as a pilot // (3) and he says that // the money aren't as good // because you have to work nights //, you have to work days // ... (4) It's a lousy job //, let's say //. (5) And you know / ... most of the money don't get to the pilot // (6) go to other ... to the company //.*

Fluency: was measured according to the number of:
Reformulations: Phrases that are repeated with some modification to syntax, morphology or word order eg

It is the most risk job ... Pilots' job is the most risky one.

Replacements: Lexical items that are immediately substituted for another eg

The two men ... the two people next to the tree ...

False starts: Utterances that are abandoned before completion and may or may not be followed by a reformulation eg

So, pilots are ... should be the most highly paid in our country.

Repetitions: Language items that are repeated with no modification eg

You can have your own ... your own ... your own ... hospital.

Pauses: A break of 1.0 second or longer within a turn or between turns. In the following data snippet there are 3 pauses, marked by a (p):

A pop-singer should do something like Beatles. Because Beatles, ... erm ... (p) I don't remember, but I think they ... (p) went to the roof of a big house and start singing ... sanging ... singing, in England and everyone saw them. Then they take a ... (p) big status ... high status.

***Silence** total*: The sum of pauses in each transcript.

Whereas Foster and Skehan only transcribed the first five minutes from each task, in my study there were some cases where a task was completed within three minutes, and other cases where the task took more than eight minutes to be completed. Therefore, in order to have a standard unit of measurement, the tabulations of the variables present values per minute.

Findings

Hypothesis 1 proposed that fluency would be greater under the planning condition.

Figures 1–6 summarize the results for fluency.

We can see that planning has indeed had a beneficial effect on fluency since there were fewer *false starts*, fewer *reformulations*, fewer *pauses* and a smaller *silence total*. Foster and Skehan (1996) report on one finding that gives an interesting comparison. In one of their tasks there were significant differences across planning conditions for *repetition* and *replacement* 'but in the opposite direction' (1996: 313). By this they mean that planning was associated with more *repetition* and *replacement*. Although they thought that this result was unexpected, interestingly, I found the same. However, it might not be coincidental that out of all the variables,

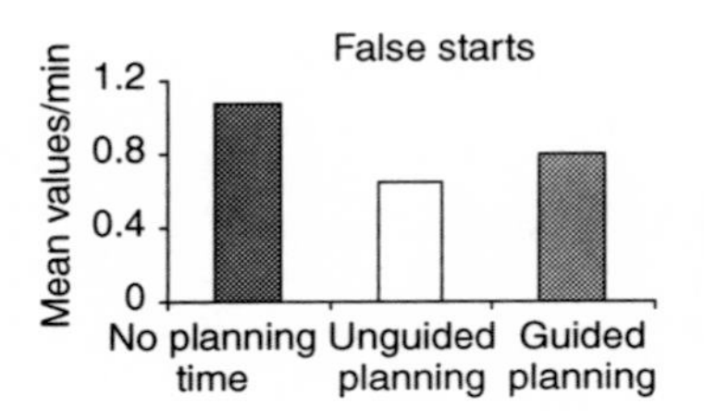

Figure 1 Mean numbers of false starts for different task planning conditions

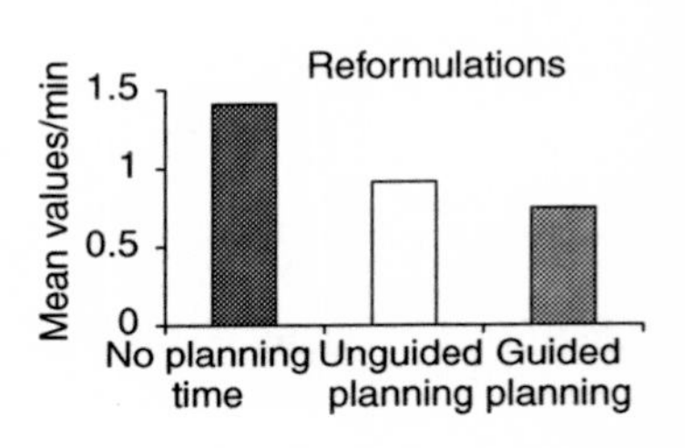

Figure 2 Mean number of reformulations for different task planning conditions

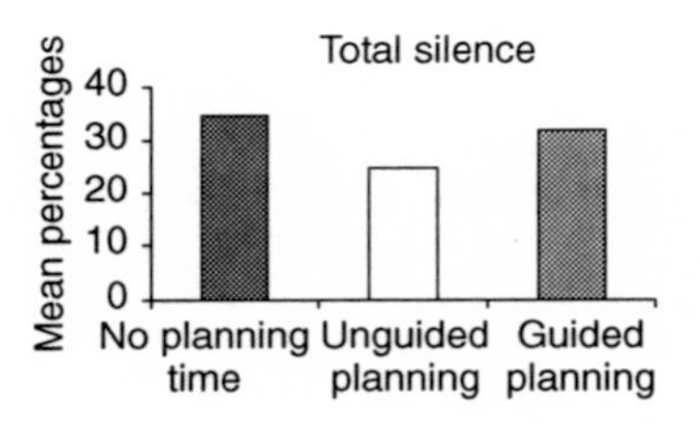

Figure 3 Mean period of silence for different task planning conditions

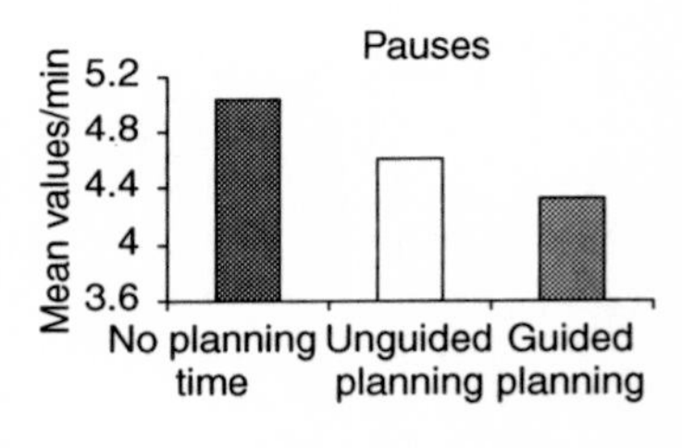

Figure 4 Mean numbers for pauses for different task planning conditions

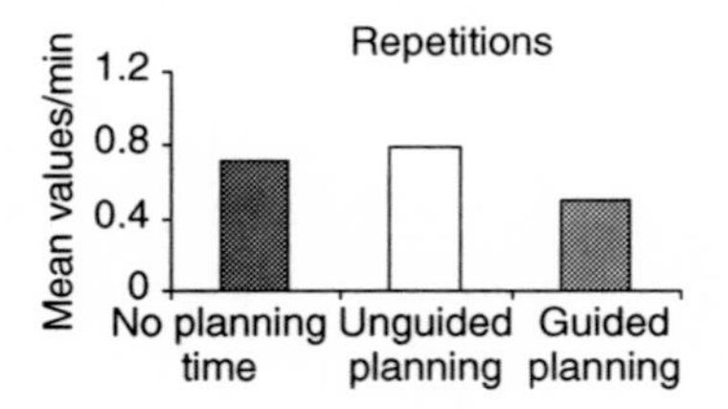

Figure 5 Mean numbers of repetitions for different task planning conditions

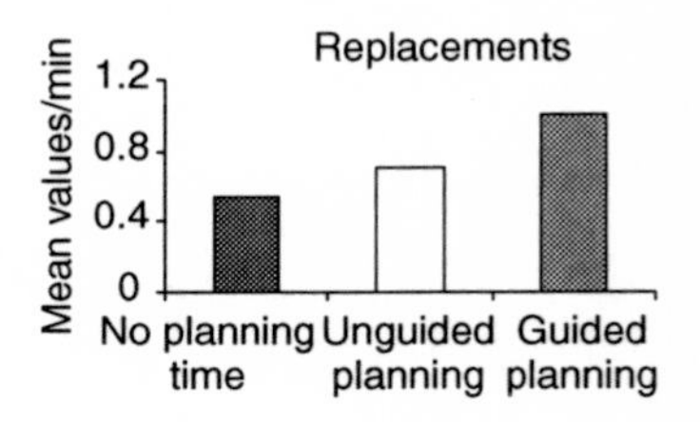

Figure 6 Mean numbers of replacements for different task planning conditions

replacements and *repetitions* were found in both studies to present a more complicated pattern. Foster and Skehan (1996: 313) suggest possible explanations as to why these two variables gave such results:

> Subjects seem to use planning time to capitalize on the use of time-creating devices (Bygate, 1987), as indexed by the effect for repetition and replacement. Such learners seem to use the planning they have done to think 'on line' and possibly to make their discourse more naturalistic.

In other words they interpret this finding to suggest learners may be aiming at naturalness of discourse. They suggest that *repetitions* and *replacements* are devices that native speakers also use in greater degree in order to cope with the problem of real time – repeating something gives them thinking time in which to compose their next utterance. Regarding *replacements,* I suggest there is another possible explanation for why planners made more use of these. Bearing in mind that *replacements* are 'lexical items that are immediately substituted for another', it might be that when students have some time to think about the task, they plan how to express their ideas. However, when they start talking they might get carried way with the conversation and say things spontaneously. Then, when they come to a point where they remember that they planned to express something in a different way, they replace what they have already said with the words they had planned to say, perhaps because they feel that it is a more appropriate way. For example one planner said *'The fireman's job is ... his occupation is very dangerous'.*

We can see that she immediately replaced *'the fireman's job'* with *'his occupation'* even though her original phrase was perfectly acceptable, maybe because that is how she had initially planned to say it.

Hypothesis 2 stated that planning would be associated with greater accuracy, that is a higher percentage of error free clauses. Relevant results are presented in Figure 7. The mean scores, for all three tasks combined, show that the non-planners have an average of 76 per cent of error free clauses, whereas the planners have 84 per cent. Although one might argue that the difference is not great, Table 3 still shows that Hypothesis 1 can be justified.

Hypothesis 3 stated that under planned conditions there would be greater complexity in language, ie there would be a greater average of clauses per c-unit. The relevant results of the data analysis are presented in Figure 8. Although there was no significant difference between the no planning and the planning condition, there is still a difference which, although small, agrees with the pattern that was observed for fluency and accuracy, that is, there is a beneficial effect for the planning condition.

The results regarding accuracy and complexity show that under planned conditions task performance was both more accurate and more complex. The implication of these findings is that when students have planning time they pay more attention to the form of the language they produce. This is what was also found in Foster and Skehan's (1996) experiment. It would be ideal if a balance between form and meaning could be achieved, especially since the concepts of fluency and accuracy are often considered to be inseparable.

It is also clear that a balance between fluency, accuracy and complexity is the desired outcome. The results of the present study show that the overall result was that planning time produced more accurate, more fluent and more complex language, demonstrating that such balance can be achieved.

Hypothesis 4 stated that the effects predicted in Hypotheses 1–3 will be greater when planning is guided, that is when there is also some

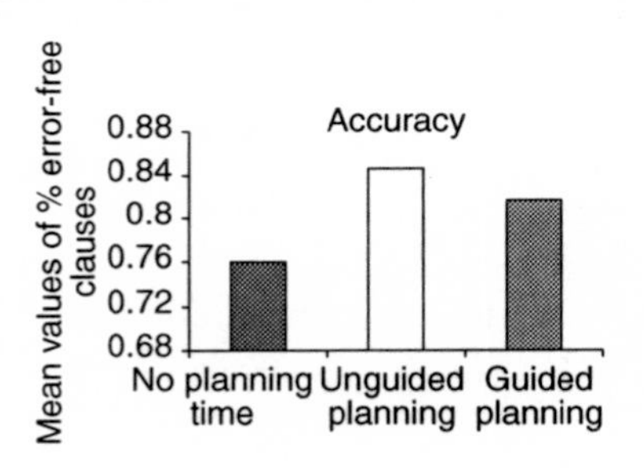

Figure 7 Mean accuracy levels for different task planning conditions

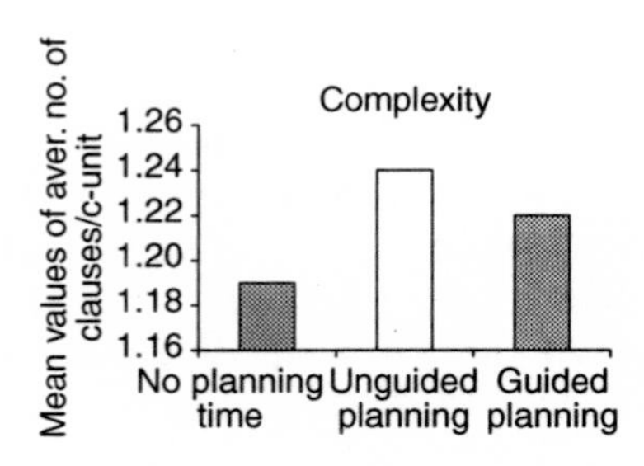

Figure 8 Mean language complexity levels for different task planning conditions

language instruction. This hypothesis cannot be supported by the data. The results were mixed and the differences between the performance of the planners and the planners who also had some language instruction were statistically insignificant (see Figures 3 and 4).

To determine the significance of the difference observed for 'false starts', 'reformulations', 'pauses' and 'total silence' across the three levels of planning time (ie no planning, unguided planning, guided planning), I performed a T-Test. This showed no statistically significant difference across the three levels of planning for any of the variables. This is perhaps at least partly due to the small scale of this research which only had nine test subjects.

One might therefore suspect that unguided planning may be more beneficial than guided planning. A possible reason for making such an assumption is that by giving students some guidance as to how to use their planning time, their planning time is actually channelled into trying to get involved with more complex ideas, which in turn demand more complex language that might be beyond their language level. In their attempt to express more interesting ideas, they cannot keep up with the demands for accuracy and complexity. Surely the precise role of guided and unguided planning is another area which needs to be investigated further.

Another issue which was not examined in my research because of its small scale, is the effect of task type. One might argue that the results presented above are such because of the type of tasks. This claim might be justifiable since, although the three tasks I used were considered to be of the same level, Task 2 (the ordering and sorting task about jobs) produced results most of which differed from those produced by Tasks 1 and 3. Therefore the task type is also a factor which can affect task performance, thus there is a need for this to be examined in a larger-scale research, which is in fact what Birch and Poupore have attempted in Chapters 18 and 19 of this volume.

Conclusion and implications

This study focuses on the relationship between task performance and the time available to plan tasks, and also examines the question of guidance. The general perspective which makes this kind of study interesting is that our attention is limited in capacity and therefore we sometimes achieve one goal at the expense of another. The task-based framework is an attempt to organize task-based instruction in a way which minimizes the chances of a disproportionate focus on meaning, and maximizes the chances that students will also produce accurate and complex language. This study has focused on one phase (*task cycle*) and one area within that phase (*pre-task planning*).

The results of this study emphasize the importance of the *planning* stage of the task-based framework, since planning time did seem to have a beneficial effect on the quality of the language produced during the tasks. It seems that the *planning* stage of the *task cycle* can work as a device to help students balance the demands of fluency, accuracy and complexity placed upon them.

Reviewing the results of this study, some practical recommendations for teaching can be made.

- Pre-task planning time is beneficial, because this ensures that attention will be drawn to language form.
- Giving learners opportunities for spontaneous language production is also desirable. Otherwise, if they get used to having time to think before speaking, they will find it difficult to cope with real life communication.
- Teachers should select and organize appropriate supplementary tasks and pre- and post-task activities, each time placing different demands on the learner.
- The fact that guided planning did not prove to be more beneficial than unguided planning suggests that although teachers might retain control of the lesson overall, they should also leave room for learner autonomy.
- A task-based teacher needs to be sensitive to individual differences. Each student is unique and works in a different way. For example, one student prefers to have guided planning, whereas another may prefer unguided planning. Teachers should offer a variety of activities in ways which will suit a range of learner preferences and styles.

It can be argued that the results of this study raise as many questions as they provide answers. Central to these questions is the issue of task conditions on which research can be most usefully conducted in the area of task-based instruction. The following questions are all possible areas for further research:

- Does the amount of planning time make a difference? (ie if the allotted planning time was something other than 10 minutes, would the effects be different?) Ellis (2003) reports on various studies, including that by Mehnert (1998), which would be good starting points for research on this area.

- Can there be an identifiable optimum combination between task conditions and task types that can lead to the 'best' performance? (Although the three tasks were considered to be of the same level, Task 2 mostly produced different results than Tasks 1 and 3. Can this be an effect of the type of task rather than an effect of planning time?)
- Is there a case to be made for varying task type/task conditions to promote eg more focus on fluency or more focus on accuracy/complexity? Or the 'right' balance between these? This is in fact what Birch investigates in Chapter 18.
- Can the teacher's input during planning time have any possible effects? (The results of the present study are very challenging, since they suggest that guided planning could perhaps have negative effects.)

As one can conclude from the above issues, there is still a lot of room for research. However, if I had to draw a conclusion linking my study with task-based theories I would say that the overall picture of the results is encouraging and allows me to suggest that task-based approaches provide second language learners with the right opportunities and confidence to face real life communication.

Appendix 1

Task 2

<table>
<tr><td colspan="2">

Ordering and sorting task

'Jobs'

Think of the following jobs and say which one is the most highly paid in your country:
– Pilot
– Actor
– Pop-singer
– Nurse
– Fireman
– Doctor
– Teacher
Discuss with your group and put these jobs in order, starting from the one that, in your opinion, should be the most highly paid and explain why.

</td></tr>
<tr><td>Non-Planners</td><td>Students start doing the task as soon as they read the instructions, without having any planning time.</td></tr>
<tr><td>Unguided planners</td><td>You have ten minutes to prepare for this task.
You can make notes during the ten minutes, but you won't be allowed to use them during the task.
Be sure you can explain the decisions that you make to your partner.</td></tr>
<tr><td>Guided planners</td><td>You have ten minutes to prepare for this task.
You can make notes during the ten minutes, but you won't be allowed to use them during the task.
These are things you can do to help you prepare:

Think of the following statement: 'It is a fact of our society that we underpay many of our most important workers' (Arnold and Harmer, 1978).
Think about the different difficulties and risks of each job.
Think about why your partners might not agree with your opinion.
Think what grammar you need to do the task.
Think what vocabulary you need to do the task.
Think how to avoid difficulties and solve problems with grammar and vocabulary.</td></tr>
</table>

Task 3

COMPARING TASK

'Spot the differences'

Work together in your group and find seven differences between picture A and picture B (Pointing is not allowed).

(*Collins Cobuild English Course Level 1*)

Non-planners	Students start doing the task as soon as they read the instructions, without having any planning time.
Unguided planners	You have ten minute to prepare for this task. You can make notes during the ten minutes, but you won't be allowed to use them during the task. Be sure you can explain the decisions that you make to your partner.
Guided planners	You have ten minute to prepare for this task. You can make notes during the ten minutes, but you won't be allowed to use them during the task. These are things you can do to help you prepare: Observe picture A carefully and try to remember numbers, sizes and positions of things. Try to predict where picture B might be different. Think what grammar you need to do the task. Think what vocabulary you need to do the task. Think how to avoid difficulties and solve problems with grammar and vocabulary.

18
Balancing Fluency, Accuracy and Complexity Through Task Characteristics

Gregory Birch

Summary *I was encouraged by the work of Skehan (1998) to examine how task characteristics can be used to predict where students may focus their attention during a task. I felt that by developing a better understanding of task characteristics, I would be more able to make informed decisions about how best to achieve a balanced development of fluency, accuracy, and complexity.*

Background and rationale

In this study, I set out to investigate how different task characteristics affected my students' oral production. A potential danger of task-based learning is that without a conscious focus on form, learners may employ communication strategies or use lexicalized language, developing their fluency, but to the detriment of accuracy. Furthermore, over time, the students may plateau at a level that is sufficient to get their meaning across but beyond which they seem unable to go, and their language does not develop further. This phenomenon is often referred to as fossilization, and Johnston (Chapter 15) had the same concern. A conscious focus on form seems to be the answer, but another problem with tasks is that students may not do this if, for example, the task is too difficult. Generally, when students speak, they are only able to concentrate fully on one of the goals of accuracy, fluency or complexity (Skehan, 1998, summarized in Chapter 1). For example, students tend to speak more slowly when they are trying to speak accurately. I was interested to see if I could select tasks with particular characteristics, to direct my students' focus onto particular goals. I hoped to find out how to make informed decisions on how to foster a balanced development of these three goals in my task-based speaking classes.

Skehan (1996, 1998) suggests that we choose tasks which focus the students' attention on *accuracy, fluency* or *complexity*. I believe that for students' language to be accurate, it also has to be linguistically appropriate (Widdowson 1989). An utterance can be grammatically correct, but if native speakers never use it, then it could be referred to as linguistically inappropriate. Accuracy was therefore a focus that I was particularly interested in for this study. Regarding complexity, although students must at times focus on language that is more complex than their current level, I did not expect complexity to play a major role in this study as I used tasks that are simple and highly-structured, and therefore do not require the students to produce overly complex language (Foster and Skehan 1996). Lastly, to establish the degree of learners' *fluency*, I used a simple measure of task-completion time in order to determine how much the students had accomplished (see Essig, Chapter 16 and Djapoura, Chapter 17 for more complex measures of fluency).

Context

At the time of this study, I was teaching 'English Communication' to 16-year-old Japanese high school students at Nagano National College of Technology. I would describe them as false beginners because although they had studied English for four years they had had limited experience in using it to communicate, like the students described by Djapoura in Chapter 17. Most of their English education to date had focused on grammar so I was using the textbook, *Alltalk 2* (Peaty, 1987), in order to provide the students with opportunities to speak. Altogether, I had five classes of 40 students who came once a week for 45 minutes. I carried out this research project with three of these classes.

Method

Procedures

I chose two tasks from the textbook for comparison since they are very similar in that they require students to describe something. One task requires the student to describe a person's appearance while the other task requires the student to describe the locations of cities. This similarity makes it easy to compare the two tasks in terms of task characteristics and the effect these characteristics might have on student production.

For the first task, the 'robbery task' (Peaty, 1987: 59–60, see Appendix 1), I got the students to work in pairs. I gave both students a picture of a robbery except that in one picture the robber was missing. I explained that the goal was to find out enough information about the robber so that the partner with only the picture of the crime scene could draw the robber. The students then switched roles and did the task again with a slightly different picture.

I refer to the second task as the 'island task' (Peaty, 1987: 83–4). In this task (Appendix 2), I gave each of the students a map of two islands but the maps differed. On one map, the student had information about the locations of cities and ferry routes on one of the islands but not the other. The purpose of the task is for each student to solicit the locations of the cities and ferry routes from his or her partner.

In the preceding, pre-task phase, I had given the students activities to familiarize them with the task itself and introduce some useful vocabulary. Before the island task, students were given a map of an island, which did not include the locations of the cities. They read a passage and wrote in the locations of the cities. For the robbery task, groups of four students were given a different picture of a person and asked to write a description. All the pictures were then taped to the blackboard and the students read their description in front of the class while the class guessed which picture was being described.

During the recording of the tasks, students worked in pairs and sat with a microphone between them. It was necessary to photocopy the tasks onto handouts so that the students were not able to turn the page of their textbook and see what was being described (permission to reproduce the tasks was received). The students who were answering the questions were asked to hold their handout in such a way that their partner could not see it. In total, I recorded three classes of approximately forty students for each task and each class was given either zero, five or ten minutes for preparation respectively. I varied the amount of preparation time as I wanted to see if this would have an effect on the students' production. Incidentally, roughly two-thirds of the students said they felt preparation time was important, and most continued to prepare even while they were being recorded.

Using task characteristics to predict student speech

Skehan suggests that we should choose tasks which '(1) are of the appropriate level of difficulty; (2) are focused in their aims between fluency, accuracy and complexity; and (3) have some basis in task-based research (1998: 131).'

Task difficulty

The level of **difficulty** must be set so that learners can cope with the requirements of the task and still focus on form, whether this is accuracy or complexity (Skehan, 1998: 134). There are two ways that teachers can do this. First, teachers can draw upon their experience and knowledge of their students' ability. Second, they can refer to current research to determine the level of difficulty of a task. This research has been summarized in Skehan (1998: 135) and is reproduced below in Table 1 (see also Chapter 1). Please note that the second condition mentioned (in italics) produces greater task difficulty.

Concerning task difficulty in this study, I would not classify either of the tasks as particularly difficult as the information is presented visually. Skehan and Foster (1997) argue that tasks with concrete information, such as the map in the island task, are less difficult than ones that contain abstract information, such as describing a childhood memory. With respect to task familiarity, the students should have less difficulty with the robbery task as they have done similar tasks before where they have had to describe the appearances of people.

Task characteristics

Skehan offers two suggestions for balancing the goals of accuracy, complexity and fluency. First, we should choose tasks 'which focus on particular goals.' For example, if we want the students to focus on accuracy, we could choose a planned task that is highly structured, such as a task where students give directions. Second, 'implement sequences of tasks so that balanced goal development occurs'. (*ibid.* 1998: 135) If we use only highly structured tasks, then it is less likely that the students will attempt to produce complex language. Therefore, we should also

Table 1 Research into task difficulty (from Skehan, 1998: 135)

Contrast	Source
Small number of participants/elements vs. *large number*	Brown *et al.* (1984)
Concrete information and task vs. *abstract*	Brown *et al.* (1984) Skehan and Foster (1997)
Immediate, here-and-now information vs. *remote, there-and-then information*	Robinson (1985) Foster and Skehan (1996)
Information requiring retrieval vs. *information requiring transformation*	Skehan and Foster (1997)
Familiar information vs. *unfamiliar information*	Foster and Skehan (1996)

include tasks which promote complexity. An example would be one that requires the students to make more complex decisions, such as deciding what to take to a desert island. The table of task characteristics found in Skehan (1998: 136) is reproduced in Table 2.

Relating the above findings to the two tasks used in this study, I predicted that the island task would lead to a more accurate and/or fluent performance, as it is more structured than the robbery task (Skehan and Foster, 1997). In the island task, the students had to ask repeatedly for the locations of cities and ferry routes and the task had a clearly defined completion point, when all the places had been located. In the robbery task, the students had to ask approximately seven different questions, and had much more flexibility in deciding when they had sufficient information for the task to end. On the other hand, the robbery task should focus the students' attention, to a greater degree than the island task, on either accuracy or fluency as the students are more familiar with the robbery task and describing the appearances of people. According to Foster and Skehan (1996), familiar tasks tend to result in more accurate and/or fluent production. It should also be noted that neither task contains any characteristic that would require the students to produce overly complex language. It is also difficult to predict which characteristic will have a larger impact on students' production. To summarize:

- the island task should allow the students to produce more accurate and/or fluent language as it is inherently more structured than the robbery task (Skehan and Foster, 1997);

Table 2 Tasks characteristics table (from Skehan, 1998: 136)

Task characteristics	Source
Accuracy Effects	
More structured tasks (especially when planned)	Skehan and Foster (1997)
Clear time line	Foster and Skehan (1996)
Familiar tasks	
Complexity Effects	
Requiring more complex decisions	Skehan and Foster (1997)
Tasks requiring transformation of elements	Skehan and Foster (1997)
Tasks requiring interpretation	Brown (1991)
Divergent tasks	Duff (1986)
Interlanguage Change Effects	
Language focusing tasks, eg dictogloss	Swain (1995)
Fluency effects	
Structured tasks (unplanned)	Skehan and Foster (1997)
Familiar tasks	Foster and Skehan (1996)

- the robbery task should achieve the same goals, as the students are more familiar with describing people than describing location (Foster and Skehan, 1996).

Findings

Evaluating task performance for fluency and accuracy

After making all the recordings, I transcribed them and closely studied the data, reading and re-reading it many times, with different focuses in mind.

Island task – fluency

Concerning fluency on the island task, I looked at how quickly the students were able to transact the task. Two factors emerge that are common among the pairs that were able to finish early. First is the fact that their production tended to be elliptical in nature; in other words, the students used extremely broken English, which is not surprising since fluency was achieved at the expense of accuracy or complexity. This was particularly true of the students who finished the earliest as these students appeared to have been more concerned with conveying meaning and less with the form it took. The following example of elliptical language is taken from a pair who finished the recording about one minute early and it is representative of other pairs who prioritized a focus on meaning at the expense of a focus on form.

A: Where is the Acton?
B: Acton is west ... from mountain. Coast.
A: Where is Southport?
B: Southeast from mountain.
A: Where is the Cliptown town?
B: North from mountain. Coast.
A: Where is the Middleford?
B: Southwest from mountain. Lake east.

The second observation is that some students were able to be fluent and, to a degree, accurate at the same time, particularly if their production employed the use of set-patterns of language or sentence frames. An example would be '*X is # kilometers (north, south, east, west) of Y.*' It became evident that the students did not start each utterance from scratch; instead they simply filled in the relevant information. The students' written preparation in the next table contains examples of these sentence frames, but it should be noted that the students did not have access to these notes while they were doing the task. Examples from the

Table 3 Examples of sentence frames used during the recordings

Written preparation	Examples from recording
—is—kilometers—of—.	The Acton town is northwest, on the northwest bay. The Southport is on the south cape. Southeast cape. There has a lake. Middleford is on the east coast. Middleford is on the east coast of the lake.
5 kilometers east from Mt.	5 kilometers east of mountains is Freetown. 50 kilometers southeast of mountain is Southport.
Go to north from Southport about 10 kilo., there is Freetown.	Freetown is north of Southport. Go 10 kilometers from Southport. Is Freetown.

recording are on the right (Table 3). It is this repeated use of sentence frames that led me to believe that the students were relying more on an exemplar-based language system (See Skehan, 1998; Widdowson, 1989).

Island task – accuracy

Mehnert (1998) reports that on her highly structured tasks, accuracy improved with as little as one minute of preparation, but there was no measurable difference in accuracy for students who had more time to prepare. This seems to hold true for my students as well. First, the highly structured nature of this task had a strong influence on accuracy since the pairs that tended to be more accurate were also the ones whose sentence frames were grammatically correct to begin with. Secondly, I also noticed that the more accurate the production tended to be, the less likely the pairs were to finish early or complete the task. Table 3 contains some examples of accurate utterances. A transcript of a full recording appears in Appendix 3.

Robbery task – fluency

I also looked at the time it took to complete the robbery task. One noticeable difference between this task and the island task is that there seemed to be less elliptical language, as a larger number of the students were able to use more complete sentences. I believe that this is due to the fact that the students are more familiar with describing appearances and clothing, and therefore, this task is less difficult. Another factor is that most students paused before asking questions. In the robbery task, the students had to ask seven questions in order to complete this task. This allowed the student answering more time to prepare. The following is an example of reasonably accurate language use.

Table 4 Example taken from a robbery recording (See Appendix 3 for whole recording.)

A: Where is he?
B: He is He is in a station.
A: When was he come there?
B: It was 11:25.
A: 11:25. What is he wearing?
B: He's wearing yellow t-shirts and jeans.
A: What What his weapon?
B: His weapon is a bat.
A: What is What was What's he doing?
B: He hit a man and steal stool a briefcase.
A: He stole a briefcase.
B: Oh yes.
A: What is his appearance?
B: He has a scar on his face.

Robbery task – accuracy

Although the students are more familiar with describing appearances than describing location, and were able to use more complete sentences, probably as a result of this familiarity, they still had some trouble with accuracy when forming questions. For example, accuracy suffered when the students had to deal with unfamiliar items such as 'stolen' or 'appearance,' which were both included on the task handout. Most students wrote questions such as 'what things stolen?' instead of 'what was stolen?' One possibility is that they simply absorbed the phrase 'things stolen' as an unanalyzed lexical chunk. Another is that they were unable to use it correctly even though they recognized stolen as the past participle of steal. Concerning the questions regarding appearance, the students with preparation time did not seem to ask the questions more accurately than the students without preparation time. Many students asked 'what is the robber's appearance?' instead of asking 'what did he look like?' It is not that the former question is ungrammatical, it has more to do with the fact that it is 'linguistically ill-formed,' a term Widdowson (1989) uses to describe utterances, such as the above-mentioned question, as 'illegitimate, rule-violations, not possible, and the native speaker knows this full well' (1989: 133).

Although the students are familiar with describing appearance, accuracy suffered when they were confronted with unfamiliar terms such as 'stolen' and the students' inability to form lexically appropriate questions. On the other hand, although the island task also had similar unfamiliar terms, the students had fewer problems as their answers tended to follow predictable patterns due to the repetitive nature of the island task. This inherent structure allowed the students to be more accurate than they would otherwise have been.

Reflection and conclusion

Although Skehan ends his section on assessing task difficulty with the advice, 'this information needs to be supplemented with teacher experience since it will be used as part of a more complex picture to make pedagogic decisions', I certainly found his two tables of factors affecting task difficulty and task characteristics (Tables 1 and 2 above) helpful in predicting how the tasks used in this study might affect student output. I correctly predicted that the robbery task would lead to a reasonably fluent and accurate performance because I felt that the students were more familiar with describing appearance. I also predicted that the island task, although far less familiar to students, would lead to reasonably accurate and fluent production because this task was more highly structured than the robbery task. I believe that for these two tasks at least, task structure had a stronger influence on student output than task familiarity.

False beginners' spoken English relates to rule-based and exemplar-based language systems in an important way. A rule-based system is one in which utterances are produced based on a knowledge of grammar. The advantage of such a system is that 'it enables maximum creativity and flexibility in what is said' (Skehan, 1998: 30). The disadvantage, however, is that it is time consuming. It takes longer to form sentences using grammatical rules than to form sentences using lexical chunks of language. An exemplar-based system, on the other hand, relies on knowledge of lexical chunks of language and these lexical chunks are strung together to form sentences. The advantage of this system is that it allows us to speak quickly, but the disadvantage is that we are more limited in what we can say. Mehnert (1998) argues that lower-level students, such as my students, do not have access to a large pool of lexical phrases and therefore, they are less likely to be able to draw upon an exemplar-based system. However, the students in this study were able to produce language that was more fluent and accurate in the island task as they were apparently able to draw upon set-patterns of language or sentence frames, which I took as evidence of the students' reliance on an exemplar-based language system.

With respect to the robbery task, I believe the students' familiarity with this task also allowed them to be fluent and, to a degree, accurate, but less so than the students' production during the island task. It seems their production during the robbery task was more grammar-based, as their questions seemed to have been formed by a strict application of grammar and to the exclusion of more lexically appropriate questions. These findings do seem to support the notion that a rule-based system diminishes the attentional resources of the students. Therefore, teachers have to be aware that in situations where the learner is less likely to be able to draw upon lexical phrases, the task should be easy enough so that some attention can be devoted to form. It should also be noted that some students were able, at times, to focus on both accuracy and fluency. It seems that the level of difficulty of the task for those students was sufficiently low that they could devote some attention to form and remain relatively fluent at the same time.

I believe task characteristics can be used to predict where the students might focus their attention, be it on accuracy, fluency or complexity. Although the characteristics found in Skehan (1998: 136) are no guarantee of how the students will perform the task, they are a valuable tool with which to evaluate tasks so that we can strive towards a balanced development of the three goals. In this study, I have used Skehan's work to evaluate tasks from a textbook with which I was familiar. It could also be used to evaluate a collection of independent tasks. Regardless of how tasks fit into the curriculum, I would recommend that fellow teachers use Skehan's work as follows to evaluate the effect of tasks in their classroom:

- Use the research findings summarized in Table 1 to determine the relative difficulty of a task.
- Use the task characteristics listed in Table 2 to determine if a task is suited to a focus on fluency, accuracy or complexity.
- Keep track of the task types you use, so that you can make informed decisions regarding the balance between fluency, accuracy, and complexity in your speaking classes.
- Keep experimenting!

Appendix 1 – Robbery task

I have included the first half of both student A's and B's handouts. On Student B's original handout, in addition to the robbery scene found on student A's handout (without the robber of course), student B had a drawing of a different robbery. The task itself was adapted with permission from *Alltalk 2* (Peaty 1987).

Student A – the robbery task

You just saw the following robbery. Your partner will ask you about the robber and the robbery. Answer his or her questions.

You will be asked questions about the following information.

About the robbery	About the robber
Time, things stolen	Male or female, age, clothes, appearance, weapon

Student B – the robbery task

Your partner has just seen a robbery. Ask him or her questions about the robber and the robbery. Later, draw the robber in the space below.
Please ask questions to get the following information.

About the robbery	About the robber
Time, things stolen	Male or female, age, clothes, appearance weapon

Appendix 2 – Island task

I have included a portion of the first half of both student A's and students B's handouts here. During the recording, the tasks were on separate sheets of paper. The task itself was adapted with permission from *Alltalk 2* (Peaty, 1987)

STUDENT A - The Island Task
You want to visit an island that your partner knows well. Ask your partner about the following information and draw the places on the map.

The locations of the towns, and ferry routes on the North Island	Acton, Southport, Clipton, Middleford, Freetown, and the ferry routes
The names of the	small island, lake, and the mountain
The height of	the mountain

o Town
△ Mountain
Bus Route
Ferry Route

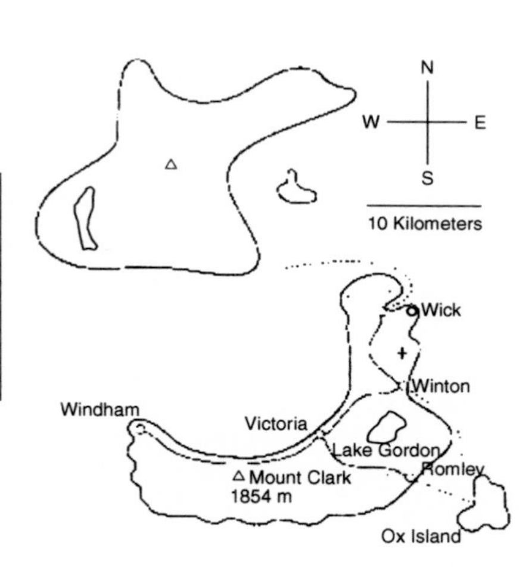

STUDENT B - The Island Task.
You want to visit an island your partner knows well. Ask your partner about the following information and draw the places on the map.

The locations of the towns, and ferry routes on the South Island	Windham, Victoria, Romley, Winton, Wick and the ferry routes.
The names of the	small island, lake, and the mountain
The height of	the mountain

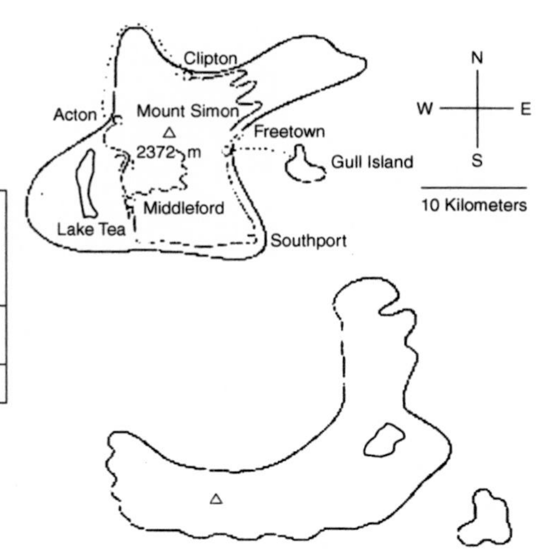

Appendix 3: excerpts from recordings of students

1. Island task

This is an example of a very accurate recording of a pair that had ten minutes to prepare. This pair did not quite finish the task in the allotted time.

Student A: Where is Acton City?
Student B: Acton city is 5 kilometers north from lake Teal.
A: Where is Southport?
B: Southport is southwest from Gull Island.
A: Where is Clipton City?
B: Clipton city is about 10 kilometers northeast from Acton.
A: Where is Middleford City?
B: Middleford City is ... Middleford is south west ... 5 kilometers southwest from Mount Simon. Middleford is Lake Teal bay side.
A: Where is Freetown City?
B: Freetown is 5 kilometers west from Gull Island.
A: And the ferry routes. Please tell me ferry routes.
B: Ferry routes is from Acton to Clipton and from Gull Island to Freetown.
A: What's the name of the small island.
B: Small island is ... Small island's name is Gull Island.
A: What's the name of the lake?
B: Lake's name is Tail lake.
A: What's the name of the mountain?
B: Mountain's name is Mount Simon.

2. Robbery task (fluency)

This is the full transcript of the data contained in Table 4.

Student A: Where is he?
Student B: He is He is in a station.
A: When was he come there?
B: It was 11:25.
A: 11:25. What is he wearing?
B: He is wearing yellow t-shirts and jeans.
A: What What his weapon?
B: His weapon is a bat.
A: What What What is What was What's he doing?
B: He hit a man and steal stool a briefcase.
A: He stole a briefcase.
B: Oh yes.
A: What is What's his hair?
B: His hair. His hair color is brown. He has not many hair.
A: Okay Okay. Enough hair
B: Enough hair.
A: He ... what he is young?
B: I think his age is between 20 and 30.

A: Okay. What is his appearance.
B: He has a scar on his face.
A: Right or left?
B: Right side. Right side face.
A: Was he running or walking?
B: He is walking.
A: Briefcase
B: Briefcase?
A: Briefcase He. Which is he have briefcase. right right hand or left hand?
B: He has a bat on right.
A: Bat on right.
B: Briefcase on left hand.
A: That's all.

3. Robbery task (accuracy)

This pair were not given time to prepare; however, Student A often paused during the recording in order to prepare the next question.

This recording exemplifies how students had difficulty forming questions but not in answering them. This happened a lot in the data.

A: What he look like?
B: (10-second pause.) He is a young man and he is a little fat.
A: What does he wearing?
B: He's wearing a yellow t-shirt and blue jeans and black shoes. She has *janakute* (that's not right) ... He has a black bag.
A: What time is it then?
B: It is ... It happened 11:25. (Long pause.)
A: Does he carrying ... carrying ... a weapon.
B: He have He have a bat.
A: A bat?
B: A bat. (one-minute pause with short Japanese exchange.)
A: Where is he? Where is he?
B: He is station. (Long pause with an exchange off mike in Japanese.)
B: Run away.

19

Quality Interaction and Types of Negotiation in Problem-solving and Jigsaw Tasks

Glen Poupore

Summary *In this study I identify some aspects of quality interaction and compare successful negotiations in learner interaction in two types of task: problem-solving/prediction and jigsaw tasks. Negotiation of meaning is thought to contribute to language development, but this study goes beyond this and examines negotiations of form, task content, task procedure, personal experience and self-initiated repair, and I argue that these too should result in greater language proficiency.*

Context and rationale

I work in a Korean university, teaching intermediate to advanced level English majors with an age range of 19 to 26. When I first began using a task-based approach with them, I was encouraged and excited by their end of lesson comments: '*Time's up already! It went by so quickly!*' As I observed my students pursuing their task goals, they looked totally engaged. It really seemed as though they had lost track of time. This led me to continue using tasks in the classroom. As time passed, I became more interested in discovering what actually occurred between the learners in the different types of tasks that I gave them. More specifically, I wanted to know if the student-to-student interaction was likely to produce L2 learning benefits.

Interaction variables

The first step was to do some reading so I could identify interaction variables that benefit L2 learning. Relying mostly on the interaction hypothesis (Long, 1983a, 1996) and on the output hypothesis (Swain,

1995), previous research identified 'negotiation of meaning' as a quality interaction variable (see Shehadeh, Chapter 1). This negotiation occurs when language learners have to clarify misunderstandings in their interactions, and work out their partner's meaning:

A: Around the house we have glass.
B: You have what?
A: uh grass, plants and grass. (From Pica *et al.*, 1996, p. 62)

Here, A's clarification contains language that is more accurate and also expands on the original utterance – an example of 'quality interaction'.

Much of the research into task interaction to date has focused on meaning negotiations since they are seen as providing vocalized evidence of L2 acquisition. However, like Van Lier (2000), I believe this narrow focus has failed to study interaction in its totality and has ignored other variables of interaction that potentially have L2 learning value.

Method

To explore interaction variables for myself, I recorded my own students engaged in various tasks. At the beginning of the semester, I told them I would occasionally bring a cassette recorder to class and choose students to record while they completed a task. At the end of the semester, I recorded six different tasks involving 21 different learners, a total of around three hours of learner interaction.

Findings

I transcribed and analysed the recordings, and, using insights derived from the work of various writers, (eg Van den Branden (1997), Shehadeh (1999), Pica *et al.* (1996)), I identified six types of **interaction variables**:

- **negotiation of meaning** (N-Meaning): interaction aimed at signaling and solving problems of message comprehensibility, as in the glass/grass example above.

  YJ: Uh, my story is, uhm, kind of ball.
  SY: Ball?
  YJ: Yeah, beer bar, she drink something.

- **negotiation of form** (N-Form): interaction aimed at drawing attention to formal aspects of language and encouraging repair.

BS: But she loves her.
HJ: He or?
BS: He, he, he loves her.

- **negotiation of task content** (N-Content): interaction aimed at pushing the speaker to provide more information related to task content.

Soon: But, uhm, Pheobe does, they, actively. Actively.
Sun: So, at that time where is Monica?
Soon: Monica? Aw, Monica is hi, hiding.

- **negotiation of task procedure** (N-Procedure): same as N-Content except in relation to task procedure.

DH: How about, uh, write the another question?
JY: Uh, this is another question, these are different.

- **negotiation of personal experience** (N-Experience): same as N-Content except in relation to personal experiences.

DH: Yeah, sometimes, when –
JY: Sometimes all naked?
DH: But, but I live in my parents, I live with my parents.

- **self-initiated repair**: a self-correction of output following the realization that one's utterance was not understood or was misunderstood, or that the utterance was incorrect in some way.

DH: But, *but I live in my parents, I live with my parents.*

Quality Interaction

All of the above transcript data for the interaction variables are taken from the tasks for this study and each one includes an example of **quality interaction.** But what is meant exactly by 'quality' interaction? For N-Meaning and N-Form, quality interaction was identified as producing a more comprehensible and more accurate utterance in response to an indicator that signalled incomplete comprehension (as in the examples above). The following N-Meaning, however, would not be measured as a quality interaction since the response is simply a repetition of the initial utterance:

JY: How to common question?
DH: I'm sorry?
JY: Common question.

For N-Content, N-Procedure, and N-Experience, meanwhile, quality interaction was identified as being a response that provided additional information (as in the examples above). The following N-Content is not an example of quality interaction because the response is only acknowledging and repeating the negotiation question in the second utterance:

JY: Or, we know the fact because of friend's reaction.
SY: TV show doesn't show?
JY: Sure of course, TV doesn't.

Van den Branden (1997), referring to the output hypothesis, claims that N-Content can help to 'push' the output of learners because provision of additional information can lead learners to generate output that is more complete and accurate, and which could include a wider range of vocabulary and grammar forms. If Van den Branden is correct concerning pushed output, I would further argue that N-Procedure and N-Experience offer the same benefits. Sociocultural theorists (eg Coughlan and Duff 1994) have claimed that learners first need to interpret tasks for themselves, and to set their own goals. By doing so, learners will negotiate task procedure and potentially produce additional output. This is also the case for N-Experience when learners engage in free conversational language about their own lives and opinions. In the tasks recorded for this study, learners engaged in both N-Procedure and N-Experience on frequent occasions and as a result I included them among the interaction variables.

A self-initiated repair is in itself a quality interaction and I simply calculated their total number. Just by being in a position to produce output, learners may realize that a portion of their production may interfere with successful communication and they will modify and improve it (as in the example of self-initiated repair above).

Comparing the interaction variables

By comparing the results for each interaction variable across all six tasks, I could identify not only their frequency but also the percentage of quality interaction (see Appendix 1, Table 1). Here is a summary of the findings:

- N-Meaning and N-Form had low success rates in producing quality interaction.
- Learners rarely negotiated for form (N-Form).

- Learners frequently negotiated for content in the performance of a task, making content negotiations more numerous than any of the other types.
- N-Content, and to a certain extent, N-Procedure and N-Experience, produced better quality negotiation than did N-Meaning and N-Form.
- Learners frequently produced self-initiated repairs.

N-Content, N-Procedure, and N-Experience can be seen as more valuable in that a response with additional information creates longer and sometimes more complex responses than the quality negotiations produced by N-Meaning and N-Form. For example:

N-Content

NS: Cause GI's face was red. Right? GI is a man.
SY: But we cannot see, in the dark. Cause, both of, if the, if patriot kissed to grandmother. Because he cannot see. So, if they, couldn't see each other, they kissed each other. The, the, men.

We can notice in this N-Content negotiation that SY is doing a considerable amount of linguistic work in trying to provide the additional information asked for by NS. Compared to the following N-Meaning example, SY seems to be experimenting a lot more with her use of language.

N-Meaning

DH: How did Joey know?
HJ: Uh, who?
BS: How did Joey get to know about Monica and Chandler?

Task types and their effects on quality interaction

Another of my research aims was to compare different types of tasks in relation to quality interaction. Pica *et al.* (1993) provide the following definitions of the different task types that I used in my study:

1. ***Jigsaw tasks***: These involve learners combining different pieces of information to form a whole (eg three individuals or groups may have different parts of a story and have to piece the story together).
2. ***Information-gap tasks***: One student or group of students has one set of information and another student or group has a complementary set

of information. They must negotiate and find out what the other party's information is in order to complete an activity.

3. ***Problem-solving tasks***: Students are given a problem and a set of information. They must arrive at a solution to the problem.

The six tasks used for the study included two problem-solving prediction tasks, two jigsaw tasks, and two information-gap tasks. Although jigsaw and information-gap tasks do have slightly different features, they are similar in that there is a gap in the information held by each participant and that they are required to share their individually held information in order to complete the task. As a result, I included them both together under the title of 'jigsaw'. Problem solving can usefully include **prediction tasks**, as J. Willis suggests (1996a: 76). She defines them as 'predicting or attempting to reconstruct the content on the basis of given clues from part of the text, without having read, heard, or seen the whole'. Unlike jigsaw tasks, participants are all presented with the same information. Past research, relying heavily on the importance of meaning negotiations, identified jigsaw and/or information-gap tasks as the most likely to produce such negotiations and therefore to generate quality interaction. I wondered if these tasks would produce the same results if applied to a wider perspective on interaction. In addition, while jigsaw and information-gap tasks have often been compared to discussion tasks in past research (eg Pica *et al.*, 1989; Pica *et al.*, 1996), problem-solving tasks, especially prediction tasks, have received little attention. I therefore thought it worthwhile to investigate these. Below is a brief description of each of the six tasks:

Task 1: 'Friends' sitcom: creating questions and predicting answers

Problem-solving prediction task

After receiving background information on an episode of the TV sitcom Friends, pairs created five questions they thought would be answered by the end of the episode. Pairs then joined another pair to form a group of four in which they would share their questions and choose the three best and provide answers to them.

Task 2: 'Friends' sitcom: predicting the ending

Problem-solving prediction task

After viewing the episode except for the final scene, pairs were asked to predict an ending together. Pairs then joined another pair and shared story predictions and chose the better one for presentation to the class.

Task 3: Vietnam story puzzle

Jigsaw task

In groups of three, each learner received two of the story's six sentences. Their first task was to put the story in chronological order. They had to read, not show their story parts to each other and no writing was allowed. The group then had to solve the mystery contained in the story (adapted from Cook, 1989).

Task 4: Fairy-tale story jigsaw

Jigsaw task

In this task, the fairy-tale 'The Princess' Suitors' was separated into four sections. In groups of three, learners were given the same story section and asked to help each other with meaning and vocabulary. Learners then made groups of four, each learner in possession of a different story section. Their task was to share the story parts and put the story in order (adapted from Taylor, 2000).

Task 5: 'Vertigo' movie scenes comparison

Jigsaw task

The class was divided into two groups. Each group watched a short scene (one to two minutes) from the Hitchcock movie *Vertigo*. The two scenes were similar, but not identical, as they represented different characters' accounts of the same incident. After watching their scene, pairs who watched the same scene were asked to share their understandings. Then, learners with different scenes were paired up and asked to make a list of similarities and differences (adapted from Helgesen, 1991).

Task 6: 'The End of the Affair' movie scenes comparison

Jigsaw task

Same procedure as 'Task 5', except that the learners were asked also to speculate on why the female character ends the affair with the male character. The scenes (between seven and eight minutes long) were from the 1999 movie *The End of the Affair* starring Ralph Fiennes and Julianne Moore.

Full instructions for Task 1 and Task 6, as given to the learners, are in Appendix 2.

Comparing the tasks

The two most significant results from the study were:

- Overall, problem-solving tasks produced more quality interaction than did jigsaw tasks.

- Jigsaw tasks produced more self-initiated repairs than did problem-solving tasks.

For greater detail, please refer to the tabulated results in Appendix 1, Table 2.

Negotiations of Meaning

Surprisingly, problem-solving tasks not only showed significantly more N-Meaning, but also a higher success rate in producing more quality interaction, i.e. more comprehensible output. This is clearly in contrast with the belief established by prior research (Pica *et al.*, 1996) that jigsaw tasks, because they require information exchange, are more likely to result in higher levels of N-Meaning.

Negotiations of Content

In relation to N-Content, problem-solving tasks had a much higher success rate in producing additional information responses. For example, notice how in the following transcript of Task 1 in which a group of five learners are negotiating for content, the clarification request initiated by JY results in a lengthy first response produced by K followed by five additional information responses (numbered in the data below):

JY: Why do you think, uh, they, were hiding, uhm, their secret.
K: Secret, aw. My partner told me, uh, Ross and Rachel are, get married, uh, before the, the, movie, uh so, at that time, at the moment uh, they, they are, Joey and Rachel, couples, the other guys don't like, uh, make fun of them, they are couples, they are kidding and, they dislike the situation, so maybe, uh, Ch, Chandler and Monica, uh, knows it, it will happen again. To, uh, to our relationship. They will make fun of me, and uh, uh, make fun of, uh, Chandler and Monica. They know. The other guys, uh, make fun of them. [1]
SY: Maybe some, uhm, girls like, like, him. [2]
JY: Chandler.
SY: Chandler and if they know that, uhm – [3]
JY: It will –
SY: Gonna be difficult to keep, the, friendship. So they are hiding. [3 continued]
JY: I, I also same idea or uh – [4]
SY: The opposite situation –

JY: The opposite situation, one of some guys, uh, liked Monica, like Monica, so, uh, Chandler – [4 continued]
DH: Uuh, hide, hide – [5]
SY: Try to keep the secret. [5 continued]
JY: Keep the secret, to the other guys. [5 continued] I think. Ok. Another? Was he really ugly?

Negotiations of Form

Although results for N-Form did not reveal large differences, problem-solving tasks did have a higher proportion of quality negotiations, suggesting perhaps that their more 'open' structure as opposed to the more 'closed' or rigid nature of jigsaw tasks provide learners with more opportunities and time to reflect and improve elements of language form. Swain (2000) has termed these occurrences as 'language-related episodes' in which learners scaffold a new language structure together. Here is an example from Task 1:

DH: Why he naked.
JY: It is very awkward question. Why does.
DH: Why does he.
DH: Why do he, why does he naked. Why does he naked.
JY: Why were you naked.
DH: But, he said, why do they. Why he naked.
JY: Uh maybe, it is very awkward grammar.
DH: Why he naked.
JY: Why
DH: Was he naked.
JY: Why, why was –
DH: Why was he naked.
JY: Was he naked.
DH: Was he naked. Why. Why was he naked.
JY: Because, we said I am naked.
DH: Ok. Oh, we, we had better hurry up.

In this excerpt, DH produces an incorrect form with 'Why he naked' which is questioned by JY. Jointly, they then experiment with possible alternatives until DH, through collaborative reflection and experimentation with JY, is able to modify his own incorrect output.

Self-initiated repairs

While most of the data favours problem-solving tasks, the exception is with self-initiated repairs, for which jigsaw tasks were noticeably more productive. The underlying cause of this result may be the preciseness of information that is demanded of the tasks since both parties needed each other's information to successfully complete the task. Following is an example from Task 6 in which SY is going to describe her movie scene to YJ (the self-initiated repairs are underlined):

SY: I explain first?
YJ: Yeah.
SY: Mmm – uh, I mean the, reading, leading character, he, read a diary, I think that its diary and he, he reads diary, and then he reminds their scene, they were, he reminds their, uh, past time. Yeah, and he, they were in, on the bed, after the relationship, they were sit, they were lying together and talking about something but I can't understand their, maybe, they, they were really love each other and that way, the story is like that way, and then there was a big lock, a big knock, very loudly, they were dressed, and then he come, he com, came down ...

We can observe here how SY, simply by being given the opportunity to speak and describe her scene, is experimenting with her language and in the process seems to notice her points of inaccuracy and corrects herself.

Reflection, analysis and classroom implications

Before offering my conclusions on the data, I would like to emphasize that the relatively small scale of this study (21 learners and six tasks), makes any findings exploratory at best.

The first interesting conclusion that emerged was how N-Content, and to a lesser degree N-Procedure and N-Experience, provided learners with L2 learning opportunities that have been underemphasized in past research. The strongest characteristic of these three types of interactions seemed to be in their capacity to 'push' learners' output toward more complete levels, which gave them increased opportunities to 'play' with their linguistic knowledge. Almost the opposite, however, could be said of N-Meaning. Meaning negotiations were low in number and showed very low success rates in producing quality negotiations. This could lead us to argue that their benefit has been overstated by past researchers. Aston (1986) has argued that one of the reasons why learners rarely negotiate for meaning lies in the fact that they will often pretend to have understood their interlocutor when in fact they have not. This argument is especially relevant to Asian cultures in which 'face-saving' assumes a high level of importance.

A second important conclusion has to do with the benefits of problem-solving prediction tasks. Maybe their more open structure gives learners more freedom to use a wider variety of language. Tightly-designed tasks such as jigsaw tasks could potentially de-motivate the learners. In fact, two of the three learners who engaged in Task 3, a jigsaw task, expressed the following comments while performing the task: 'I don't like this kind of puzzle' and ' I don't like this kind of game which makes it so difficult'.

Learner motivation, therefore, is clearly important. On this matter, Williams and Burden (1997) advise teachers to consider not only what they call learners' 'intrinsic interest of activity' but also their 'locus of control'. In other words, not only do tasks need to arouse learners' curiosity and be at an optimal level of challenge, they should also provide learners with a certain amount of control in making their own decisions about how to perform the tasks. Based on this study, I would argue that problem-solving prediction tasks have higher levels of 'intrinsic interest of activity' and place the 'locus of control' firmly with the learners.

This does not mean, however, that jigsaw tasks cannot be interesting and motivating. They involve cooperation and they naturally contain an element of mystery that could enhance learners' motivation. However, if they are excessively challenging and/or if they take away a learner's sense of control on how to perform the task, then their value may decrease. On a more positive note, the jigsaw tasks did produce a high number of self-initiated repairs. By requiring learners to exchange individually held information, they create the need for learners to be more precise in what they say. The value of jigsaw tasks may therefore lie not in producing N-Meaning but in producing self-initiated repairs.

The key to understanding the value of problem-solving and jigsaw tasks, then, is in their specific task features. In problem-solving tasks, the same information is provided to the participants, which gives them more freedom to control the task and to control the language that they want to use. In jigsaws, the tasks are more 'closed' and structured as different information is provided to the participants which they must mutually exchange. A good 'third' way would be to create tasks that somehow incorporate both of these task features. For example, in Task 6, a jigsaw task, I had students who viewed the same scene first pair up to help each other with their understandings (same information) and only then split up and move to another student who had viewed a different scene (different information).

As for N-Form, while these were few in number, what was interesting was how learners sometimes collaboratively helped one another to scaffold a potentially new language form. Creating within tasks the opportunity for learners to engage in these discussions is most certainly a positive direction. The TBL framework described by J. Willis (1996a, 1996b), in which learners are given time to prepare a public report of their task findings, creates such an opportunity. However, there are certain considerations we must keep in mind in relation to the planning and report stages. For example, even though the six tasks used in my study contained these stages, N-Form was still rare. This result, however, may have been more positive if I had:

- given more time to the learners to plan their public reports.
- more strongly encouraged learners to negotiate for form.
- created a higher level of expectation concerning the accuracy of learners' reports.

Conclusion

There is obviously more to the positive dimensions of interaction than just the negotiation of meaning. By giving students more freedom to control tasks we are also giving them more opportunities to experiment with their language and to naturally discuss and negotiate elements related to task content, procedures, and personal experiences. These are examples of language that naturally occur in the real world and for this reason we must provide these opportunities to our learners. By only presenting tasks that are designed to maximize negotiations of meaning, we are not only creating conditions that may restrict free use of language, we are also creating conditions of language use that may be unnatural. I therefore recommend teachers to further explore the benefits of problem-solving tasks, especially prediction tasks, as they have been underemphasized if not overlooked in the past. As for TBL, through my experience I can confidently state that this offers a great deal of promise as a teaching framework, even in cultural contexts such as that in Korea, where students are accustomed to a more traditional and formal learning atmosphere. Through feedback sessions, my students have expressed how refreshing, liberating, and motivating the approach was for their language learning.

Appendix 1: Tabulated results

Table 1 Results for each interaction variable across all six tasks

Negotiation Types	Number of quality negotiations	Total number of negotiations	% quality negotiations
N-Content	115	215	53
N-Meaning	29	107	27
N-Form	4	19	21
N-Procedure	21	49	43
N-Experience	19	45	42
Total Negotiations	186	435	43
Total self-initiated repairs	231		

Table 2 Problem Solving Prediction versus Jigsaw tasks[1]

Negotiation Types	Problem solving prediction			Jigsaw		
	Number of quality negotiations	Total number of negotiations	% quality negotiations	Number of quality negotiations	Total number of negotiations	% quality negotiations
N-Content	65	100	65	67	152	44
N-Meaning	24	73	33	8	36	22
N-Form	3	10	30	1	10	10
N-Procedure	14	34	41	7	15	47
N-Experience	6	15	40	1	1	100
Total negotiations		240			214	
Total self-initiated repairs		91			148	

[1] Total time for the problem-solving tasks amounted to 86 minutes while jigsaw tasks amounted to a total of 100 minutes. For comparative purposes, the interaction variables for problem-solving tasks were therefore adjusted to correspond to 100 minutes.

Appendix 2: Task instructions for Task 1 and Task 6

Task 1: Problem-solving prediction

'Friends' sitcom: creating questions and predicting answers

1. Now you know the background to the popular sitcom "Friends". Find a partner and do the following activity:

- Write five questions that you think will be answered by the end of the episode.

2. Now, find another pair and make a group of four. Share and compare your questions. Choose the three best questions and think of possible answers. Prepare to present to the class.

Task 6: Jigsaw

'The End of the Affair' movie scenes comparison

1. Find a partner (one is A, the other is B).
2. A students stay in this classroom and watch a scene from the movie. B students go to another classroom and watch a similar but different scene.
3. Watch your movie scene twice and try to remember everything that happens (you can take notes if you wish). Also think about why Sarah ends the affair. Then discuss your understandings with a partner.
4. Return to your original partner and discuss in detail what you saw and make a list of similarities and differences. Also, try to agree on why Sarah ends the affair. Prepare to present your findings to the class.

Epilogue: Teachers Exploring Research

Corony Edwards

Summary *To conclude the collection of 'explorations' that make up this book, I decided to ask the contributors for their views on doing research. From the responses to my small-scale survey I identified a number of key qualities and conditions that are considered necessary for carrying out classroom explorations and research, and compiled a list of the contributors' 'top ten tips' for getting started with explorations like those described in this book.*

Rationale: teachers and research – some questions

Although this book has as its main focus task-based language learning, it is also a book about teachers doing research. On these pages you have 18 examples of classroom-based experiments, investigations and small-scale research projects carried out by teachers, and a further chapter that provides some of the theoretical background to these projects and places them in the context of the wider body of second language acquisition research (Shehadeh, Chapter 1).

I was interested to find out from these teachers what they felt about doing classroom research, and what advice they might offer others embarking on this for the first time. I therefore conducted my own small research project, in which I asked the 19 other contributors to this book to fill in a questionnaire on the topic of 'teachers and research'. I wanted to find out what they consider counts as research (is their contribution to this volume, for example, a research report, or something different in their view?), what they get out of doing classroom research, and what the disadvantages are; what knowledge, skills, facilities and other factors they think someone should have to carry out research successfully. Finally, I asked them specifically about how they came to research aspects of task-based learning, and what they had learned from undertaking their projects for this volume. I hoped that their responses will give readers some insight into what it is like to do the sort of research that can result in reports like the ones presented in this book, and to be encouraged to try similar work for themselves.

I also hoped that in completing the questionnaires, our contributors would be prompted into reflecting on their work as *researchers*. Doing research as a means of professional development is now widely accepted by teacher educators as a legitimate part of a teacher's activities. This makes it just a much a candidate for reflective scrutiny as classroom teaching. One respondent said in the email that accompanied his completed questionnaire, 'I enjoyed reminiscing on some of my experiences!' and another commented, 'It was quite interesting to fill out', comments which suggest to me that some reflection was taking place.

Findings

What is classroom research?

One of my first questions to our 19 teachers was whether they thought that their contribution to this book counted as a 'research'. The majority said 'definitely' (ten) or 'probably' (six), with only one (Patricia Pullin Stark) saying that her chapter was not a research report, 'because it is based on experience and reflection ... [without] the collection and analysis of data'. Patricia's comment reflects the way that many of our teachers define research, as something involving **data** (eg recordings made in classrooms) that can be **analysed** to allow us to observe and understand how something behaves under certain conditions, to discover something new to us, to provide answers to questions, or possibly a structured plan of action to solve a problem. Nunan (1992: 18) gives a similar, minimalist definition of **research**, but Freeman (1998: 5) claims that 'to truly make research a central part of teaching, we must redefine research', and suggests that it can be seen as 'an **orientation** toward one's practice. It is a questioning attitude toward the world, leading to **inquiry** conducted with a **disciplined** framework.' (*ibid.* 8) (my emphasis).

I also asked the teachers whether they thought that the sort of classroom *experimenting* that most teachers regularly do, eg trying out a new activity, technique or set of materials, could count as *research*. Several thought that experimenting was more spur-of-the-moment, less planned than research 'proper', but William (Bill) Essig makes a useful point:

> I view these as two distinct elements along an informal/formal continuum with experimenting at the informal end, research at the other, and action research somewhere in the middle. In other words, experimenting is what I do every day in the classroom while research is a well-thought out and time-consuming process containing reportable results.

This should be encouraging if you think that classroom research is not for you: by seeing it as a more formalised extension of what you already do, but bringing enhanced understanding and helping you to more systematically develop your teaching skills, you may be more prepared to engage in it yourself. Of course, as Ali Shehadeh points out (personal email, 26 June 2003) you should not get the impression that 'research is an easy matter at the expense of standard procedures, research design, and other well established conventions that researchers should follow', and Patricia Pullin Stark (personal email, 26 June 2003) emphasises that we are working in a serious academic field that is increasingly based on scientific research. Where she works, 'the ... policy is that all research ... should relate directly to learning and/or teaching, and ... [whilst] no one here is a dry academic ... some of the researchers have done some enormous quantitative studies, [while] many of us are working on qualitative[1] work.'

Small is beautiful

One thing that is clear both from the chapters in this book and from the teachers' responses, is that not all classroom research has to be done on a grand scale. It does not have to involve formal experiments or statistical analysis of large amounts of data; you don't need a budget for it (although many thought this would be nice!) nor does it have to be done by academics working in universities. Eight of our contributors do not work in universities, and fourteen said they thought this was irrelevant or not really necessary; no-one thought it was essential. However, as we will see later in this chapter, in reality it is often easier to get started on an investigation if this is a required part of your job or studies, and this seems to have been true for most of the contributors to this volume. Whatever your work context though, the advice of several of the teachers was to keep it small and simple, especially if you are relatively new to doing research. Maria Leedham, says very simply: 'Have a go. Start small. Tape a class and see what comes out of this that is useful', and Raymond Sheehan says, 'Just do it!' The section below on 'essential skills and qualities' suggests a very simple way of doing 'micro-research' that would be ideal for getting started.

Ten tips

Based on what our teachers said they had learned themselves while doing research, and the advice they would give to colleagues new to research, I have compiled this list:

Our contributors' top ten tips for getting started on classroom research:

1. Keep it small and simple.
2. Keep it relevant, to both you and your learners.
3. Have a clear aim (a specific question you want to answer, a clearly identified problem you want to solve, or a hypothesis that you want to test).
4. Talk: discuss what you are doing with colleagues, sound out ideas with someone who has already done some classroom research.
5. Read, especially reports of previous research into your topic.
6. Write: keep notes; write down all your ideas and observations; keep a diary or journal.
7. Listen to your learners; ask for their views (as Annamaria Pinter shows, even young learners can do this!) and include these as part of your data.
8. Be honest. It is rare for research to go exactly to plan: methods may not work and results are often not what you expected, but don't be afraid to say so! You and others can learn from your mistakes and surprises. As Bill Essig says, 'Even the unexpected is valuable'.
9. Remember there is no 'right answer': research involves interpretation of facts, so two people with the same information could arrive at two different conclusions.
10. Share your findings with others: tell colleagues, give talks, publish.

As I compiled this list I noticed that it had remarkable overlaps with a list of seven aims that Dick Allwright devised for an approach to teacher-research, or 'exploration of puzzles', that he calls 'Exploratory Practice' (Allwright, 1993). I have included Allwright's list of aims in Appendix 1 for comparison. Exploratory Practice is an approach that aims at 'the development of situational understanding', in contrast with Action Research, which aims to 'produce practical solutions to isolated problems'[2] (Allwright, 2003: 116). Exploratory Practice is concerned with 'quality of life' rather than 'quality of work' in a given situation, and its starting point is therefore not identification of practical problems, but of 'bringing puzzling issues of classroom life to consciousness' (*ibid.* 124).

Time

Allwright (1993) identifies three problems – time, skills learning and threat to self esteem – associated with exploratory practice (see Appendix 1). Time was the number one problem identified by our teachers, too (incidentally, no-one mentioned either of Allwright's other two problems). Having plenty of spare time in which to do research was considered a useful asset by our teachers, although Patrick Kiernan more pragmatically suggests that 'in practice, classroom research is the art of making the most of a little spare time'. Lamprini (Lana) Loumpourdi tells us that research 'takes time from the lesson and maybe distracts you a bit from your 'actual' objective, at least for those teaching in a demanding exam-focused context'; Greg Birch similarly warns that research can 'take your focus away from your students in the short term'.

It strikes me that if teachers follow our tip number 2, and Allwright's first aim, of researching topics that are relevant to both themselves and their learners, then the potential clash of interests between research and teaching becomes less of an issue, and the time used should be seen as a worthwhile investment because of the future gains to be reaped. At the very least, we should be careful that our research goals and classroom goals do not conflict – a potential problem identified by both James Hobbs and Maggie Baigent. At best, the students can become involved in the research process itself as this becomes part of their learning activity, as for example, in Maria Leedham's project, where the students compare transcripts of themselves doing exam speaking tasks with those of native speakers. Research need not be something that is done 'to' or 'about' the students, but something done 'with' them. Task-based lessons that use transcripts of fluent speakers doing tasks as the basis for language awareness-raising, and other types of 'data-driven' learning, are approaches to teaching that already place the students in the role of 'researcher', and therefore present great opportunities for smoothly blending an 'exploratory practice' approach to classroom research to exploratory ways of learning.

Of course, classroom research does not only take up time in the classroom. Doing action research nearly always involves extra planning and reflection time (Wallace, 1998, Burns, 1999) and if you've ever had a go at transcribing recordings you'll know what Antigone Djapoura means when she says this 'takes a great amount of time and patience'. Don't be put off though – you rarely need to transcribe all the data you have recorded, and you (and your students) can learn a lot from just a couple of minutes worth, which you should be able to transcribe in about 20 minutes (although depending on the nature of your study, you may need more than this). If you go on to write a report of your project, this, though rewarding, takes yet more time. Theron Muller notes that 'my job calls for me to teach, and offers no compensation or time for ... research, making one-time, occasional research difficult, and ongoing research impossible.' All this helps us to understand why 'keeping it small and simple' is appropriately placed as the number one tip!

The rewards of research

So if doing classroom research is so time-consuming, why do teachers do it at all? Our contributors had a huge list of reasons that far outnumber the disadvantages and problems they gave. David Cox, Bill Essig, Seung-Min Lee and Ali Shehadeh all feel they have become better teachers through doing research. Greg Birch (personal email to Jane Willis, 26 June 2003) provides a specific example:

> One thing I have gotten out of this whole project is an appreciation for how writing truly is a process. For the first time, I have had to teach writing and this experience has definitely influenced how I teach my class.

And Craig Johnston talks of

> excitement about what I've learned; satisfaction at the depth of understanding and clarity of articulation I've achieved; confidence that I can approach professional challenges in a principled way and eventually overcome them; awareness about what I'm doing; a deeper appreciation for and more critical eye when reading other people's research.

Many others mentioned similar benefits, including a deeper sense of professionalism, a respect for other researchers, better appreciation of their students' abilities and skills, 'the natural joy of learning and discovering' (Glen Poupore), motivation, greater sense of purpose, confidence in ability to do something about problems or 'deal proactively with constraints' (Raymond Sheehan), insight, a sense of achievement or accomplishment, more enjoyment of teaching, and prevention of stagnation and 'routinisation' (Raymond Sheehan). Jason Moser tells us that for him, 'doing research however small it is, is so crucial to maintaining my interest in the profession and giving me a sense of pride about being a "real teacher".' Finally, David Coulson says,

> I am first a teacher, but in the job I have with comparatively few teaching hours, I also have to justify my position by producing some published material. In that utilitarian sense, research has helped my career. But that's not why I do it. I do it because it is an interesting and important part of being a language teacher ... responsible teaching can probably only be viewed as an ongoing process of research, whether that is formal or informal. The act of being in the classroom becomes research since we observe what is happening, and we inevitably have a reaction to that after class. Once a teacher gets into a more formal cycle of research, I think it becomes self-evident that observing and making small changes is an integral part of language teaching.

Incentives and inspiration

Of course, many of our teachers started doing research because it was a requirement of their job or a course they were enrolled on, a researcher's equivalent to the 'extrinsic motivation' that language teachers often read about. For some, this is still the case. James Hobbs confesses:

> It can be difficult to keep a dual focus on a) research goals, and b) teaching goals such as finishing chapter X, getting homework checked, giving grades, etc. I've got no end of ideas for research projects, but I need an incentive (such as another 20 credits on the MSc, or the chance to have a paper published in your book) to persuade me to actually carry out a project.

I'm sure this is true for many teacher-researchers – it certainly is for me! What is clear is that for most, once you've had a go, the benefits are such that even a relatively small incentive is enough to set you off on another project. Once you've started, it can become quite addictive! I find that it helps me enormously if I find a colleague to act as a project partner, either in my own institution or based elsewhere, because having made a commitment to someone else to undertake a project I'm much more likely to actually do something. Annamaria Pinter also advocates doing action research together with others, and more generally, Greg Birch, Jason Moser and Theron Muller all mention support, from colleagues and other researchers, as being a key factor for success (both Allwright,

2003: 131–5 and Burns, 1999: 12–14, highlight the importance collaborative research).

Another approach I've found that helps me when doing small-scale action research (for example when I ask my students for feedback or evaluation on something we do in class) is to tell the students at the time of collecting my data that I will write a summary of what I find and give them each a copy. They are usually very interested to receive this, and will often badger me for it; when I do produce it, they get an authentic reading text (in the richest possible sense of the term) into the bargain.

Apart from external incentives, what inspires people to embark on a particular project? In other words, what sort of 'intrinsic motivation' do researchers have? The desire to address a particular problem seems to be a common reason, according to our teachers. Lana Loumpourdi, Raymond Sheehan, Maria Leedham, Jason Moser and David Coulson were all dissatisfied with aspects of their teaching or students' performance, and were testing out solutions when they did the studies reported in this book.

In other cases, reading something that has been published[3] provides the impetus. Often, having read about a phenomenon, teachers begin to relate this to their own students and want to investigate more objectively. Theron Muller had read that process approaches ('Type B syllabuses', in White's 1988:110 terminology) such as TBL might be unsuitable for beginner students, but White also suggested that such approaches might be the best-suited of available methods for developing spontaneous language ability – an aim of Theron's beginner level course! Theron 'wanted to get to the bottom of this paradox, and thought [his] students were more intelligent and able than they were given credit for.' Annamaria Pinter gives a similar reason: '… fluency tasks never seem to be used with children's classes. I felt that children's abilities are underestimated.' So both tried out aspects of TBL with their students in spite of the received wisdom, in both cases with positive results.

For others, published work simply inspired the teachers, rather than presenting ideas for them to challenge. Craig Johnston writes that he was inspired by 'Pauline Foster's paper on planning time in 'Challenge and Change' (Willis and Willis, 1996)' and adds 'really, that whole book was inspiring.' Bill Essig was inspired by the same book, and Patrick Kiernan 'felt there was a gap between narratives produced by tasks and those described in the literature on conversational narrative' and wanted to adapt tasks to encourage language that was closer to everyday conversation.

Some further sources of inspiration for our teachers were a 'desire to help my students' (Bill Essig), wanting to know what learners thought about lessons, using research as a learning vehicle, because 'I was dissatisfied with my current level of understanding (Greg Birch) and plain curiosity 'to discover what my students actually did in the process of completing the tasks and to see if there were any language learning benefits' (Glen Poupore).

You can get a more complete idea of why each of our teachers embarked on the projects reported in this book by looking at the table at the end of the Introduction to this book.

Personal qualities and essential skills

One section of my questionnaire asked the teachers to rate a number of different personal qualities, skills and other factors according to how necessary each is for someone to be able to do classroom research successfully. Our teachers said that you need to be patient, determined, interested in how people learn languages and new ways of teaching and learning, and to approach things in a logical way. Flexibility (especially when things do not go to plan) also got a frequent mention. These qualities were all considered to be far more important than being academic or 'brainy', which were rated by most as being just 'useful' or 'not really necessary'.

Enthusiasm for doing research is important, but it isn't enough on its own. The majority of our teachers agreed that having some knowledge of theory and previous research findings relevant to your topic is useful, maybe essential. They also agreed that you should know something about the research methods used in previous research, which is no doubt why so many went on to recommend that you read reports of previous research projects. Specifically, they thought that being able to design research instruments, such as questionnaires or evaluation forms, is a very useful skill. But these 'instruments' do not always have to be complicated to design or time-consuming to fill in. I often do what I would call '**micro-research**', when I give out those very small sticky notes ('Post-Its') in my classes and ask the students to write their response to a single question on one of these. For example, I recently asked a rather quiet class how they felt when I made an open invitation to ask questions or comment on something; the twenty-one anonymous responses I received, written on slips just 3cm by 5cm, were enough for me to write a three page report for the students, told me a lot about the way I was managing the group, and resulted in much more interactive classes from then on.

If you have the chance to get some training in how to do research, this is of course useful, but most of teachers thought it was not essential. As Bill Essig says, 'with effort, it can be self-taught', and learning by trying out methods reported by others is a good way to do this. You can see a list summarizing the different research methods and instruments used for each of the studies described in this book in Appendix 2, and you can find suggestions and expert advice on how to use these and others in many of the resources recommended in Appendix 4.

Although it's more easily said than done, our group of teachers agreed that you should be able to describe what you observe clearly. You should also, as a minimum, be able to analyse your data in a qualitative way, by identifying general trends or patterns of results for example, and be able to explain your observations and discuss the implications for teaching. This does not necessarily mean using statistical techniques, although counting tallies and scores and presenting them as tables or charts can be a useful way to spot trends, as long as such quantitative work is not presented as 'proving' a result or being of 'significance' without appropriate statistical tests having been applied.

Where quantitative approaches are used, Antigone Djapoura (who ran a T-Test to determine whether her results were statistically significant: see Chapter 17) points out the desirability of complementing these with qualitative findings:

> Although a quantitative analysis might look more 'professional', numbers can be meaningless and boring without any attempt at a qualitative analysis as well.

Indeed, classroom research frequently uses mixed or hybrid qualitative-quantitative methods (see, eg, Robson, 2002: 372–3, who lists eleven approaches to combining qualitative and quantitative research).

So while quantitative analysis may sometimes be desirable, often it is not necessary or even possible for small-scale classroom research, and when it is used, it has to be done carefully and with appropriate interpretation of results.

When it comes to qualitative approaches, on describing your methods and observations clearly Bill Essig says,

> [This is] very, very important because who ever reads or listens to your report of the results will not have been with you as you carried out your research. You need to help them imagine that they were there with you.

and on discussing the implications of your findings, he says,

> This is the whole purpose of doing research. How can what we learn by doing research help us to understand how our students learn or how we can be more effective teachers? This is the question that needs to be answered.

Ethics, or what to tell your students

Many of our teachers recorded their students in order to get the data they needed for their investigations. This raises the ethical issue of what to tell your subjects, i.e., your students or colleagues who are participating in the project. Nearly everyone thought that it is essential to get consent from those who will be subjects in your study. David Coulson feels that subjects have a right to know, if, for example, they are being recorded, and Patrick Kiernan thinks that 'doing it surreptitiously is possible but unethical'. However, in terms of how much to say on the details of the project, Antigone Djapoura says, 'I think that it might actually be better for them not to know (what the study is about), in order not to change anything in their behaviour on purpose.' James Hobbs also warns against possible devaluation of data if you tell informants exactly what you are looking for before you collect this. So the message is, get permission to record / observe / analyse written work, but be vague about the precise reasons until after you've got the data.[4]

Views of beginner teacher–researchers

As well as the contributors to this book, who are already committed researchers, I asked some other teachers about their attitudes to doing classroom research. I wanted to find out what sorts of concerns teachers had as first-time, soon-to-be researchers, or, in the case of teachers who have never done research and have no plans to, why not! As far as non-researchers went, I got hardly any replies (you see what I mean about research not always going to plan!). But on reflection, perhaps this is not so surprising. Teachers who do not already do classroom research probably do not see this as relevant to them, and are therefore not motivated to fill in questionnaires on this topic, so I have to leave this particular question for a future study (see also Hancock, 1997, for a speculative article on why class teachers are reluctant to become researchers).

I did receive 12 responses from teachers embarking on research for the first time. Although there is not the space here to give a full report of this part of my study, my main findings were that most of these teachers do have a number of concerns. They reported feeling enthusiastic, somewhat excited, but also, worried, lacking in confidence, even a little scared. Several said they were quite confused about how to proceed.

Conclusion: teacher or researcher?

One of the questions I put to the teachers who wrote chapters for this book was where they would place themselves on this continuum:

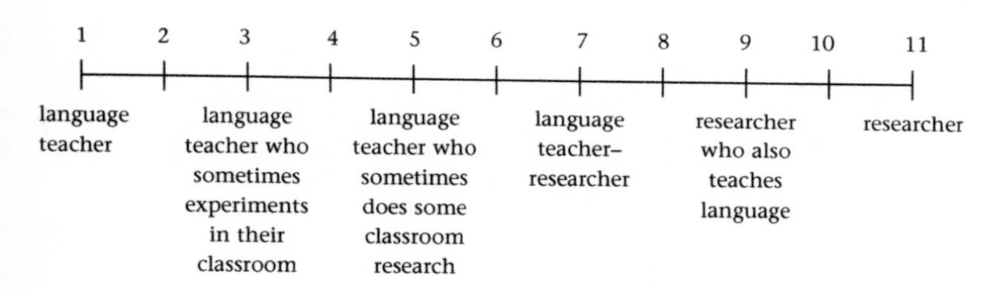

Given what you know of the teachers from their chapters and from this one, you probably won't be surprised to learn that by far the most popular responses (15 in all) were 5, 6 and 7, and everyone was within the range 3 to 9. Patrick Kiernan adds a note that he started out as 1, and sees himself as having moved along the scale (he's at 6 now). For most teachers, 6 or 7 is probably the sort of teaching-research balance they will be happy to maintain. The one person who saw himself as being more of a researcher than a teacher was Ali Shehadeh, who now holds a university post. He explains, 'these days my academic responsibilities, besides teaching, include advising on linguistic courses, supervising research (MA and PhD) students, and doing research. However, looking at my career in general, I would really give myself 7' (Shehadeh, 2003).

The point of this scale is not to suggest that we should be striving to reach a particular point on it, but to show that there is a whole range of degrees to which teachers can engage with research, or adopt a 'research stance on their practice' (Hancock, 1997: 91). You might find it a useful device to decide where you stand at present in relation to teaching and research, and to consider whether this is the balance that is right for you. If, like Patrick, you see yourself as moving along the scale from left to right, we hope that this book will have given you some ideas and inspiration to do so.

Appendix 1

Allwright's (1993) 10 criteria for exploratory practice
Summarized from Allwright, 1993: 128–30

Aims	
1. Relevance	What teachers explore should be relevant to themselves and their learners.
2. Reflection	Integration of research and pedagogy should promote reflection by learners and teachers, as reflection is seen as a powerful force for development.
3. Continuity	Integrated research and pedagogy should be continuous, not something to 'try once and then drop forever'.
4. Collegiality	Integration of research and pedagogy should reduce professional isolation between teachers, and bring teachers and learners, teachers and academics closer together.
5. Learner development	Questions asked should be relevant to learners, and learners should be prompted to reflect on their experiences to foster learner development; 'exploratory learning' is also a possibility.
6. Teacher development	Integrated research and pedagogy should contribute to the teacher–researcher's own development and to the more general professional development of the field.
7. Theory-building	Integrated research and pedagogy should help us develop general understanding of classroom learning and teaching.
Problems	
1. Time	Classroom research is time consuming; preparing lessons to accommodate research, doing research during lessons, sorting and analysing all take extra time. If excessive, teachers will stop researching.
2. Skills learning	New research skills have to be learned, taking time and intellectual effort (but NB that exploratory teaching aims to minimise the need for specialist skills, eg questionnaire design, by basing investigative activities on familiar pedagogic activities).
3. Threat to self-esteem	Research may reveal problematic aspects of your teaching which can threaten self-esteem.

Appendix 2

Methods and techniques for classroom research

Method / technique / data type	Who used this?	How did they use it, and why?
Recordings of students doing tasks *Note here the different ways that these recordings are used.*	Theron Muller	**Theron's** short transcripts of task recordings show how his students' language developed in complexity as they moved from the task to the report stage of the lesson. By including this data in his report, and linking it to theory (Skehan's 'complexity'), his study begins to take on a slightly more formal 'research' flavour.
Nearly all are at least partly transcribed as this makes analysis much easier. In fact, the very act of transcribing helps us to notice features.	Patrick Kiernan	**Patrick** recorded his students doing their narrative tasks, so he could later transcribe some of their performances at various stages of the project, see what progress they had made, and what problems they were still having. He also recorded the students doing the tasks in their native Japanese, so he could check their comprehension and compare their L1 and L2 performances, although he does not report the findings of this part of his study here.
Some are used to make qualitative judgements about students' performance. In this case, illustrative examples are usually included in the report.	Maria Leedham	**Maria** gave transcripts of her recordings to her intermediate level students, so they could compare their own performance of exam speaking tasks with those of native speakers. She also recorded the students after this awareness-raising exercise to see what effect it had had. In other words, she used transcripts of her recordings both as learning material for her students and as data for her research.
	Seung-Min Lee	**Seung-Min** uses some of the transcribed material from his recordings in his chapter to illustrate the way his pupils were (not) using meaning negotiation skill before training, and how these had developed after training. But as he recorded all the pupils doing all the tasks in the study, he is also able to analyse this data quantitatively, and he presents tables showing how many of each type of negotiation device is used by each group.
Some are analysed systematically using one or more techniques so that quantitative statements can	Annamaria Pinter	**Annamaria** recorded children doing similar tasks on repeated occasions, so she

Appendix 2: Continued

Method / technique / data type	**Who used this?**	**How did they use it, and why?**
be made about the number of instances of a feature that appear in a set of transcripts. In these cases, results are usually presented as tables or graphs, supported by illustrative extracts from the transcripts.		could compare the recordings for signs of improvement in performance. She reproduces some transcribed extracts in her chapter to illustrate the changes she observed.
	David Coulson	**David** initially used recordings to help him understand a problem his students had reported, but in doing so he noticed that they sometimes used a collaborative strategy to help each other maintain conversations. This would turn out to be the basis of the solution. In trying out his solution with his class, he made further recordings, which he transcribed, to study their progress.
Some are used as learning materials for the students, to raise awareness of problems in their performance.	Maggie Baigent	**Maggie** recorded her advanced level students doing tasks and transcribed her recordings. From these she was able to find out to what extent they used multi-word chunks in their spoken language compared with the production of native speakers. She worked out both the numbers of incorrect chunks produced by the students and the 'chunk density' of their language – measures which she presents numerically.
	Craig Johnston	**Craig** recorded students doing tasks and later giving their public reports of these. His transciptions allowed him to analyse the students' spoken output at the two stages for features such as grammatical accuracy, complexity and variety and appropriateness of vocabulary, which he expresses either as numerical scores, or in more qualitative terms, as appropriate for the feature in question.
	William Essig	By recording the students giving their eight original narratives and the eight retellings, **Bill** could see what differences the task repetition and the private or public context had made to the students' performances. Although Bill analysed

		all his data quantitatively, he does not present all his numerical data here, since he looked at a large number of features, but instead gives us a more reader-friendly narrative account.
	Antigone Djapoura	**Antigone** made nine recordings. Each of her three groups of students did three tasks; when the three groups all did a task, they each did it slightly differently, either with no planning, or with ten minutes planning time, or with both planning time and some guidance on an instruction sheet. By the end of the three tasks, each group had done a task under each of the three conditions. Antigone could then compare the three sets of three recordings to see if planning time resulted in improved performance, and whether guided planning further enhanced this. She presents her quantitatively analysed data mainly in the form of bar charts.
	Greg Birch	**Greg** recorded 60 pairs of students doing two different tasks, giving 120 recordings. Unlike Antigone, Greg does not analyse the language recorded and transcribed in quantitative terms, but gives a qualitative account of the differences in performance that he observed, supported by examples.
	Glen Poupore	**Glen's** recordings of learners doing six different tasks gave him plenty of data for a quantitative analysis of different negotiation types used by the learners. His findings are summarized in two tables in an appendix, and described more qualitatively in his report.
Recordings of fluent speakers doing tasks / speaking in natural settings	Maria Leedham	**Maria** asked some English native speaker colleagues to do a task that she recorded and transcribed. Maria's students studied these transcripts in class, to raise their awareness of turn-taking devices and backchannelling.
	James Hobbs	**James** recorded native speakers of English doing tasks so he could extract from the recordings a syllabus of interactive phrases. He later used some of the recordings, with their transcripts, in class, as a way of focusing his students' attention on such phrases.

Appendix 2: Continued

Method / technique / data type	Who used this?	How did they use it, and why?
As for recordings of students, recordings of fluent speakers can be used for both teaching and data analysis, and can be qualitatively and / or quantitatively analysed.	Maggie Baigent	**Maggie** made her own recordings of native speakers doing tasks with two colleagues (who she also asked to look at all the transcripts for chunks) and had her students do the same tasks so she could make comparisons. She used both sets of transcripts to test her students' awareness of multi-word chunks by asking them to read through and mark all the chunks they found. She also found published recordings and transcripts of native speakers doing tasks, and used a short extract from these as an example for the students looking at their own transcripts.
	David Cox	**David** made recordings of 25 pairs of native speakers doing tasks so he could check whether the language predicted for the tasks by experienced teachers actually occurred. He transcribed and then analysed these using a concordancing programme on his computer to search for how many predicted language items actually occurred, and also to find the commonly occurring items that had not been predicted. He reports these as tables of numerical data along with short examples in his chapter.
Examples of students' written work, teaching materials, etc. *Including examples of students' written output and / or prompt materials used for speaking tasks supports and enriches the accounts given here.*	Raymond Sheehan	**Raymond** includes, as appendices, an example set of concordance lines that he used with his students. He also includes in his report an annotated framework to show how concordance-based language tasks can be incorporated into a lesson.
	Jason Moser	**Jason** includes some samples of completed lesson journals in his appendices. These allow us to see exactly what form the journal took, in case we want to try it in our own classes, and also demonstrates what type of language the students were using, and how their language developed as the lesson progressed.

Although none of our contributors used students' written work or learning materials as part of their data for analysis purposes, other studies may well do so, eg an evaluation of a task-based course book, or an exploration of writing tasks.	Seung-Min Lee Maggie Baigent David Cox Antigone Djapoura Greg Birch	**Seung-Min** includes copies of the tasks his students did for the study, which helps readers to make sense of the transcribed recordings. **Maggie** includes instructions and materials for the four tasks used in her study. **David** gives us precise descriptions of the tasks and materials used in his study, so it could be exactly repeated if desired. **Antigone** includes her task material and instructions in full in an appendix. Like Maggie and Antigone, **Greg** reproduces the visual stimuli and task instructions from his study in an appendix.
Observing students in class (informally) *Noticing how our learners react to what they are doing in class is essential if we are to evaluate our own teaching and develop this in an appropriate way.* *Informal observations often allow us to notice important and interesting things that we had not expected, and which our formal recording techniques might miss.*	Lamprini (Lana) Loumpourdi Theron Muller James Hobbs Most of the other contributors!	**Lana** and **Theron** both make informal observations on how their students' reacted to what they were doing in class, eg Theron notes that his students were 'showing interest in script correction and practice', and Lana, having previously noticed 'how the teaching of just theory and rules confused and bored my students and failed to achieve the desired results' observes that in her task-based 'quiz' lessons, 'a group of boys who never really participated in the Grammar classes before came up with the more original ideas and were so eager to utter them first, that they started speaking in English really fast.' **James** notes at the end of his chapter that he was not able to conduct a formal survey of his students' views, but his own informal observations give us a useful idea of how successful his approach was. Look out for other contributors reporting their informal observations.
Observing students in class (formally – eg by		None of the contributors to this collection used the tally sheets or checklists often suggested in books on doing classroom research. In some cases,

Appendix 2: Continued

Method / technique / data type	Who used this?	How did they use it, and why?
using checklists, tally sheets or in-class note-taking)		eg studies looking at interaction types or patterns, this is because using transcribed recordings of classroom language allows for more accurate analysis of data than real-time observation and classification. However, the main reason here is because in all cases our contributors were acting in the dual role of teacher and researcher. A third party observer may be able to fill in sheets during class, but a teacher researching their own classroom almost certainly cannot!
Informal feedback from students *Like informal observation, informal and unsolicited feedback from students can give us insights that formal procedures may miss.*	Patricia Pullin Stark Craig Johnston	In addition to quoting from formal feedback (see below), **Patricia** also reports ad hoc comments from students during the course, eg the student who 'commented that the project had taken a disproportionate amount of time for a five-minute presentation'. **Craig** tells us that he 'spoke briefly' with his three students after his experiment, to get feedback from them, and thus discovered that his positive assessment of their improved language output during their reports should be tempered by the fact that they found it more difficult to understand each other at this stage.
Interviews / formal, recorded feedback with students, evaluation forms and surveys *These are useful to show what the students thought*	Patricia Pullin Stark Jason Moser Annamaria Pinter	**Patricia** starts her paper with some comments collected from students after their course. **Jason** conducted a survey among his students to see how they reacted to his lesson journals. He summarises the survey results at the end of his chapter. **Annamaria** interviewed her pupils (in their native Hungarian) after the task-repetition experiment to see how they felt they had done. She tape-recorded

of things, balancing what could otherwise be a rather one-sided (biased?) view from you, the teacher.		the interviews and translated them into English so she could directly report their views in her chapter.
Questionnaires for students		No-one in our group used questionnaires for purposes other than course feedback. However, they are widely used for purposes such as self-assessment of level, needs analysis, learner styles and strategies. Books on doing classroom research, such as those listed in Appendix IV, give plenty of examples.
Learner diaries or other records kept by learners	Jason Moser	**Jason** got his students to fill in a pro-forma sheet during each lesson so at each stage they could write down examples of the language they had used, and sum up at the end by saying what they had learned. These 'lesson journals' were not primarily for his own data collection purposes, but were intended as genuine learning devices to raise students' awareness of the nature and purpose of each stage of the lesson, and to create a record they could take away of what was otherwise an unrecorded speaking class.
Teacher diary / journal / notes or recall and reflection	Jason Moser	**Jason** includes a 'reflection' section, the final stage of his action research cycle, where he discusses the insights he has gained. In other chapters, you can find writers reporting a similar process under the heading of 'discussion' or 'implications'. The important point is that exploratory practice or research does not stop at observing results – we have to think about them too!
Other	David Cox	**David** asked experienced teachers to look at task instructions and write down the language (in a questionnaire) they predicted would occur when native speakers did the task. Colleagues can often be useful sources of opinions and other data.

Appendix 2: Continued

Method / technique / data type	Who used this?	How did they use it, and why?
Triangulation *Using more than one way of collecting data enables us to check results against each other, or use different types of results to illuminate different aspects of an issue.*	Jason Moser Annamaria Pinter Craig Johnston	**Jason** summarizes the findings of evaluation surveys conducted among his students in addition to his own analyses. **Annamaria** not only evaluates the effectiveness of task repetition on the basis of her own judgment of improvements observed in task transcripts: she also interviews her pupils to seek their view of the experience. **Craig's** assessment of the value of a report stage in a task-based lesson is mainly based on his analysis of his students' language. However, at the end of his report he does tell us what his students' said during informal feedback, in contrast to his own more positive view. Many of the other studies reported in this collection balance the teacher–researcher's verdict with observations of how the students reacted.

Appendix 3

Examples of other classroom experiments and research carried out by our contributors: (some of these are directly related to tasks, others to different specific areas such as relevance of a syllabus, but most are on topics that are of relevance to any communicative, learner-centred classroom).

Exploring task language and variables

- Looking at how the nature of the task affects the language produced. (Djapoura)
- Comparing 'before' and 'after' recordings of students performing interview tasks to evaluate progress after a series of lessons focusing on communicative micro strategies (Hobbs)
- Comparing L1 and L2 narratives produced by learners doing narrative tasks (Kiernan)

Learner and teacher language (general)

- Finding out why learners relied so heavily on L1 in class to resolve vocabulary difficulties (Cox)
- Looking at ways of increasing students' spoken output (Essig)
- Investigating teacher–student interaction in oral interviews (Baigent)
- Classifying face-threatening acts in teacher–learner interaction based on recordings of classes and transcripts donated by colleagues (Hobbs)
- Experimenting with teacher's use of questions, to see if this helped students to become less reticent in class (Birch)
- Analysing the English compositions of Korean university students to find out the nature of their problems in constructing written discourse (Poupore)

Syllabus, materials, and learning activity design and evaluation

- Investigating the relevance of a business English syllabus to the workplace (Pullin Stark)
- Researching, creating, piloting and evaluating materials to supplement a text-book of medical terminology (Hobbs)
- Developing a co-operative version of the 'hangman' game to give students meaningful reading, pronunciation and listening comprehension opportunities (Coulson) (Published as Coulson, D, 2001, 'Motivating Junior High School Students to Participate through Directed, Consciousness-Raising Activities'. The Proceedings of the 26th Annual International Conference of the Japan Association for Language Teaching. October, 2000.
- Developing and evaluating a task-based assessment model for assessing primary school pupils' communicative competence (Lee)
- Looking at how parallel concordancing (using two corpora, one in L1, and the other in L2, containing sets of translations or 'parallel' texts) can be used in second language classes (Djapoura)
- Investigating whether rhyming patterns help Japanese children retain English words (Johnston)

- Comparing vocabulary recall with and without overt teaching (Baigent)
- Observing how drills work with junior level students (Loumpourdi)
- Investigating whether using a 'discovery' process would allow learners to write better memos (Sheehan)
- Exploring process writing techniques in an FCE context (Baigent)

Learner views and perceptions

- Investigating what motivates a group of learners (Essig)
- Conducting informal interviews with students to find out what their experiences with authentic input were (Poupore)
- Investigating children's perceptions of assessment and testing in EFL (Pinter)
- Investigating MA students' views and perceptions of their written feedback on assignments (Pinter)
- Finding our why learners were having problems using learner dictionaries (Sheehan)

Other

- Reflectively analysing a teaching diary (Kiernan)
- Learning strategies (Pullin Stark)
- Weak learners (Pullin Stark)

Appendix 4

Books and other resources recommended by our contributors

Allwright, D. and K. Bailey 1991 *Focus on the language classroom* Cambridge: Cambridge University Press.
Altrichter, H. 1993 *Teachers investigate their work: an introduction to the methods of action research* London: Routledge.
Bailey, K. and D. Nunan 1996 *Voices from the language classroom* Cambridge: Cambridge University Press.
Brown, J. D. 1988 *Understanding research in second language learning: a teacher's guide to statistics and research design* Cambridge: Cambridge University Press.
Brown, H. D. and S. Gonzo (eds) 1995 *Readings on Second language acquisition* London: Prentice Hall Regents.
Brown, J. D. and T. Rodgers 2002 *Doing second language research* Oxford: Oxford University Press.
English Teaching Professional magazine (a great blend of information).
Freeman, D. 1998 *Doing teacher research* Boston MA: Heinle and Heinle.
Frankfort-Nachmias, C. and D. Nachmias 1996 (6th edn) *Research Methods in the social sciences* New York: Worth Publishers.
Genesee, F. and J. Upshur 1996 *Classroom-based evaluation in second language education* Cambridge: Cambridge University Press.
Holliday, A. 2002 *Doing and writing qualitative research* London: Sage.
Kemmis, S. and R. McTaggert (eds) 1998 (3rd edn) *The action research planner* Victoria: Deakin University.
McCarthy, M. 1991 *Discourse analysis for language teachers* Cambridge University Press.

McDonough, J. and S. McDonough 1997 *Research methods for English language teachers* London: Arnold.
Modern English Teacher and other journals where practising teachers describe small-scale experiments.
Nunan, D. 1989 *Understanding language classrooms: a guide for teacher-initiated action* Hemel Hempstead: Prentice Hall.
Nunan, D. 1992 *Research methods in language learning* Cambridge: Cambridge University Press.
Prabhu, N. 1990 'There is no best method – why?' *TESOL Quarterly* 24 161–76.
Richards, K. 2003 *Qualitative Inquiry in TESOL* Basingstoke: Palgrave Macmillan.
Richards, J. and C. Lockhart 1994 *Reflective teaching in second language classrooms* Cambridge: Cambridge University Press.
Tarone, E., S. Gass and A. Cohen 1994 *Research methodology in SLA* Hillsdale: Lawrence Erlbaum.
Wajnryb, R. 1992 *Classroom observation tasks: a resource book for language teachers and trainers* Cambridge: Cambridge University Press.
Wallace, M. 1998 *Action research for language teachers* Cambridge: Cambridge University Press.
Willis, J. and D. Willis (eds) 1996 *Challenge and change in language teaching* Oxford: Heinemann.
Wray, A., K. Trott and A. Bloomer 1998 *Projects in linguistics* London: Arnold.

Other resources

Small battery-operated tape recorders with reasonable microphones.
An online group for support, getting opinions.
Internet – do searches for articles on your topic (type keywords into a Google search).

Notes

1 While there is no clear-cut distinction between **qualitative** and **quantitative research** (see Larsen-Freeman and Long, 1991: 15), the former term usually applies to approaches that are concerned mainly with descriptive data, and the latter with data which can be counted, normally in sufficient quantities to be subjected to statistical analysis. See also Holliday 2002: 6.
2 For a skeleton outline of the stages of action research see p. 6 in the introduction to this volume.
3 Incidentally, on reading published work, David Coulson says 'Recently I have got into the habit of looking up on 'Google' the academic who wrote the latest paper I have read. It literally puts a face, and important background information, to a name.' (Coulson, personal email, 24 June 2003)
4 These views broadly conform with the guidelines given in sections 6.2 and 6.5 of the *Recommendations on Good Practice* published by BAAL (The British Association for Applied Linguistics) 1994.

References

Allwright, D. 1993 'Integrating "research" and "pedagogy": appropriate criteria.' *Teachers develop teachers research: Papers on research and teacher development.* Edge, J. and K. Richards (eds) Oxford: Heinemann.

Allwright, D. 2000 *Exploratory practice: an 'appropriate methodology' for language teacher development?* The Exploratory Practice Centre www.ling.lancs.ac.uk/groups/crile/EPCentre/readings/IALS%20PAPER%20DRAFT.htm accessed May 30 2003.

Allwright, D. 2003 'Exploratory practice: rethinking practitioner research in language teaching' *Language Teaching Research* 7(2): 113–41.

Anderson, A. and T. Lynch 1988 *Listening* Oxford: Oxford University Press.

Aston, G. 1986 'Trouble-shooting in interaction with learners: the more the merrier?' *Applied Linguistics* 7(2): 128–43.

Aston, G. 1998 'Learning English with the British National Corpus.' Paper presented at 6th Jornada de Corpus, UPF, Barcelona, May 1998 http://www.sslmit.unibo.it/guy/barc.htm

BAAL (British Association of Applied Linguistics) 1994 *Recommendations on good practice in applied linguistics* http://www.baal.org.uk/goodprac.htm#intro

Bardovi-Harlig, K. 2000 *Tense and aspect in second language acquisition: form, meaning, and use* Malden, MA: Blackwell.

Bialystok, E. 1983 'Some factors in selection and implementation of communication strategies' in C. Faerch and G. Kasper (eds) *Strategies in interlanguage communication* London: Longman: 100–18.

Bolinger, D. 1975 *Aspects of language* (2nd edn) New York: Harcourt Brace Jovanovich.

Breen, M. and C. Candlin 2001 'The essentials of a communicative curriculum in language teaching' in Hall, D. and A. Hewings (eds) *Innovation in English language teaching: a reader* New York: Routledge: 9–26.

Brown, H. D.1994 *Principles of language learning and teaching* (3rd edn) New Jersey: Prentice Hall.

Burns, A. 1999 *Collaborative action research for English language teachers* Cambridge: Cambridge University Press.

Bygate, M. 1994 'Adjusting the focus: teacher roles in task-based learning of grammar' in Bygate, M., A. Tonkyn and E. Williams (eds) *Grammar and the language teacher* Hemel Hempstead: Prentice Hall: 237–59.

Bygate, M. 1996 'Effects of task repetition: appraising the developing language of learners' in Willis, J. and D. Willis (eds) *Challenge and change in language teaching* Oxford: Heinemann: 136–46.

Bygate, M. 2001 'Effects of task repetition on the structure and control of oral language' in Bygate, M., P. Skehan, and M. Swain (eds) *Researching pedagogic tasks: second language learning, teaching, and testing* Harlow: Longman: 23–48.

Bygate, M., P. Skehan, and M. Swain (eds) 2001 *Researching pedagogic tasks: second language learning, teaching, and testing* Harlow: Longman.

Carless, D. 2002 'Implementing task-based learning with young learners' *ELT Journal* 56(4): 389–96.

Carter, R. 1998 'Orders of reality: CANCODE, communication and culture' *ELT Journal* 52(1): 43–56.

Channell, J. 1994 *Vague language* Oxford: Oxford University Press.

Cook, G. 1989 *Discourse* Oxford: Oxford University Press.

COBUILD 2000 *Corpus concordance sampler*: http://titania.cobuild.collins.co.uk/form.html

Coughlan, P. and P. Duff 1994 'Same task, different activities: analysis of SLA from an activity theory perspective' in Lantolf, J. and G. Appel (eds) Norwood, N.J: Ablex Publishing Corporation: 173–93.

Dekeyser, R. 1998 'Beyond focus on form: cognitive perspectives on learning and practicing second language grammar' in Doughty, C. and J. Williams (eds) *Focus on form in classroom second language acquisition* Cambridge: Cambridge University Press: 42–63

Donato, R. 1994 'Collective scaffolding in second language learning' in Lantolf, J. and G. Appel (eds) Norwood, N.J: Ablex Publishing Corporation: 33–56.

Doughty, C., and J. Williams 1998 'Pedagogical choices in focus on form' in Doughty, C. and J. Williams (eds) *Focus on form in classroom second language acquisition* Cambridge: Cambridge University Press: 197–261.

Edge, J. (ed.) 2001 *Action research* Alexandria, VA: TESOL Inc.

Edwards, C. 2004 'Module 4, activity cycle 4.2: What counts as a task?' http://www.delphi.bham.ac.uk.

Eggins, S. and D. Slade 1997 *Analyzing casual conversation* London: Cassell.

Eldridge, J. 1996 'Code-switching in a Turkish secondary school' *ELT Journal* 50(4): 303–11.

Ellis, R. 2000 'Task-based research and language pedagogy' *Language Teaching Research* 4(3): 193–220.

Ellis, R. 2002 'The place of grammar instruction in the second/foreign language curriculum' in Hinkel, E. and S. Fotos (eds) *New perspectives on grammar teaching in the language classroom* London: Lawrence Erlbaum Associates: 17–34.

Ellis, R. 2003 *Task-based language learning and teaching*. Oxford: Oxford University Press.

Ellis, R., Y. Tanaka and A. Yamazaki 1994 'Classroom interaction, comprehension and L2 vocabulary acquisition' *Language Learning* 44: 449–91.

Feez, S. 1998 *Text-based syllabus design* Sydney: National Center for English Teaching and Research.

Fielding, R. 1996 *Students' use of lexical phrases in written work as indicators of degrees of exposure to the target language* Unpublished MSc dissertation, Aston University, Birmingham, UK.

Foster, P. 1996 'Doing the task better: how planning time influences students' performance' in Willis, J. and D. Willis (eds) 1996.

Foster, P. 1999 Key concepts in ELT: task based learning and pedagogy *ELT Journal*, 53(1): 69–70.

Foster, P. 2001 'Rules and routines: a consideration of their role in task-based language production of native and non-native speakers' in Bygate, M., P. Skehan and M. Swain (eds) *Researching pedagogic tasks: second language learning, teaching, and testing* Harlow: Longman: 75–93.

Foster, P. and P. Skehan 1994 *The influence of planning on performance in task-based learning* Paper presented at the British Association of Applied Linguistics, Leeds, September 1994.

Foster, P. and P. Skehan 1996 'The influence of planning and task type on second language performance' *Studies in second language acquisition* 18: 299–324.

Frankel, I. and V. Kimbrough 1998 *Gateways* Oxford: Oxford University Press.

Freeman, D. 1998 *Doing teacher research: from inquiry to understanding* Boston MA: Heinle and Heinle.

Fuller, D. and C. Fuller 1999 *Face to Face – English for today's generation* Tokyo: Macmillan Language house.

Gairns, R. and S. Redman 2002 *Natural English* Oxford: Oxford University Press.

Graddol, D. 1997 *The future of English* London: The British Council.

Halliday, M. A. K. 1975 *Learning how to mean: explorations in the development of language* London: Edward Arnold.

Hancock, R. 1997 'Why are class teachers reluctant to become researchers?' *British Journal of In-service Education* 23(1): 85–99.

Harley, B. 1998 'The role of focus-on-form tasks in promoting child L2 acquisition' in Doughty, C. and J. Williams (eds) *Focus on form in classroom second language acquisition* Cambridge: Cambridge University Press: 156–74.

Helgesen, M. 1991 'Video Rising' *Newsletter of the Japan Association for Language Teaching* Video SIG. 3(2).

Helgesen, M., S. Brown, and T. Mandeville 1999 *English firsthand 2 student book* Singapore: Addison Wesley Longman.

Heyder, S. 1994 *Easy true stories: a picture based beginning reader.* New York: Pearson's Education (Longman).

Hinds, J. 1982 *Ellipsis in Japanese.* Edmonton, Alberta: Linguistic Research Inc.

Holliday, A. 2002 *Doing and writing qualitative research* London: Sage.

Iwashita, N. 1999 'Tasks and learners' output in nonnative-nonnative interaction' in Kanno, K. (ed.) *Studies on the acquisition of Japanese as a second language.* Amsterdam: John Benjamin: 31–53.

Izumi, S. 2002 'Output, input enhancement, and the noticing hypothesis: an experimental study on ESL relativization' *Studies in Second Language Acquisition* 24(4): 541–77.

Johns, T. 1988 'Whence and whither classroom concordancing?' in Bongaerts, T., P. de Haan, S. Lobbe and H. Wekker (eds) *Computer applications in language learning* Dordrecht, The Netherlands: Foris: 9–27.

Ketko, H. 2000 'The importance of multi-word chunks in facilitating communicative competence' *The Language Teacher* 24(12): 5–11.

Krashen, S. 1982 *Principles and practices in second language acquisition* Oxford: Pergamon Press.

Krashen, S. 1985 *The input hypothesis: issues and implications* London: Longman.

Krashen, S. and T. Terrell 1983 *The natural approach: language acquisition in the classroom* New York: Prentice-Hall.

Labov, W. 1997 'Some further steps in narrative analysis' in Bamberg, M.G.W. (ed.) *Journal of Narrative and Life History: special issue oral versions of personal experience: three decades of narrative analysis* 7(1–4): Mahwah, NJ: Lawrence Erlbaum Associates: 395–415.

Lantolf, J. 1996 'Second language acquisition theory-building: letting all the flowers fly!' *Language Learning* 46: 713–49.

LaPierre, D. 1994 *Language output in a cooperative learning setting: determining its effects on second language learning* Unpublished M.A. dissertation, University of Toronto, Toronto, Canada.

Larsen-Freeman, D. 2000 *Techniques and principles in language teaching* Oxford: Oxford University Press.

Larsen-Freeman, D. and M. H. Long 1991 *An introduction to second language research* London: Longman.

Leaver, B. L. and M. Kaplan (forthcoming 2004) 'Task-based instruction in US Government Slavic language programs' in Leaver, B. L. and J. R. Willis *Task-based instruction in foreign language education: practices and programs* Washington: Georgetown University Press.

Leaver, B. L. and J. R. Willis 2004 *Task-based instruction in foreign language education: practices and programs* Washington: Georgetown University Press.

Lee, S. M. 2002 *Development of students' meaning negotiation skill in English classes at primary school* Unpublished MA dissertation, University of Birmingham, UK.

Lewis, M. 1993 *The lexical approach: the state of ELT and a way forward* London: Language Teaching Publications.

Lewis, M. 1997 *Implementing the lexical approach* London: Language Teaching Publications.

Lewis, M. (ed.) 2000 *Teaching collocation: further developments in the lexical approach* London: Language Teaching Publications.

Lightbown, P. M. and N. Spada 1999 *How languages are learned* Oxford: Oxford University Press.

Lloyd, P. 1991 'Strategies to communicate route directions by telephone; a comparison of the performance of 7-year olds, 10-year olds and adults' *Journal of Child Language* 18: 171–89.

Long, M. 1983a 'Linguistic and conversational adjustments to non-native speakers' *Studies in Second Language Acquisition* 5: 177–93.

Long, M. 1983b 'Native speaker/non-native speaker conversation and the negotiation of comprehensible input' *Applied Linguistics* 4(2): 126–41.

Long, M. 1989 'Task, group, and task-group interaction' *University of Hawaii Working Papers in English as a Second Language* 8(2): 1–26.

Long, M. 1996 'The role of the linguistic environment in second language acquisition' in Ritchie, W. and T. J. Bhatia (eds) *Handbook of second language acquisition* Orlando: Academic Press: 413–68.

Long, M. and G. Crookes 1991 'Three approaches to task-based syllabus design' *TESOL Quarterly* 26(1): 27–55.

Long, M. and P. Robinson 1998 'Focus on form: theory, research, and practice' in Doughty, C. and J. Williams (eds) *Focus on form in classroom second language acquisition* Cambridge: Cambridge University Press: 15–41.

Lopez, J. 2004 'Introducing task-based instruction for teaching English in Brazil: learning how to leap the hurdles' in Leaver, B. L. and J. R. Willis (eds) *Task-based instruction in foreign language education: programs and practices* Washington: Georgetown University Press.

Passos de Oliveira, C. 2004 'Implementing task-based assessment in a TEFL Environment' in Leaver, B. L. and J. R. Willis (eds) *Task-based instruction in foreign language educating: programs and practices* Washington: Georgetown University Press.

Lynch, T. and J. Maclean 2000 'Exploring the benefits of task repetition and recycling for classroom language learning' *Language Teaching Research* 4(3): 221–49.

Lynch, T. and J. Maclean 2001 'A case of exercising: effects of immediate task repetition on learners' performance' in Bygate, M., P. Skehan, and M. Swain (eds) *Researching pedagogic tasks: second language learning, teaching, and testing* Harlow: Longman: 141–62.

Markee, N. 2000 *Conversation analysis* Mahwah, NJ: Lawrence Erlbaum Associates.

Mehnert, U. 1998 'The effects of different lengths of time for planning on second language performance' *Studies in Second Language Acquisition* 20: 83–108.

Moon, R. 1998 'Vocabulary connection: multi-word items in English' in Schmitt, N. and M. J. McCarthy (eds) *Vocabulary: description, acquisition and pedagogy* Cambridge: Cambridge University Press.

Morris, S. and A. Stanton 1998 *Practice tests for FCE* Harlow: Longman.

Murata, K. 1994 'Intrusive or co-operative? a cross-cultural study of interruption' *Journal of Pragmatics* 21: 385–400.

Nattinger, J. and J. DeCarrico 1992 *Lexical phrases and language teaching* Oxford: Oxford University Press.

Norrick, N. 2000 *Conversational narrative: storytelling in everyday talk* Amsterdam/Philadelphia: John Benjamins.

Nunan, D. 1989a *Designing tasks for the communicative classroom* Cambridge: Cambridge University Press.

Nunan, D. 1989b *Understanding language classrooms* Hemel Hempstead: Prentice Hall International.

Nunan, D 1992 *Research methods in language learning* Cambridge: Cambridge University Press.

Nunan, D. 1995a *Atlas: learning-centered communication* Boston: Heinle and Heinle.

Nunan, D. 1995b *Atlas: learning-centered communication: teacher's extended edition* Boston: Heinle and Heinle.

Ochs, E. and L. Capps 2001 *Living narrative: creating lives in everyday storytelling* Cambridge, MA: Harvard University Press.

OUP/ELT debate, 2003 http://www.oup.com/elt/global/teachersclub/teaching/debate/tasks/ (accessed, May, 2003).

Pawley, A. and F. H. Syder 1983 'Two puzzles for linguistic theory: nativelike selection and nativelike fluency' in Richards, J. C. and R. W. Schmidt (eds) *Language and communication* London: Longman: 191–226.

Peaty, D. 1987 *Alltalk 2* Tokyo: Macmillan Language House.

Perlman, J. 1997 *Dinner for two* Montreal: National Film Board of Canada.

Pica, T. 1989 University of Pennsylvania. personal communication, 20 October 1989.

Pica, T. 1997 'Second language teaching and research relationships: a North American view' *Language Teaching Research* 1(1): 48–72.

Pica, T. 2001 'The content based curriculum: does it provide an optimal or optional approach to language learning?' in Renandya, W. and N. Sunga (eds) *Language curriculum and instruction in multicultural societies* Singapore: SEAMEO Regional Language Center: 145–74.

Pica, T., L. Holliday, N. Lewis and L. Morgenthaler 1989 'Comprehensible output as an outcome of linguistic demands on the learner' *Studies in Second Language Acquisition* 11(1): 63–90.

Pica, T., R. Kanagy and J. Falodun 1993 'Choosing and using communication tasks for second language research and instruction' in Crookes, G. and S. Gass (eds) *Tasks and language learning: integrating theory and practice* Clevedon, Avon: Multilingual Matters: 9–34.

Pica, T., F. Lincoln-Porter, D. Paninos, and J. Linnell 1996 'Language learners interaction: how does it address the input, output, and feedback needs of L2 learners?' *TESOL Quarterly* 30(1): 59–84.

Prabhu, N. S. 1987 *Second language pedagogy* Oxford: Oxford University Press.

Richards, J. 2000 *New interchange* Cambridge: Cambridge University Press.

Richards, J. and T. Rodgers 2001 *Approaches and methods in language Teaching* (2nd edn) Cambridge: Cambridge University Press.

Richards, K. 2003 *Qualitative inquiry in TESOL* Basingstoke: Palgrave Macmillan.

Robinson, P. 2001 'Task complexity, cognitive resources, and syllabus design: a triadic framework for examining task influences on SLA' in Robinson, P. (ed.) *Cognition and second language learning* Cambridge: Cambridge University Press: 287–318.

Robson, C. 2002 *Real world research* (2nd edn) Oxford: Blackwell.

Sacks, H. 1995 *Lectures on conversation: one volume edition of UCLA lectures given between fall 1964 and spring 1972* Oxford: Blackwell.

Samuda, V. 2001 'Guiding relationships between form and meaning during task performance: the role of the teacher' in Bygate, M., P. Skehan, and M. Swain (eds) *Researching pedagogic tasks: second language learning, teaching, and testing* Harlow: Longman: 119–40.

Seedhouse, P. 1999 'Task-based interaction' *ELT Journal* 53(1) 49–156.

Shehadeh, A. 1999 'Non-native speakers' production of modified comprehensible output and second language learning' *Language Learning* 49(4): 627–75.

Sinclair, J. 1991 *Corpus, concordance, collocation* Oxford: Oxford University Press.

Skehan, P. 1996a 'Second language acquisition research and task-based instruction' in Willis, J. and D. Willis (eds) *Challenge and change in language teaching* (eds) Oxford: Heinemann: 17–30.

Skehan, P. 1996b 'A framework for the implementation of task-based instruction' *Applied Linguistics* 17(1): 38–62.

Skehan, P. 1998 *A cognitive approach to language learning* Oxford: Oxford University Press.

Skehan, P. 2002 'A non-marginal role for tasks' *ELT Journal* 56(3): 289–95.

Skehan, P. 2003 'Tasks in L2 learning and teaching' *Language Teaching* 36(1): 1–14.

Skehan, P. and P. Foster 1997 'The influence of planning and post-task activities on accuracy and complexity in task based learning' *Language Teaching Research* 1(3): 185–211.

Skehan, P. and P. Foster 1999 'The influence of task structure and processing conditions on narrative retellings' *Language Learning* 49(1): 93–120.

Skehan, P. and P. Foster 2001 'Cognition and tasks' in Robinson, P. (ed.) *Cognition and second language instruction* Cambridge: Cambridge University Press: 183–205.

Skehan, P. and P. Foster 2002 *The effect of post task activities on the accuracy of language during task performance* unpublished manuscript, King's College London.

Stern, H. H. 1983 *Fundamental concepts of language teaching* Oxford: Oxford University Press.

Stevens, V. 1995 'Concordancing with language learners: why? when? what?' *CAELL Journal* 6(2): 2–10. Available at http://www.ruf.rice.edu/~barlow/stevens.html

Storch, N. 2002 'Patterns of interaction in ESL pair work' *Language Learning* 52(1): 119–58.

Swain, M. 1988 'Manipulating and complementing content teaching to maximise second language learning' *TESL Canada Journal* 6(1): 68–93.

Swain, M. 1995 'Three functions of output in second language learning' in Cook, G. and B. Seidlhofer (eds) *Principle and practice in applied linguistics: studies in honor of H. G. Widdowson* Oxford: Oxford University Press: 125–44.

Swain, M. 1997 'Collaborative dialogue: its contribution to second language learning' *Revista Canaria de Estudios Ingleses* 34: 115–32.

Swain, M. 1998 'Focus on form through conscious reflection' in Doughty, C. and J. Williams, (eds) *Focus on form in classroom second language acquisition* Cambridge: Cambridge University Press: 64–81.

Swain, M. 2000 'The output hypothesis and beyond: mediating acquisition through collaborative dialogue' in Lantolf, C. (ed.) *Sociocultural theory and second language learning* Oxford: Oxford University Press: 97–114.

Swain, M. and S. Lapkin 1995 'Problems in output and the cognitive processes they generate: a step towards second language learning' *Applied Linguistics* 16(3): 371–91.

Swain, M. and S. Lapkin 1998 'Interaction and second language learning: two adolescent French immersion students working together' *The Modern Language Journal* 82(3): 320–37.

Swain, M. and S. Lapkin 2001 'Focus on form through collaborative dialogue: exploring task effects' in Bygate, M., P. Skehan, and M. Swain (eds) *Researching pedagogic tasks: second language learning, teaching, and testing*. Harlow: Longman: 99–118.

Taylor, E. K. 2000 *Using folktales* Cambridge: Cambridge University Press.

Thornbury, S. 1999 *How to teach grammar* Harlow: Longman.

Tsui, A. 1995 *Introducing classroom interaction* London: Penguin English.

Van den Branden, K. 1997 'Effects of negotiation on language learners' output' *Language Learning* 47(4): 589–636.

Van Lier, L. 2000 'From input to affordance: social interactive learning from an ecological perspective' in Lantolf J. (ed.) *Sociocultural theory and second language learning: recent advances* Oxford: Oxford University Press: 245–59.

Vygotsky, L. S. 1986 *Thought and language* Cambridge, MA: MIT Press.

Vygotsky, L. S. 1987 'Thinking and speech' in Rieber, R. W. and A. S. Carton (eds) N. Minick (trans.) *The collected works of L. S. Vygotsky: volume 1* New York: Plenum: 39–285.

Wajnryb, R. 2003 *Stories: narrative activities in the language classroom* Cambridge: Cambridge University Press.

Wallace, M. 1998 *Action research for language teachers* Williams, M. and T. Wright (eds) Cambridge: Cambridge University Press.

Waters, A. 1997 'Theory and practice in LSP course design' in Pique, J. and D. Viera (eds) *Theory and practice in ESP* Universitad de Valencia.

White, R. V. 1998 *The ELT Curriculum: design, innovation and management* Oxford: Blackwell.

White, S. 1989 'Backchannels across cultures: a study of Americans and Japanese' *Language in Society* 18: 59–76.

Widdowson, H. G. 1989 'Knowledge of language and ability for use' *Applied Linguistics* 10(2) 128–37.

Wigglesworth, G. 2001 'Influences on performance in task-based oral assessments' in Bygate, M., P. Skehan, and M. Swain (eds) *Researching pedagogic tasks: second language learning, teaching, and testing* Harlow: Longman : 186–209.

Williams, M. and R. L. Burden 1997 *Psychology for language teachers: a social constructivist approach* Cambridge: Cambridge University Press.

Willis, D. and J. Willis 1987 'Varied activities for variable language' *ELT Journal* 41(1): 12–18.

Willis, D. 1990 *The lexical syllabus* Birmingham: Collins COBUILD.

Willis, D. 1996a 'Accuracy, fluency and conformity' in Willis, J. and D. Willis (eds) *Challenge and change in language teaching* Oxford: Heinemann: 44–51.

Willis D, 1996b 'Introduction' in Willis, J. and D. Willis (eds) *Challenge and change in language teaching* Oxford: Heinemann: iv–vi.

Willis D. 2003 *Rules, patterns and words: grammar and lexis in English language teaching* Cambridge: Cambridge University Press.

Willis, D. and J. Willis 1996 'Consciousness-raising activities in the language classroom' in Willis, J. and D. Willis (eds) *Challenge and change in language teaching* Oxford: Heinemann: 63–76.

Willis, J. 1996a A framework for task-based learning Harlow: Longman Addison-Wesley.

Willis, J. 1996b 'A flexible framework for task-based learning' in Willis, J. and D. Willis (eds) *Challenge and change in language teaching* Oxford: Heinemann: 52–62.

Willis, J. 1998a 'Concordances in the classroom without a computer: assembling and exploiting concordances of common words' in Tomlinson, B. (ed.) *Materials development in second language teaching* Cambridge: Cambridge University Press 44–66.

Willis, J. 1998b 'Task-based learning: what kind of adventure?' internet article http://langue.hyper.chubu.ac.jp/jalt/pub/tlt/98jul/willis.html accessed 28 March 2003.

Willis, J. and D. Willis 1989 *The Collins Cobuild English course, level 1* London: Collins.

Willis, J. and D. Willis (eds) 1996 *Challenge and change in language teaching* Oxford: Heinemann.

Willis, J. 1994 'Perspectives on task-based instruction: understanding our practices acknowledging different practitioners', in Leaver, B. L. and J. R. Willis (eds) 2004 (forthcoming) *Task-based instruction in foreign language education: practices and programs* Washington: Georgetown University Press.

Index

Where there are multiple page references, those shown in **bold** indicate the place in the text where the word is defined.